Housing, Social
Policy and
the State

Housing, Social Policy and the State

Edited by Joseph Melling

CROOM HELM LONDON

© 1980 Joseph Melling
Croom Helm Ltd, 2-10 St John's Road, London SW11

British Library Cataloguing in Publication Data

Housing, social policy and the state.
   1. Housing policy – Great Britain – History
   I. Melling, Joseph
   301.5'4'0941   HD7333.A3

   ISBN 0-85664-918-X

Reproduced from copy supplied
printed and bound in Great Britain
by Billing and Sons Limited
Guildford, London, Oxford, Worcester

CONTENTS

Preface

PREFACE

The original inspiration for this collection of essays came from the Conference on Social Policy, held at the University of Glasgow in May 1978. The Conference was financed by the Social Sciences Research Council, to whom our thanks are due. Particularly helpful were Mr David Levy and Dr Derek Oddy, of the Economic and Social History Committee. The organisation of the Conference was greatly assisted by the help of Keith Burgess, Jason Ditton, Jim Emery, Colin Filer, Paul Littlewood and Iain McIntosh.

Thanks are also due to our friends and colleagues at the Universities and Polytechnics where we work. Personal thanks to John Butt, Roger Davidson, Alan Macgregor, Bob Morris, and Pat Thane for their encouraging comments. Roy Hay provided support from his outback department in Australia, and the flying doctors gave us many enjoyable Moroccan evenings.

Formal acknowledgements are due to the Public Record Office and the various publishers, for permission to reproduce documents and extracts.

Finally, thanks to Kathy for the good times.

J.L.M.

1 INTRODUCTION

Joseph Melling

There now exists an extensive and in many ways impressive literature
on the history of housing and housing policies in Britain. Besides forming an important area of economic theory, sociology and social administration, there are an increasing number of studies within social and
urban history.[1] Historians have focused upon local conditions as well
as national developments, whilst social administration studies have
approached housing politics largely through its central formulation and
implementation.[2] In every field there has been some recognition of the
importance of 'local' influences, whether it is regional building cycles,
peculiarities of local provisions, or the role of local government in
housing provision.[3] Yet there have been few systematic attempts to
relate local amenities to general policy, or to link the different methods
devised within each discipline for the study of housing. Significant
differences, not merely of terminology and methods but of theory and
interpretation, survive with little reference to parallel debates within
neighbouring fields.[4]

Both these divisions and these debates are of importance to our
understanding of past and present literature upon housing in Britain,
since it is through them that we can trace changing perceptions of the
'housing question'. As many writers have emphasised, the 'scientific'
approach to social phenomenon and the consequent academic
specialisations seen since the later nineteenth century, were closely
linked to the material changes which society was undergoing and the
social investigations carried out during this period.[5] These years saw
a wide range of Royal Commissions appointed by the state to collect
information on various subjects, and the 'discovery' of social problems
by pioneering investigators dedicated to the principles of empirical
validation and quantification through their monumental surveys.[6]
These studies in turn resulted in 'changing approaches to the efficacy
and scope of government and administration', as the real dimensions
of the various 'problems' facing society became clear.[7]

It is also apparent, however, that these ventures into 'darkest
England' were as concerned with colonising the poorer groups in
society, as with investigating their condition. Even when not acting on
behalf of the state, the early reformers were often committed to re-
creating the 'idea and reality of a moral community' within the class

context of industrial Britain.[8] The Charity Organisation Society
became a powerful advocate of moral action as well as social casework,
and many housing reformers shared a strong religious commitment.
This work also made a substantial contribution to the prevailing
ideology and the intellectual traditions of British society, reinforcing
the principles of empirical enquiry and utilitarian administration. Such
contributions complemented the increasing influence of American and
German social theory, from the pragmatism of James to the works of
Wilhemine Germany.[9] Even powerful critics of social inequalities, such
as the Webbs, tended to accept the pluralistic and institution-orientated
views of history which such methods implied.

It is arguable that many such influences continue to shape the
accounts of social policy in general and housing in particular. Whilst
the cruder versions of optimistic progress, the Whig history of welfare
reform, have been effectively challenged in recent years, they have
often been replaced by pluralist analyses which emphasise the
evolution of policy through conflicting pressures and the 'pragmatic'
response of government to problematic situations.[10] The Whig vision
of progressive enlightenment and improvement through reform, has
been largely discarded for an interpretation which shows history as a
learning process – the consolidation of experience through pragmatic
experiments.

Rarely do we find historians of social policy aligned in such simple
fashion, but it is noticeable that almost every arm of state power and
each political grouping within the state has its own school of apolo-
gists. The great men of social politics, usually the Conservative and
Liberal leaders moved by the passion for government, continue to
receive a large amount of personal attention. Close behind are the
bureaucratic élite of senior civil servants, operating according to the
hidden imperatives of continued expansion and optimum efficiency.
There are also the self-acknowledged experts and intellectuals, utilising
both social enquiry and government growth to become the 'pioneers of
the welfare state'.[11] With such groups of élites jostling for historical
significance, it is easy to relegate the role of class struggles and material
interests to secondary importance or to the 'background' of social unrest. This is greatly helped by the meticulous attention to biographical
detail, whilst often ignoring the economic and social forces which
create the conditions in which groups and individuals operate.[12] The
formal processes of policy and administration are elevated to a historical role which consigns the 'problem' with which they are dealing to
rather lesser significance.

These tendencies are nowhere more apparent than in some of the most influential works on the history of housing policy in Britain. The best known contribution since the Second World War is perhaps Marion Bowley's *Housing and the State* published on the eve of Labour's victory in 1945.[13] It gave an account of housing legislation since Addison's Act of 1919, and characterised the progress of housing policy as a series of pragmatic 'experiments' by state and society to its changing housing needs. Although such phrases as 'moral responsibility', 'social conscience' and 'housing need' are used quite freely by Bowley, it becomes clear that she fully accepts the conditions imposed by the market economy and sees the necessity for maintaining housing standards within this context.[14]

Bowley emphasises the important role of different 'schools' of housing expert in shaping interwar housing policies, although she does recognise the importance of different pressures on government. Thus she portrays the final 'radical' phase of housing intervention during the later 1930s as the 'offspring of the union between public conscience and the desire for public economy' in British society.[15] Although the influential middle-class and skilled groups had left the 'housing movement' by then, argues Bowley, the power of public opinion was sufficient to ensure fresh measures despite the stringencies of Treasury finance.

The author concludes that the 'root cause' of the housing problem stemmed not so much from fundamental social and economic conditions, as from the 'absence of any clearly defined purpose or intention on the part of the government' in dealing with proven difficulties.[16] The key to solving the country's housing problems was to find the correct principles of administration, and in this light Bowley advocates greater state intervention guided by expert advice and rational administration.[17]

More recent work than Bowley's enjoys the advantages of modern research and considerable hindsight, as is evident in Paul Wilding's major contributions on Exchequer subsidies and the evolution of the Ministry of Health.[18] Whilst Wilding has illuminated many areas of housing policy, however, it is clear that he shares many of his predecessor's premises concerning pluralist politics and administrative reform, within his 'incrementalist' analysis of housing reform.[19] Wilding suggests for example, that Exchequer subsidies to local authorities for housing purposes would 'almost certainly' have arrived before 1919, had the war not intervened.[20] This was clear from the strong movement amongst backbenchers (particularly Conservatives like Walter Long), despite the resistance of politicians, bureaucracy and public opinion to the necessary innovations.

In speaking of the progressive social reformers amongst the Unionist opposition, one can even see Wilding identify with their 'severely pragmatic . . . approach', arguing that it was 'this concentration on the realities of the situation which is so refreshing and marks a new approach'.[21] Those who perceive the practical realities of any social problem are clearly favoured in such an analysis, irrespective of Conservative hostility to tangential campaigns such as Lloyd George's land reform movement. In concentrating upon the specifics of housing, Wilding is able to suggest that the Addison Act was the belated fruit of a long political struggle rather than a response to the critical conditions of postwar Britain.[22]

Both Bowley and Wilding tend to highlight initiatives of policy formulation within the state itself, rather than locating state control in a context of class relations and class struggle. The state is portrayed as operating above class interests, whilst being subject to a plurality of pressures from social interests. Housing policy is therefore the gradual recognition of pressing housing needs by a large section of the population, as voiced in various housing 'movements'.

It was partly in response to such interpretations, as well as to the claims of 'urban sociology', that a powerful Marxist critique of social policy and urban studies has arisen during the last few years. Many such works have been primarily concerned with the nature of the state in capitalist society, including state welfare provision, although a few are direct treatments of housing.[23] One of the more important studies is Manuel Castells' *The Urban Question*, focusing as it does on the French urban experience of the present day.[24]

Castells is primarily concerned to destroy the 'myth of urban culture', and those conservative interpretations of urban life which argue for a cultural experience attached to this ecological form.[25] The writer replaces such views with his own analysis of the urban environment as the point of consumption — as that context necessary for the reproduction of the labour force, and of the productive relations which form the basis of capitalist society. Housing is therefore a crucial element in the maintenance of efficient production and stable social relations, although it is threatened by the same contradictions and conflicts as capitalist production itself.

This analysis is extended to Castells' treatment of the state's role in sustaining both the process and the relations of production, hence the importance of state intervention. John Foster writes of Castells' critique:[26]

the state is seen as the central integrating element of a mode of
production, and one which constantly intervenes to reproduce its
basic preconditions in the face of unfolding contradictions . . . It
responds to, and itself incorporates and expresses, the changing
balance of class power in a social formation . . . not because it acts
as its instrument but because the class itself expresses the structural
ripeness of the system's contradictions.

Such structuralist views of the state have already been attacked by
Thompson and others,[27] but Foster takes the argument against Castells
further. He suggests that Castells' formalistic treatment of urban movements distorts the highly specific and complex situations in which
different struggles occur, and that he virtually reduces class conflict to
effective action within the ambit of the state. The consequence is an
account where, 'class struggle is validated, the balance of class forces
is seen to have been altered, to the extent that policy has been changed'.[28]
We thereby arrive at a position not very different from that of Bowley
and Wilding, with the state acting as the barometer of political pressures
upon it.

Whilst Foster is undoubtedly correct in many of his criticisms, his
own survey of imperial London's slums suffers from necessary trunca-
tion and a failure to systematically relate housing conditions to much
wider market forces.[29] For unless we appreciate the highly specific
situations in which housing is provided and housing struggles occur,
we cannot explain the fragmentary development of housing policy at
both national and local levels.

These contributory factors were no more purely 'national' in
character, any more than they were purely urban in origin. Foster has
emphasised the strategic importance of London developments, whilst
Wilding has shown the significance of rural areas in pre-1914 proposals.[30]
Nor is it possible to reduce housing to a few simple functions, given the
changing context in which it may be constructed, occupied and
struggled over. It is in the dialectical relation between general developments and specific situations, between objective conditions and subjec-
tive experiences, that we must trace the development of housing and
housing policy in these years.[31]

What follows is an attempt to outline the main characteristics of
housing in a capitalist economy and to trace the historical development
of housing investment over the years 1880-1939. It is suggested that the
multi-faceted nature of housing explains its importance to the economy
during these years, and the scale of state intervention required to resolve

those conflicts which economic dislocation produced.

Housing investment and state intervention, 1880-1939

Within the capitalist economy, housing performs a number of vital
functions, indicating the level of general activity as well as generating
fresh investment and enterprise. As a form of investment, housing still
accounted for the largest single share of gross domestic capital formation before 1914, whilst a building boom employed thousands of
workers throughout the country.[32] For the working population, housing
provided the basic shelter and the obvious facilities for the reproduction of the labour force. It thereby formed part of the economic
infrastructure for both industry and agriculture, serving the needs of
local capital as well as constituting a major point of consumption for
the working class. [33]

Despite its parasitic status in both classical and Georgian economics, housing land ranked amongst the most 'real' of all forms of
property and provided a major link between land rents and the rentier
profits from housing and mortgages. [34] Just as important were the
contractual and legal obligations in which the occupation of houses
involved the great majority of working-class tenants, during these
years. Such bonds overlaid the unequal position and power of owner
and tenant in the housing market, whilst legal provisions overlaid the
inequalities of the labour market. [35]

Housing also maintained certain divisions within the working class,
with its gradations of housing standards and areas. Whilst it is important to remember the existence of considerable mobility within the
housing stock and between different areas, there is substantial evidence
for the existence of distinct 'artisan' areas and even 'occupational
communities' of particular skill groups. [36] Whether or not settlement
patterns sustained sectional values and divisions, it is undeniable that
housing formed one of the most powerful supports for bourgeois
hegemony with its principles of individual contract, civil obligations
and political rights attached to the occupation of particular property.[37]
Above all, housing fulfilled a key role in maintaining the economic
and social relations of a class society. Housing and property relations
must therefore be located within the fabric of an economy and society
dominated by the capitalist mode of production.

Like every other industry operating within the market economy, the
building industry depended upon factors, goods and services that were
themselves subject to the pressure of market forces at a number of
different levels. It was from a desire to secure an adequate labour

supply and thereby stabilise the local market, that encouraged so many employers to sponsor housing during the early stages of industrialisation, when the whole economy was passing through its infrastructural stage. Alongside housebuilding went the provision of railways, dockyards and urban amenities to meet the needs of the expanding economy.

Caroline Bedale's essay on Oldham bears out the arguments of Gauldie concerning the early involvement of industrialists in providing housing during the textiles revolution. The case of employer housing on Clydeside during the years 1870-1920 also illustrates the role of private firms in providing accommodation for an expanding regional economy when local builders failed to supply their needs. [38] Such large-scale capital projects were a worthwhile investment as long as the profitability of local industry offset the relatively low returns which could be expected from housing. The importance of local industry and commerce in shaping building activities throughout the nineteenth century helps to account for the regional variations in the national building cycle during these years. [39] In the case of shipbuilding areas, the extreme oscillations of the shipbuilding and housebuilding cycles interacted to produce the eccentric pattern of house construction in regions like Clydeside.

This uncertainty was greatly exacerbated by the organisation of the house building trades themselves. The construction of houses involves practices which are both relatively simple and extremely complex, established often by centuries of tradition and yet dependent on unstable forces of supply and demand. Construction techniques grew out of craft skills and customs not easily displaced or diluted by technical innovation and labour-saving devices. [40] In common with a substantial section of the Edwardian economy, the building industry depended on 'skill intensive' methods of production before 1914, with a high proportion of craftsmen engaged in the labour process. [41]

Such constraints enabled a host of small builders to flourish in the industry, frequently specialising in one or two trades, despite the growth of the Victorian master builders and their powerful foremen. [42] Such small firms could weather the violent movements of the building cycle by operating with few capital overheads and quickly shedding labour in bad times. This itself encouraged the rapid oscillations between low troughs of depression and high waves of frantic speculation, which made life for the workmen so unpredictable. [43] For unlike many other industries, the skilled craftsmen were not effectively organised in the trades and there were constant pressures upon their employers to cut

costs by cheapening and driving the workers, break local rates where
they existed, and scamp jobs whenever possible.

The fortunes of the building industry depended on a complicated
array of supply and demand factors that change according to local,
national and international market conditions. Much of the finance for
the speculative construction continued to come from local capital
markets, as various institutions and individuals advanced credit and
funds to builders and purchasers alike. As the infrastructure of the
British economy was built up during the nineteenth century, so the
building cycles came to reflect the increasing sophistication of the
market economy. The international economy emerged during the later
decades of the century, facilitating the flow of capital, labour and
credit as well as trade of goods and services. Britain became the centrepiece of an international economic system, distributing its massive
resources of goods as well as various factors of production around the
world.[44]

Such a role brought an increasing sophistication of the capital markets, whilst creating the conditions for a series of infrastructural
building cycles overseas. This led to the inverse relationship between
building activities in Britain and America and to the long-term movement of domestic finance capital away from such investments.[45]
Whilst disagreements persist as to the nature and significance of these
long cycles, there is little doubt that the growing importance of the
international economy strongly affected building investments.[46]

The increasing 'perfection' of the British capital markets around the
City of London,[47] allowed the export of capital overseas to increase
steadily after the 1870s reaching a climax before 1914. Only in periods
of financial crisis or generally low interest rates on the London market
did the 'staples' of mortgages, railway bonds and other domestic securities regain their former popularity amongst the investors.[48]

The fact that the London brokers were increasingly geared to
meeting the needs of the foreign borrowers may partly account for the
marked retardation in domestic industrial growth, which continued
throughout the Great Depression and down to 1914.[49] Falling prices
and squeezed profits led to the restriction of industrial expansion
during the Depression years, and the deceleration in the rate of growth
only worsened in the better conditions of the new century.[50] By that
time British financiers and investors were sending a third of all savings
overseas, and it is likely that this massive export of capital weakened
domestic industry still further.[51]

Whether or not the home economy was able to absorb the great amounts of capital it generated in these decades is uncertain, but the realities were that Britain found increasing difficulty in competing with those countries whose industrialisation it was helping to finance through the export of capital, labour and credit. [52] There was a decline in the volume of goods exported and a marked shift towards imperial markets and investment.[53] Where the investment *did* stimulate domestic production, it was usually in those established sectors of the economy such as coal, textiles and shipbuilding rather than more advanced industries.[54]

These trends were to have profound implications for British society and its building industry during these decades. The general impact of overseas investment was to distort the income structure still further, by encouraging the concentration of wealth amongst particular groups of capitalists. Growth of the national income was not to decelarate until the 'climacteric' of the 1890s, but industrial profits had diminished relative to both wages and other forms of income since the 1870s. Both J.A. Hobson and Chiozza Money emphasised the degree to which overseas investment arose from, and in turn encouraged, the concentration of wealth and income in the imperial society of their day, Money estimating an annual income of over £100 million from capital exports before 1914.[55] Recent research on wealth distribution confirms their picture of increasing wealth amongst the financial élite of London's rentier classes, in sharp contrast to the provincial industrial regions.[56]

Such riches were even more starkly contrasted with the condition of the wage-earners in London and elsewhere, as studies of urban life revealed one-third of the population existing below a minimum poverty line. The situation deteriorated after 1896, when the upward climb of real wages during the Great Depression was reversed and wages fell amidst rising profits and increasing rentier investments.[57] It is interesting that Hobson should have cited Rowntree's work in his study of imperialism, for both Rowntree and Pigou went on to identify the real housing problem as 'the general fact of poverty, whereof inadequate housing is merely a manifestation'.[58]

This highlights a crucial element in the paradoxical housing problems before 1914, as insanitation and overcrowding continued despite the housing booms and 'surpluses' of these years. The same social inequalities which made massive rentier investments possible overseas, were preventing working class tenants from presenting an effective housing demand at home. Whilst overseas lending boomed, industrial growth declined, real wages fell, unemployment continued and poverty increased. In response to declining incomes and worsening conditions, many working-class families moved into inferior accommodation or 'doubled up' with their neighbours, thereby exacerbating the problem of overcrowding which formed the main housing blight before the First World War.[59] The fundamental problem was one of underconsumption by those tenants inhabiting privately rented dwellings, unable to pay the increased rents demanded in better accommodation.

There were also difficulties in the distribution and allocation of capital amongst the various rentier groups involved in the provision of housing at this period. Four main elements can be identified: the land-owning rentiers who exacted rent from letting the ground on which houses stood; the financial interests who usually provided a mortgage for those small scale investors purchasing houses; the speculative builders who operated on short-term capital and credit and sold quickly to continue their activities; and the owners themselves, who were most often petty bourgeois savers investing in a few houses. There were tendencies towards the concentration of housing and building interests, as the chapters on Glasgow and the North East indicate, but the predominant pattern seems to have been for a large number of small owners to purchase from an equally large number of small builders.

With the evolution of central capital markets and overseas lending, there seems to have been a long-term trend away from low-interest mortgage bonds by finance capital. Only during the panics and *general* decline in interest rates, as during the 1870s and 1890s booms in building, were there sufficient incentives for owners to purchase houses, and financiers to loan on mortgage bonds.[60] When interest rates rose they carried up mortgage rates, and thereby diminished the margin of profit available to owners and builders.[61] The decline in building activity was often delayed and distorted by the 'stickiness' of rents and the optimism of speculative builders, but the trends acting against the industry finally brought it to a complete halt in the early years of the twentieth century. It was not simply a problem of inadequate demand due to poverty and the maldistribution of income, but also to the profits creamed off the industry by the land and financial rentiers and the movement of large-scale capital out of building.[62]

Such progress in the building industry and the construction cycles could cause tensions not merely between owners and occupants, but also between the different sections of capital involved in housing provision. This is well illustrated in Caroline Bedale's study of housing in Oldham during the nineteenth and early twentieth centuries. The close interdependence of economic expansion and building activity characterised the years before the Great Depression, but thereafter employers responded to increasing competition by intensifying labour exploitation. Industrialists continued to be primarily interested in labour supply and minimum running costs, hence their participation in early housing ventures, whilst the landed groups were determined to maximise their rentier profits.

The rentiers and builders provided housing for the 'better quality' artisans of Oldham in the 1890s boom, but by the next decade the local industry was in stagnation. Since most of the housing was provided during the years of prosperity, the problems of insanitation and overcrowding were not of the same scale as those faced in other British cities. On Clydeside, the inadequacies of tenement and backlands accommodation was clear by the 1880s, as indicated in Seán Damer's chapter on p.73. There were also clear tensions between the large employers, particularly the shipbuilders, who wished to expand along the river front, and the various rentier groups controlling the housing market. Employers faced high rents and inadequate facilities in areas like Clydebank, Greenock, Partick and Govan, making their own overheads and the cost of attracting the necessary workforce heavier in certain localities.[63] This ultimately forced many employers into providing company housing for skilled workers unable to pay inflated rents and unwilling to travel to work without payments.

In each case there were housing movements that drew support from those experiencing the deprivations of the pre-war years. Amongst the Oldham working class there emerged two distinct currents: on one side there were trends towards the increasing incorporation of the more affluent workers who joined building societies, purchased joint stock shares and generally supported the 'urban bourgeoisie'; on the other, there was a strong resistance campaign protesting against overcrowded conditions and inferior standards of accommodation. The latter drew support from amongst the lesser grades of worker and the poorer class of tenant, and it was on their support that the Independent Labour Party depended for their housing campaigns.

In North Shields and Clydeside there was a similar differentiation of skilled and unskilled worker in housing, with the slopes to the river showing a housing stratification in areas of both Tyne and Clyde. On the north east coast the housing campaign of the ILP drew support from the semi-skilled unions, whilst on Clydeside the skilled engineers were prominent in the early party. This may be accounted for by the pressures on the tenement dwellers of Glasgow and district, as described in Damer's essay, with diminishing space and rising rents in many shipbuilding and engineering districts.

Such campaigns must be set within the context of broader industrial

and political developments of these years, as industrial unrest and rank
and file agitations challenged the established leaders of the working
class. Widespread support for the ILP campaigns at local level must be
distinguished from the endorsement of parliamentary democracy. In
fact, these years saw the genesis of those 'syndicalist' agitations which
came to light during the First World War, not only at Singers of Clydebank but at other localities throughout the country. As Sydney Buxton
told the Cabinet in 1912:[64]

> There are two clear features of the present industrial position which
> also make for unrest.
>   The first is the change for the worse which has come over the
> Trade Union movement in respect of the attitude of the men
> towards their leaders and towards agreements . . .
>   The second feature is the almost complete collapse of the Labour
> Party in the House as an effective influence in labour disputes . . .
> Their elimination is a distinct loss to industrial peace.

Such memoranda as Buxton and Askwith submitted, insisted on the
strategic importance of rank and file action amongst the railwaymen,
miners and transport workers. The support for the ILP and its housing
campaigns amongst such workers testifies rather to the local appeal and
militant campaigns of the Party, than to the deferential politics of the
workforce in Edwardian Britain.

It is in the light of these economic contradictions, industrial campaigns and political agitations, that we must trace the moves towards
greater state intervention in the housing question. State regulation
began to affect housing provision from the 1870s, as the Bank of
England (with Treasury support) responded to the monetary crises by
raising its lending rate in London.[65] Such action was followed by
periodic intervention over the longer term whenever infrastructural
upswings overseas, and other demands on investments, led to a dangerous loss of gold at the City. In order to protect the gold standard and
the whole system of multi-lateral payments, the increase in interest
rates was introduced as a means of attracting funds back to Britain.[66]
In certain situations this directed investment into mortgages, but rising
interest also cut into rentier profits for the owner and after 1890 there
seems to have been a progressive diminution in the owners' margins.[67]
This also contributed to the transfer of resources away from domestic
building before 1914, possibly reflecting the increased power of financiers' interests upon the Bank and the overriding concern with a stable

monetary system.

Much more direct influences upon housing came through the social policies pursued by governments from the 1880s. Damer's essay stresses the significance of the Royal Commission on Housing, appointed amidst the growing unrest and class mobilisation of that decade. The most noticeable consequence was the important Housing Act of 1890, providing for the construction of housing by local authorities on a permissory and utilitarian basis.[68] It is perhaps fitting that the Unionists should have supported housing reforms before 1914, as the representatives of the great landed and financial interests of London and elsewhere. They were willing to campaign for any measures which would shift the burden of housing on to ratepayers and taxpayers — a reasonable ransom for the privileges of imperial wealth and social stability. For both the critics and supporters of imperialism were sensitive to the needs of national efficiency and social order, whether in the metropolis or the industrial centres around the country. J.A. Hobson commented in his own work:[69]

> Imperialism is the fruit of this false economy; 'social reform' is its remedy. The primary purpose of 'social reform' . . . is to raise the wholesome standard of private and public consumption for a nation, so as to enable the nation to live up to its highest standard of production.

The consequences of overcommitment to foreign and imperial investment whilst neglecting national manpower had been demonstrated during the Boer War, when military defeats convinced many politicians of the need for an effective social reform platform.[70] Although the Unionist crusade for social imperialism linked to tariff reform failed in 1906, many of their proposals were implemented under the Liberal administration. The state came to intervene not only in social reform, but in industry and the financial questions concerned with national income distribution during this period.

Industrial arbitration and conciliation had been provided since the 1890s, and had provided the owners with a valuable means of containing unrest.[71] After 1907 however, militant action began to create serious problems in industries such as mining, forcing the state to regulate the hours, wages and conditions of men employed in the pits. The Cabinet even considered the suggestions that compulsory arbitration and nationalisation should be introduced as means of resolving the unrest.[72]

The Finance Act of 1909, and the social legislation which followed it,

was partly a response to the same unrest in industry and society, for as
Askwith informed the Cabinet, all 'classes are seeking to secure some of
the amenities of existence, and are becoming more impatient of the
bare struggle for a livelihood'.[73] The internal challenges to the imperial
society were just as dangerous as its external challenges, whether from
Germany or subject territories. Gradually, the state was taking responsibility for the casualties of the imperial economy, or as the Labour
paper *Forward* said in 1914:[74]

> The Insurance Act is forcing upon the State the problems of pov-
> erty, of casual labour, of under-employment. For the first time the
> State has assumed a certain direct responsibility in regard to these
> questions, such obligations will be the starting point of the social
> legislation of tomorrow.

Each of these areas of reform – industry, finance and social insurance – was related to the pre-war housing movements in Britain. It was
in the strike-torn mining industry, especially the Scottish fields, that
housing unrest was most prevalent and best organised before 1914.
Dissatisfaction at company housing and colliery settlements became so
powerful that the Asquith government felt compelled to appoint a
Royal Commission to investigate the whole subject of Scottish housing from 1911. This Commission did not report until 1917, but its findings were to influence the post-war housing legislation that greatly extended state responsibility.[75]

On the other hand, the Finance Act of 1909 failed to make any
serious impact on income distribution and only succeeded in encouraging the drift away from low-interest mortgage investment into the
safer or more lucrative securities.[76] The taxes on 'unearned income' as
a factor in stifling housing investment should not be exaggerated, but
it certainly did little to alleviate the building famine of these years.
Whilst financial measures tended to discourage construction, social
legislation suggested ways in which some of the worst problems and
shortages might be resolved. It is in this context of increasing problems
and tensions that the moves towards state subsidies should be viewed,
with a groundswell of rank and file militancy in both industry and political organisations throughout the country. By posing fundamental
social problems as capable of political solution, the state had itself
helped to politicise the housing question and to encourage demands
for substantial intervention by government.

The outbreak of war in 1914 was to radically change the nature of the housing problem, and the character of class struggle in British society. Industrial conflicts and housing struggles were to remain largely localised in organisation and methods of resistance, but their objectives and their power for dislocation were considerably greater. It was the *strategic* importance of the housing unrest on Clydeside, in Belfast, Birmingham, London and elsewhere, that proved their greatest strength since the tenants and workers effectively threatened the whole war machine by 1915.

The two essays on Glasgow indicate the vulnerability of the state in Scotland at this time, and the government responded to industrial disturbances and low output by passing the Munitions Acts of 1915. Opposition to dilution, wage restraint and employment conditions now turned against the state as well as the employers, and by the Autumn there occured the fusion of tenants' and workers' organisations — again at the level of vigilance committees and local Trade Councils — that ultimately defeated the forces of coercion.

Whether the Rent and Mortgage Interest Restriction Act signified a shift in the balance of class forces in the state, or merely restricted class action to state reforms, is one of the differences between the two chapters about which the reader must decide. What is clear, is that the act gave only temporary respite both for the besieged owners and the suffering tenants during the war. It ensured that fresh investment avoided mortgages and housing in favour of industrial securities or the government's own War Loan stock. Nor did the legislation quell the housing unrest, which the Commissioners on Industrial Unrest reported during 1917.[77] In the same year, the Royal Commission appointed in 1912 to investigate Scottish housing conditions reported, emphasising the deterioration of the situation since 1914. The Majority Report stated that:[78]

In the developments that have been forced on us by the war, one truth has been made abundantly clear: the housing of the industrial workers can no longer be regarded as a problem merely for the localities; it is essentially a question of national interest and must be dealt with from the national standpoint.

With the upsurge of militancy during 1917-18, a powerful movement for nationalisation and workshop control developed in a range of industries. One of the key areas of conflict was the Scottish coalfields, where the peacetime discontent had precipitated the appointment of the Ballantyne Commission.[79] Amongst the major grievances placed before the Sankey Commission later, and one of the most telling argu-

ments in favour of nationalisation, was the condition of miner's housing.[80] The coalowners could only reply that the Ballantyne Report had
committed the state to housing the working class, and it was the government which should 'at once take steps to make good the housing
shortage and . . . improve the housing conditions'.[81] Scottish coal masters not only accepted the need for state intervention, but went on to
claim that the miners' criticisms, 'although intended to be, and accepted as, an indictment of the private management of the mining industry', were really 'an indictment of the public management by the State
of the Housing problem'.[82] As in 1915 therefore, the large employers
were unwilling to accept any responsibility for bad housing conditions
and were anxious that state action should alleviate the unrest that
threatened the whole industry. Only by acting on this front could the
much more serious campaign for nationalisation and workshop control
be weakened.

The Royal Commission Report of 1917 had in fact recommended
that state action must be forthcoming, but there were dangers inherent
in the granting to central or local government sole responsibility for
housing.[83] They suggested therefore, that the local authorities should
be the 'executive authorities for the realisation of the national policy',
whilst funding should come from a new central department sensitive to
the needs and views of the Treasury.[84] The latter was to have a large
say in the future of state housing reforms, and should have 'definite
control over all capital outlays' in order to protect national finances.[85]

In 1919, as industrial and social disturbances reached fresh peaks,
the government passed Addison's legislation creating the Ministry of
Health and providing for central housing subsidies.[86] The same politician
had been responsible for various other reconstruction projects, such as
Whitley Councils, and was eminently suited for dealing with the difficult post-war conditions. Whilst agreeing with Sean Damer's comment
on the radical departure which the Addison Housing Act represented, it is
important to stress the limitations which it placed on local authorities and
initiatives by giving central administration such a powerful influence on
policy.

Although state intervention made a major contribution to housing
provision in the inter-war years, it could not insulate the industry from
the market forces which had influenced its previous history so dramatically. The First World War had seen the virtual collapse of private
house building, particularly after the Rent and Mortgage Restriction
Act of 1915, as funds flooded into domestic and state securities and
builders faced rising costs of labour, capital and materials. Only the

penalties imposed by the legislation upon mortgage sales and transactions prevented the ruin of the owners and the various trusts and individuals holding mortgage bonds. The state's own need for capital had driven up the rates of interest and so created many of the pressures on mortgage rates, owners, and tenants, that had led to the crisis of 1915. By restricting interest and rents it merely secured its further commitment to an industry which could not survive on the demand generated by working-class tenants. Only by further action could the government liberate housing from the manifold contradictions which its past action had helped to create, and it is in this light that the Addison Act becomes significant.

The economic consequences of the peace were to be almost as disastrous for private building as those of war, once the deterioration in conditions set in during 1921. After a brief post-war boom, investment began to flow overseas and government securities once again, and with the spread of financial uncertainty the City made a determined campaign for a return to the gold standard, along with drastic cuts in public expenditure.[87] At the same time, the over-expansion of the boom years had created serious overcapacity in British industry, as well as concentrating industrial wealth and power in fewer hands.[88] These difficulties were only gradually approached during the 1920s when employers, financiers and key officials projected substantial rationalisation of production in the heavier industries.

Although there emerged a closer relationship between industry, finance capital, and Bank officials as a consequence of this, the tensions between the different sections of capital — which had been evident at both national and local level before 1914 — continued to appear. On the one side investors were maximising returns from domestic, foreign and government securities and investments, whilst safeguarding their capital. On the other, the industrialists were concerned to improve national efficiency whilst maintaining a viable infrastructure in those traditional centres of industry and the newer areas of production. The City elements were generally in favour of high interest rates, the return to gold and tight control of state budgeting, whilst industry would clearly benefit from low rates and cheap exports. When the return to gold was attempted, however, it led to a serious loss of both reserves and confidence.[89]

These developments directly affected the building industry and the capacity of the state to intervene in the provision of housing. High interest rates combined with post-war increases in labour and materials costs to weigh down the building revival, and only after 1921 was the situation to change substantially.[90] Growing depression and unemployment allowed the builders to reduce costs and intensify labour exploitation within the industry.[91] In those areas of expansion, benefiting both salaried and skilled groups in many parts of south England and the Midlands, a distinct revival began. But it was not until the great monetary crisis of 1931 and its aftermath, that the housing industry was really liberated from many of its post-war restraints. Cheaper money was assured as Britain left the gold standard and the government carried through the 'great conversion' of lowering interest rates on state securities and sent massive funds pouring into the building societies and thereby fuelling the great housing boom of the 1930s.[92]

As the various supply factors began to favour the industry, demand for building came from the growing towns in the south which were exploiting the new technology and consumer industries of the inter-war period. Their affluence was shared by the black-coated and white-collar grades enjoying the advantages of security from unemployment and a stable income during years of falling prices. It was from these groups of affluent workers that the demand for privately owned dwellings came, aided by the agency of the building societies. For the first time really, the housing industry began to construct very large numbers of private houses for owner occupation, as the societies' growing funds made mortgages easily available. There were some signs of a revival in privately rented accommodation during the 1930s, but this was almost eclipsed by the waves of home ownership.[93]

This prosperity arrived only gradually, however, and never reached certain regions of Britain during rhe inter-war Depression. Those established centres of heavy industry, particularly in the North and Scotland, declined into stagnant pools of depression and unemployment until rearmament finally salvaged them. The whole environment deteriorated along with the shipyards, engine shops and steelworks on the shores of the Tyne and Clyde, which became industrial backwaters after decades of rapid growth. It was these areas which saw only a stunted growth of building, and where state subsidies to both local authorities and private builders was so critical after 1919.[94] The government could not allow the strategic centres of heavy industrial production, and the 'human capital' manning the works, to collapse beyond repair. Nor were the powerful industrialists such as Lithgow willing to accept the serious debilitation of their interests and infrastructure, without some effort by the state to resolve their difficulties. They were joined in their concern for preservation of older areas by those building interests involved, and their financial supporters.

There were also the political implications of housing reform to consider, and the consequences of a return to unregulated market conditions. The years 1914-19 demonstrated the central importance of the housing issue in working-class struggles for the improvement of conditions, nationalisation of industry, and local control of production and services. During this period of sharpened class-consciousness, the strategies of industrial organisation and direct action were highly effective. This could be combined, after the arrival of mass democracy in 1918, with formal political activity at both national and local level.

Amongst those workers most active in the housing campaigns of the post-war years were the skilled workers, who had experienced a decline in their differentials and a diminution in trade sectionalism during the First World War. The erosion of their relatively priviliged position, and the articulation of demands for rank and file control, pushed them into the leadership of the local housing campaigns which were usually organised by the ILP. Rent strikes continued at Glasgow, Clydebank and elsewhere during the 1920s, as the government sought to relax rent controls without protecting tenants against scarcity increases.

After 1921 the impetus for offensive action had passed in both industry and localities, as the miners (strongest campaigners for housing reform during the previous decade) faced isolation and defeat. Rising unemployment placed workers and tenants on the defensive, with the focus of class struggle shifting to the local and national elections. Victories in the latter enabled the Labour Party to pass the Wheatley legislation of 1924, and to forestall the cuts intended by the Tories in 1929. Yet the financial crisis of 1930 to 1931 was to shatter the parliamentary party as effectively as the General Strike had destroyed the challenge of direct action. In this situation, local resistance through rent strikes, municipal government and judicial contests, became more significant. Through Labour control in cities like Glasgow, or the Communist-dominated 'Little Moscows' in the more isolated communities like Leven and Chopwell, the working class could maintain a measure of control over their housing and other social conditions.[95]

It is out of this complex interplay of economic and social forces, evident at both national and local level, that housing legislation emerged during these years. After 1921 the minor housing boom stimulated by the Addison Act began to deflate, and the Chamberlain measure of 1923 failed to resuscitate private enterprise. Whilst the Wheatley Act was in many respects a victory for Labour's housing platform, local authorities continued to borrow at high interest rates on the capital market — despite the 1920 Conference resolution of the Party for low-

interest loans to the authorities.[96] Labour governments encouraged
building interests by managing subsidies efficiently, during this transition period of uncertainty and instability.

The chapters on Leeds, North Shields and Manchester illustrate these
general themes as well as the considerable differences between localities. All of the studies are set in the industrial north of England and
Scotland, which experienced the greatest problems in replacing existing
stock and encouraging fresh building. Each town saw, along with Oldham and Clydeside, the genesis of a housing movement before and during the First World War, despite their contrasting conditions.

Robert Finnigan's essay on Leeds housing shows how the Conservative administration collaborated with the Labour Party in establishing a
housing committee to supervise the construction of a projected 6,000
dwellings under the Addison Act. Despite the bitter controversies which
the implementation of the legislation and the rents issue caused in post-
war Leeds, the local authorities had succeeded in providing a mere 200
dwellings by 1921. After the initial fears of social unrest and rent
strikes had passed, the Tories made only limited moves towards meeting
local needs and gave only qualified support to Chamberlain's initiative of
1923. The local authority made relatively little use of the measures introduced by 1925, and it was not until Labour's local victory of 1928
that rapid progress was made towards improving the city's housing
stock (almost 60 per cent of which was back-to-back accommodation).
The experience of Leeds indicates the success with which local Conservatism could mobilise building interests, lower middle-class groups and
even working-class tenants on issues such as differential rents, compensation and the reconditioning of slums. To this extent it contrasts sharply with the progress of Manchester under the enlightened Conservatism discussed below.

Although the Tory propaganda in Leeds exploited the popular anti-
pathy to the Poor Law by linking it with a 'means test' of differential
rents, this cannot be the whole answer. They were also able to incorporate greater numbers of people into the propertied camp by encouraging owner-occupation amongst the ratepayers, and thereby 'making
Tories'. This combination of material acquisition and ideological fragmentation allowed the party of reaction to regain control of Leeds during the early 1930s, reflecting broader divisions in British society.

The case of North Shields is discussed by David Byrne, who argues
convincingly for the existence of an identifiable 'urban bourgeoisie' in
that area, made up of a variety of propertied, building, and building
society interests. This group had been responsible for the pre-war

housing, which had sharply differentiated working-class tenants between the better housing of skilled artisans and those occupying the base of the housing pyramid. It was the inadequacies of the latter accommodation which had sustained the ILP's housing campaign, that led to the drafting of the Balkwell blueprint in 1913.

The post-Addison period saw the dilution of housing standards at North Shields, and the entrenchment of urban interests as the local authorities sold off developed land at very cheap rates, and subsidised over two-thirds of private sector building during the later 1920s. At the same time the rent levels and preference controls of the local authorities encouraged the fresh pattern of segregation between white collar and affluent workers inhabiting the good quality Balkwell estate, and the poorer groups left to rent the inferior dwellings built during the stringent conditions of the thirties. Whilst some 'filtering up' of lesser groups did occur, the predominant trends towards differentiation confirmed those in private dwellings and reproduced the ideological values attached to such accommodation. Similar points are made in Bedale's investigation of Oldham's housing, and suggest the existence of national trends within the allocation of local government housing.

Jennifer Dale's essay discusses the general issues of local-central relations during the inter-war years, but concentrates upon the example of Manchester as an area for research. She shows that the Manchester Conservatives, operating from a broader industrial base and with a much greater diversity of economic and financial interests than the urban bourgeoisie of Oldham, North Shields and Leeds, pursued an enlightened and persistently progressive housing policy through much of the inter-war period. Standards were compromised during the thirties, but only after negotiation between local and central Conservative administrations.

In highlighting the importance of a dynamic civic gospel at Manchester, Dale indicates the complex and creative role of ideology in effective housing administration. It is only by recognising the importance of such enlightened perceptions of class interests, that we can adequately explain the legislation of 1890 and 1935. Within specific situations, such as Leeds in the 1930s, the Tories could obstruct progressive reforms but more powerful groups realised the benefits of social equipoise and negotiated concession.

The political consequences of gradualist reform was remarkably similar in each locale, despite the differences in relative strength of the parties at each. In the case of North Shields the ILP's own ranks were colonised by the white-collar groups, strong in technical expertise and professional ability, but reluctant to engage in militant action and increasingly concerned with the administrative paraphenalia of housing provision. In Leeds the reformers were led by an evangelical minister and strongly committed to radical action, but enjoyed power only intermittently and were effectively contained by the forces of reaction. In Manchester the Conservatives were progressive enough to ensure that Labour never presented a serious alternative programme, and were thereby able to stifle substantial criticism of their policies. Only in Glasgow did Labour seize and hold power from 1931, introducing their own housing programme to reinforce the political machine which was rapidly established in the city.

Whether defeated and fragmented by opposition, excluded by moderate initiatives, or incorporated within the fabric of local government, Labour did not present the same threat after 1931 that it had previously. The growing affluence of white-collar and new industrial grades, expressed in home ownership and improved accommodation, helps to account for the stabilisation of class relations during the 1930s. Where serious problems of insanitation and overcrowding persisted was in the older industrial areas suffering unemployment and lower incomes.

It is quite true, as Bowley points out, that the major legislation of 1935 (dealing specifically with overcrowding and compelling local authorities to operate minimum standards) came when the more affluent groups had been catered for. But its implementation must be viewed in the light of accelerating industrial revival, the strategic importance of these areas for rearmament, and the pressures from building and financial interests to encourage 'safe' expansion of the economy. After 1936 the private housing boom began to subside, and its significance as an economic stimulant meant that to allow deflation of the boom might throw the whole system into recession. The effective attack on cancerous housing conditions in areas like Clydeside, Tyneside and Lancashire was not only advisable in the late 1930s, it was politically and economically necessary. This is not to deny the importance of ideology, but to suggest that the arrival of radical reform for those who had been the worst housed for decades, was not merely due to the belated appearance of a British public conscience.

This ultimately leads us back to an investigation of the nature of state policy, and the forces which lead to changes in the direction of policy formulation and implementation. Each of the contributors make their underlying assumptions concerning the nature of the state fairly clear in their chapters, and it is unnecessary to repeat them here. Certain themes do emerge from the essays, however, which raise many questions concerning the theoretical concepts and methods of analysis currently being used in the study of housing development. Firstly, it is clear that any study of housing simply in terms of neutral pragmatic responses by either owners or government to imposed conditions, is inadequate and simplistic. History may be written by experts, administrators and academics, but it is not made by them. On the other hand, to see housing as the blunt instrument for the reproduction of labour and the relations of production, is equally crude and mechanistic. The detailed study of Oldham's property relations indicates how complex and fluid were house ownership and property control.

These property relations must be set in the broader context of an international market economy, which created tensions and contradictions between different sections of capital as well as between producers and consumers in the housing market. Increasing housing difficulties and the imbalance between oversupply and underconsumption, was as much a product of an imperial economy and society as was the massive poverty uncovered by Booth and Rowntree.

The close relationship between the rise of industrial, political and housing unrest before 1914, testifies to the importance of housing in class relations and points to the necessity for state intervention. But the actual shape which this intervention took was determined by the events and conflicts of 1914 to 1919, and not by the imperatives of administrative growth or rational pragmatism. Direct action in rent strikes and housing resistance was as great a challenge to propertied rights, as the rank and file militancy of these years. When they fused, as they did in 1915 and threatened to do during 1919-21, labour organisations could threaten the state itself.

To this extent, Castells is surely correct in his interpretation of 'urban revolution', with the unification of working people at the points of production and consumption. Only his formalistic account of class struggle and state action restricts and distorts his study of housing struggles. In Castells, as Foster comments:[97]

We lose the critical interplay between capitalism's economic law of motion — its recurring need to reduce the share of the product received by labour — and the particular cultural, political and ideological identities which specific historical levels of consumption sustain.

Only by examining these specific situations, as these contributions attempt to do, can we appreciate the historical significance of housing conflicts and legislation.

The second major difficulty with such a critique, is its restriction of housing struggles to changes in the 'balance of class forces' within the state. To do this, however many levels we give the state, is to limit effective class action to those shifts in social policy which can be construed as advances or retreats by the working class.[98] The experiences of the years 1880 to 1939, show that direct action was taken before state action. Although housing reforms may have been valuable concessions to the tenants, they did nothing in themselves to change the composition or the character of state power. Indeed, some of the most important measures were introduced by Conservatives in periods of relative stability. Perhaps the most dangerous movements were those which derived from local organisation, and which threatened to carry through direct action in both industry and locality at a time of increasing class-consciousness.

Such questions are only raised by these essays as a possible basis for further research. Each of the contributors is still actively engaged in the study of housing, and hopes to sustain these preliminary essays with further discussions.

Notes

1. J.R. Hay, *The Development of the British Welfare State, 1880-1975* (Edward Arnold, London, 1978), pp. 1-12.

2. S.D. Chapman, (ed.), *The History of Working Class Housing* (David & Charles, Newton Abbot, 1971); Marion Bowley, *Housing and the State, 1919-1944* (George Allen & Unwin, London, 1966); J.B. Cullingworth, *Housing and Local Government in England and Wales* (George Allen & Unwin, London, 1966).

3. Excellent surveys of building cycles are found in J. Parry Lewis, *Building Cycles and Britain's Growth* (Macmillan, London, 1965); and A.K. Cairncross, *Home and Foreign Investment, 1870-1913* (CUP, Cambridge, 1953).

4. Asa Briggs, 'The History of Changing Approaches to Social Welfare', in E.W. Martin, (ed.), *Comparative Development in Social Welfare* (George Allen & Unwin, London, 1972), p. 11.

5. H. Stuart Hughes, *Consciousness and Society* (MacGibbon & Kee, St Albans, 1967), emphasises the revolt against positivism also, and the critique of Marxism developed from 1890s. See p. 41 and ch. 3.

6. J.R. Hay, *The Origins of the Liberal Welfare Reforms, 1906-1914* (Macmillan, London, 1975), for discussion.

7. Briggs, 'The History of Changing Approaches to Social Welfare'.

8. Robert Pinker, *Social Theory and Social Policy* (Heinemann, London, 1971), p. 9.

9. See Bernard Bosanquet, *The Philosophical Theory of the State* (Macmillan, London, 1902), pp. xxxi-xxxix, pp. 191-9, for contemporary discussion of state policy.

10. Asa Briggs, 'The Welfare State in Historical Perspective', *Archives Européennes de Sociologie*, 2 (1961) for critique of evolutionism. Derek Fraser, *The Evolution*

of the British Welfare State (Macmillan, London, 1973), p. 1, argues for an analysis of social policy development as 'an erratic and pragmatic response of government and people to the practical individual and community problems of an industrialised society'.

11. John Vincent, 'Welfare State Pioneer', *The Observer* 13.11.1977, a review of Jose Harris's biography of William Beveridge; cf. J.R. Hay, *Social History* (1978).

12. See Pat Thane (ed.), *The Origins of British Social Policy* (Croom Helm, London, 1978), for discussion.

13. Marion Bowley, *Housing and the State*.

14. Ibid., pp. 34-7.

15. Ibid., pp. 185-6.

16. Ibid., pp. 132-3, 182-3.

17. Ibid., pp. 190-3.

18. Paul Wilding, 'The Genesis of the Ministry of Health', *Public Administration*, vol. 45 (1967); and 'Towards Exchequer Subsidies for Housing 1906-1914', *Economic and Social Administration*, vol. 6, no. 1 (1972).

19. Wilding, 'Towards Exchequer Subsidies' (1972) writes that the proposals and initiatives of 1909-13 'confirm and substantiate the evidence of widespread dissatisfaction with the 1909 Act, and they make the legislation of 1919 and the granting of Exchequer subsidies for housing look much less radical and much more a product of the incrementalism which is the most obvious characteristic of the development of housing policy in this country', pp. 15-16.

20. Ibid., p. 3.

21. Ibid., p. 15 on Boscawen's Bill.

22. Ibid., p. 10.

23. Michael Barratt Brown, 'The Welfare State in Britain', *The Socialist Register* (Merlin, London, 1971), pp. 185-223, is one good example.

24. Manuel Castells, *The Urban Question: A Marxist Approach*, trans. Sheridan (Edward Arnold, London, 1976).

25. Ibid., p. 81, where Castells writes: 'Now it is this fusion-confusion, between the connotation of a certain ecological form and the assignment of a specific cultural content that is at the root of the whole problematic of urban culture.'

26. John Foster, 'How imperial London preserved its slums', *Regional Research*, Book Reviews (1979), p. 658.

27. E.P. Thompson, *The Poverty of Theory* (Merlin, London, 1978); and 'Recovering the Libertarian Tradition', *The Leveller*, no. 22 (January 1979), p. 21, 'Class struggle does not happen because of the existence of classes but, on the contrary, it is because people commence to struggle in a class way that then one can begin to talk about class formations. That is not to say that there aren't objective reasons within production relations why people define their interests in class ways.'

28. Foster, 'How imperial London preserved its slums', p. 659.

29. Ibid., p. 653 where Foster comments that, 'it is necessary to conceive the wider social forces which link a particular housing market to the development of society at large'.

30. Ibid; Wilding (1972), p. 7.

31. See Georg Lukacs, *History and Class Consciousness* (Merlin, London, 1971), p. 3, criticism of Engels conception of the dialectic, that 'he does not even mention the most vital interaction, namely the *dialectical relation between subject and object in the historical process*'.

32. A.K. Cairncross, *Home and Foreign Investment*, p. 123; C.H. Feinstein, 'Income and Investment in the United Kingdom, 1856-1914', *Economic Journal*, vol. 71 (1961), p. 368.

33. See Lady Bell, *At the Works: A Study of a Manufacturing Town* (Edward Arnold, London, 1907), p. 3, for a contemporary account.

34. H.W. Singer, 'An index of urban land rents and house rents in England and Wales, 1845-1913', *Econometrica*, vol. 9 (1941), pp. 223-8.

35. See Keith Burgess, *The Origins of British Industrial Relations* (Croom Helm, London, 1975), pp. iii-iv, and in general for this argument in context of nineteenth-century industrial conflict.

36. R.Q. Gray, 'Styles of Life, the "Labour Aristocracy" and Class Relations in later Nineteenth-Century Edinburgh', *International Review of Social History*, vol. XVIII (1973), pp. 442-3.

37. See H.F. Moorhouse, 'The Political Incorporation of the British Working Class', *Sociology*, vol. VII, no. 3 (1973), pp. 341-3, for a discussion of 'incorporation' thesis.

38. Joseph Melling, Employers, Labour and the Glasgow Housing Market, 1880-1920', SSRC Conference paper, Glasgow (May 1978).

39. S.B. Saul, 'House Building in England, 1890-1914', *Economic History Review*, vol. XV (1962), pp. 120-3; Parry Lewis, *Building Cycles and Britain's Growth*, pp. 106-7.

40. Raphael Samuel, 'The Workshop of the World: Steam Power and Hand Technology in mid-Victorian Britain', *History Workshop*, no. 3 (Spring 1977), p. 14; Burgess, *The Origins of British Industrial Relations*, pp. 86-97.

41. C.K. Harley, 'Skilled Labour and the Choice of Technique in Edwardian Industry', *Explorations in Economic History*, vol. XI (1974), p. 404.

42. E.W. Cooney, 'The Origins of the Victorian Master Builders', *Economic History Review*, vol. VIII (1955-6), p. 170; Robert Tressell, *The Ragged Trousered Philanthropists* (Panther, St Albans, 1977), pp. 31-2 for foremen.

43. Saul, 'House Building in England, 1890-1914', p. 123.

44. Brinley Thomas, 'Demographic determinants of British and American building cycles, 1870-1913', in Donald N. McCloskey (ed.), *Essays on a Mature Economy* (Princeton UP, Princeton, NJ, 1971), p. 58; and H.J. Habakkuk, 'Fluctuations in House-Building in Britain and the United States' in A.R. Hall (ed.), *The Export of Capital from Britain, 1870-1914*, (Methuen, London, 1968), p. 108.

45. Parry Lewis, *Building Cycles and Britain's Growth*, pp. 106-7; Saul, 'House Building in England', p. 120.

46. Habakkuk, 'Fluctuations in House-Building', pp. 107-11; Brinley Thomas, 'Demographic determinants', p. 49; P.L. Cottrell, *British Overseas Investment in the Nineteenth Century* (Macmillan, London, 1975), p. 60, for general survey of debate.

47. Cottrell, *British Overseas Investment*.

48. S.B. Saul, *The Myth of the Great Depression* (Macmillan, London, 1968), p. 40; Saul, 'House Huilding in England', p. 130.

49. Saul, *The Myth of the Great Depression*, p. 39; cf. D.N. McCloskey, 'Did Victorian Britain Fail?' *Economic History Review*, vol. XXIII, no. 3 (December 1970), pp. 446-8.

50. Saul, *The Myth of the Great Depression*, pp. 42-53 for discussion of profits.

51. W.P. Kennedy, 'Foreign Investment, Trade and Growth in the United Kingdom, 1870-1913', *Explorations in Economic History*, vol. XI (1974) p. 434; cf. McCloskey, 'Did Victorian Britain Fail?' pp. 451-5.

52. Kennedy, *Foreign Investment*, p. 435 for argument on savings.

53. Ibid., p. 429; Saul, *The Myth of the Great Depression*, pp. 49-50; cf. McCloskey, 'Did Victorian Britain Fail?' p. 448.

54. Kennedy, *Foreign Investment*, p. 426.

55. J.A. Hobson, *Imperialism: A Study* (Constable, London, 1905), pp. 44,

75-6, 83-5; Chiozza Money, *Poverty and Riches* (Constable, London, 1907), pp. 146-7; cf. C.K. Hobson, *The Export of Capital* (Constable, London, 1914), p. xvi.

56. W.D. Rubinstein, 'The Victorian Middle Classes: Wealth, Occupation and Geography', *Economic History Review*, vol. XXX, 4 (1977). See Cairncross, *Home and Foreign Investment*, p. 123; and C.H. Feinstein, 'Income and Investment in the United Kingdom, 1856-1914', *Economic Journal*, vol. LXXI (1961), p. 368, for economic background.

57. Chiozza Money, *Poverty and Riches*, p. 146; Feinstein, 'Income and Investment', on relative significance of profit in national income.

58. J.A. Hobson, *Imperialism*, pp. 76-7; Pigou, 'Some Aspects of the Housing Problem' in Seebohm Rowntree and A.C. Pigou, *Housing: The Warburton Lectures* (Manchester University Press, 1914), pp. 54-5.

59. For rent levels see H.W. Singer, 'An index of urban land rents', p. 228; and Robert Baird, 'Housing' chapter in A.K. Cairncross, *The Scottish Economy* (CUP, 1954), p. 228. For overcrowding, Saul, 'House Building in England', p. 130; Pigou, 'Some Aspects of the Housing Problem', p. 54; and John Butt, Glasgow Housing, 1900-1939' in Ian MacDougall (ed.), *Essays in Scottish Labour History* (John Donald, Edinburgh, 1978), p. 5 of draft. All give some comparison of English and Scottish experience.

60. Saul, 'House Building in England'.

61. Ibid., p. 131; Cairncross, *Home and Foreign Investment* for discussion.

62. Singer, 'An index of urban land rents', p. 225.

63. Melling, 'Company Housing and Company Welfare Policy, 1880-1920', (mimeo, University of Glasgow 1976).

64. Public Record Office, CAB 37 110, 'Memorandum on Industrial Unrest' by Sydney Buxton, 13.4.1912, pp. 4-5.

65. Parry Lewis, *Building Cycles and Britain's Growth*, p. 109.

66. C.K. Hobson, *The Export of Capital*, pp. xv-xviii; Brinley Thomas, 'Demographic determinants', p. 60; Cottrell, *British Overseas Investment in the Nineteenth Century*, p. 28.

67. Kennedy, 'Foreign Investment, Trade and Growth', p. 435.

68. Laurence Gomme, *Principles of Local Government* (Constable, London, 1897), pp. 1-2 defined local government as elected independently of central authorities, by persons 'qualified resident, or having property, in certain localities ... formed by communities having common interests and common history'. This was a fairly typical view of nineteenth-century local authorities' powers.

69. J.A. Hobson, *Imperialism*, pp. 77-8.

70. G.R. Searle, *The Quest for National Efficiency* (Blackwell, Oxford, 1973); Roy Hay, 'Employers and social policy in Britain: the evolution of welfare legislation, 1905-14', *Social History* (1977).

71. Roger Davidson, 'The Board of Trade and Industrial Relations 1896-1914', *The Historical Journal*, vol. XXI, 3 (1978), p. 380, which indicates the context in which individuals like Buxton were operating.

72. Public Record Office, CAB 37 110, Buxton Memorandum, pp. 5-6.

73. Public Record Office, CAB 37 107, G.R. Askwith, 'Memorandum on the Present Unrest in the Labour World', 25.7.1911, p. 4.

74. *Forward*, 14.3.1914.

75. *Report of the Royal Commission on the Housing of the Industrial Population in Scotland, Rural and Urban*, Cd. 8731, paras 1932, 2223-30 for the Commission's own account of its origins — which it largely attributes to mining unrest.

76. Cd. 8731, *Minority Report*, para. 84; F.E. Fremantle, *The Housing of the Nation* (Philip Allan, 1925), pp. 22-3; Wilding, 'Towards Exchequer Subsidies',

p. 14. All discuss impact of finance legislation.

77. *Report of the Commission of Enquiry into Industrial Unrest*, no. 8 Division: Scotland. Cd. 8669, para 8.

78. Cd. 8731, para 2203.

79. Cd. 8731, para 1938 and *passim*.

80. Scottish Coal Masters' Association, Scottish Record Office, CB 7 5/40 file on housing.

81. Cd. 8731, para 1938. The Commission itself accepted urgent necessity of state intervention. It was this which SCMA was referring to.

82. CB 7 5/40, 'Notes and Suggestions'.

83. Cd. 8731, para 1938.

84. Cd. 8731, paras 2203, 2222 (4).

85. Cd. 8731, para 2220.

86. Frank Honigsbaum, *The Struggle for the Ministry of Health*, Occasional Papers on Social Administration, no. 37 (1970), pp. 52-3; Bentley B. Gilbert, *British Social Policy 1914 – 1939* (Batsford, London, 1970), pp. 149-53, 200-1, for housing unrest. Addison, at the LGB, was responsible for steering both these important Bills.

87. Andrew Boyle, *Montagu* (Norman Cassel, London, 1967), p. 182; Sir Henry Clay, *Lord Norman* (Macmillan, London, 1957), pp. 318-59, give some insights into individuals involved in shifting relationships between different sections and institutions of capital.

88. P.L. Payne, 'Rationality and Personality', *Business History*, XIX, no. 2 (July 1977), shows developments in heavy industrial sectors of Scottish industry 1916 to 1936.

89. Sidney Pollard, *The Gold Standard and Employment Policies between Wars* (Methuen, London, 1970), p. 2.

90. Ibid., pp. 7-8 for Norman, Niemayer and Bradford.

91. Arthur Peter Becker, 'Housing in England and Wales during the Business Depression of the 1930s', *Economic History Review*, vol. III (1950-1), p. 332.

92. W.F. Stolper, 'British Monetary Policy and the Housing Boom of the 1930s', *Quarterly Journal of Economics*, vol. 56, part 1, ii (1941). A neglected but excellent and generally convincing study.

93. Cullingworth, *Housing and Local Government in England and Wales*, ch. 1.

94. Gilbert, *British Social Policy 1914-1939*, pp. 197-204.

95. Stuart Macintyre, 'Red Strongholds Between the Wars', *Marxism Today* (March 1979), pp. 85-90.

96. I owe this point to Keith Burgess.

97. Foster, 'How imperial London preserved its slums', p. 658.

98. Foster makes a similar point at ibid., p. 659, where he argues that: 'Because for Castells it is only the overall system and its ongoing contradictions which can ultimately "explain" and because the state acts above classes to contain these contradictions . . . so state policy, and the changes within it, provides the only litmus test for class struggle. Class struggle is validated, the balance of class forces is seen to have altered, to the extent that policy has been changed . . . class struggle ends up being expressed, registered and indeed located *within* the state.' It might be added that the aim of policy-makers is precisely to incorporate struggles within a formal political and legal framework, thereby neutralising the challenges to state power as a whole.

2 PROPERTY RELATIONS AND HOUSING POLICY: OLDHAM IN THE LATE NINETEENTH AND EARLY TWENTIETH CENTURIES

Caroline Bedale

Introduction: What is Meant By State Intervention

This paper is concerned with working-class housing in Oldham from about 1880 to the 1920s. In it I look at who was providing housing during this period, why new building ceased almost completely by the First World War, the beginning of provision of housing by the state, and the implications of this.

When discussing state intervention, the danger of taking a case study approach, that is concentrating on a town or area, is that issues may be taken out of context and viewed as being peculiar to that town. However, if one wishes to look in detail at the implementation of a policy it is usually impracticable to do this for the whole of the country. Thus it is important to make clear the theoretical framework within which such a case study is based. The aim is not to try and prove some hypothesis by means of the empirical data collected, but rather to try and explain the data in the light of the theory. Within a theory of the nature of the state in capitalist society the intention is to explain the form that this intervention takes at the local level, and to examine the relationship between local struggles and class struggles at the national level of the state.

It is not only on grounds of impracticability of national research that a small area is taken. If one is studying where a national policy comes from, how it gains support, and is put into practice, local studies can prove very illuminating. While existing within the overall context of a capitalist society, there have been, and still are, important economic, social and political differences between towns and regions. Not least of these is the presence of one dominant industry or company, and the effect this has on the development of an area. (One then, of course, ought to look at the reasons why different industries concentrated in different areas, and why different areas developed differentially, but this is beyond the scope of this paper.) In the same context, the way that local government has responded to initiatives from the central government is also worthy of study: particularly to see how its response reflects and reinforces the local class formation and interests, or to what extent it is merely an agent for the central government.

It is vital to be clear about what is meant by 'the state'. It is by no means just the government, whether central or local, nor such governments plus their paid officials (Civil Service or local authority officers). These are all *part* of 'the state', but there are other parts. It seems misleading to use the terms 'central state' and 'local state', mainly because they imply two separate and autonomous bodies.

To talk of the 'local state' implies that there are within it the range of agencies that one would expect to find within 'the state', i.e. forces of repression (the army, police, the law), a legislature, means of ideological control (religious institutions, education). While local governments do have some control over some of these functions, it is obviously not the case that one can talk about 'a state' in the locality.[1] Basically I would agree with Cockburn (1977, p. 2) that 'local councils don't spring from some ancient right of self-government but are, and under capitalism have always been, an aspect of national government which in turn is a part of the state'. It is not only a matter of functions: another criticism of the term 'local state' is that it is at the national level of the state that class struggle is ultimately focused in terms of political power, although this does not deny the importance of local struggle in shaping policies at a local level.

In analysing what is meant by the state one should not just concentrate on the institutions which constitute it, but rather what it is that the state represents in capitalist society. The state is not something separate from society, having an independent existence; it must be defined within a particular historical context in order not merely to explain the changes in its nature, but also to make that nature clear. That is, that it represents a relation between, an expression of, forces in society; it is not a force in its own right.

In their early works Marx and Engels wrote that, 'The executive of the modern state is but a committee for managing the common affairs of the whole bourgeoisie' (1848, p. 44), and, 'The state is the form in which the individuals of a ruling class assert their common interests, and in which the whole civil society of an epoch is epitomised.' (1845-6, p. 80). This implies that the state is merely an instrument in the hands of the bourgeoisie. However, not only in later works but also in this earlier period they presented a more complex view of the state:

The material life of individuals, which certainly does not depend on their mere 'will', their mode of production, and their form of intercourse, which reciprocally influence each other, are the real basis of the state. . . . These real conditions are not created by the state power; they are rather the power which creates it. The state does not rest on a dominating will, but the state which arises out of the material mode of life of individuals has also the form of a dominating will. (1845-6, p. 357)

The same point was made later by Engels:

As the state arose from the need to hold class antagonisms in check, but as it arose, at the same time, in the midst of the conflict of these classes, it is, as a rule, the state of the most powerful, economically dominant class, which, through the medium of the state, becomes also the politically dominant class, and thus acquires new means of holding and exploiting the oppressed class. (Engels, 1884)

These passages bring out the essential nature of the state, as rooted in the particular material base of society at a given time, as reflecting the level of conflict between classes at that time, and thereby generally representing the interests of the dominant class.

Poulantzas sums this up in a similar manner, as resulting from the fact that the state is not an agent of one or other class, but rather that it is the location of conflict between classes, i.e. it represents the relative strength of class forces.[2] As such, the state generally represents the interests of the dominant class, and so state intervention has tended to reproduce the conditions for capitalist production and accumulation.

However, in particular situations the working class (or certain fractions of capital) have been able to exert their influence, and have brought about changes which have altered the ground on which struggle continues to take place. Thus there can be significant shifts in the relative positions of capital and labour even while the capitalist system remains. This is apparent when one looks at the formulation of policies concerned with the reproduction of labour power (i.e. what are generally referred to as social policies). The reproduction of labour power involves not only the more obvious aspect of the physical reproduction of a skilled and healthy labour force, through the provision of housing, health and social services, insurance and sickness benefits and education. It also involves the reproduction of the relations of production: the class structure, the private ownership of property, and the reproduction of the hegemony of the ruling class in the widespread acceptance of the legitimacy of these relations of production.[3]

Partly as a result of working-class pressure certain gains have been made: unemployment and sickness benefits, council housing, free education, etc. While these may be, and have been, reduced at certain times, it is virtually unthinkable that they could be withdrawn altogether. Yet, such gains also exhibit clearly the contradictions facing the working class in their struggle against the bourgeoisie: while representing things that the latter have been forced to concede, these policies were, in fact, also required to ensure the adequate reproduction of labour power, and through them the dominance of capital has been reproduced and reinforced.

The reproduction of the dominance of the ruling class is not just an abstract concept, it may be found in the concrete form that the physical reproduction of labour power by the state takes. Thus in much state intervention one can see not only its economic role in reproducing labour power, but also its ideological role in reproducing and reinforcing ruling-class hegemony. The building of state housing, was, until after the Second World War, specifically for 'the working classes', and as the working class for whom it was intended became more and more marginal (i.e. slum dwellers or those in overcrowded houses) in the 1930s, so the physical standard of the houses built was reduced. More recently, the economic and status advantages of owner-occupation as compared with council housing have strengthened the notion that council housing is inferior, and that its residents are also in some way inferior. One effect of welfare measures, including housing, has certainly been to raise the living conditions of the working class. What is more, many council tenants appear to feel that they have experienced a *qualitative* change in their lives through being housed by the state. Yet capital has continued to find in council housing a means of extracting surplus value, both through the actual production of houses, and through the loans necessary for their production.

State intervention can take two, not necessarily mutually exclusive, forms in relation to housing: either in demand/consumption by creating 'solvent demand', that is by ensuring that people can afford to purchase or rent the housing built; or in supply, by intervening in the construction process including the restructuring of building capital (Castells, 1972, p. 158). Both these elements can be seen in the type of subsidies and housing policies in Britain over the last century. It will be argued, however, that the state has concentrated on the former, and this is of major significance in its failure to solve 'the housing problem' both for capital in general and for the working class.[4] If money is given by the state to enable people to afford to buy or rent housing or to subsidise private builders, this does not alter in any way the commodity form of housing. Council housing does challenge the commodity form to some extent because its allocation and consumption is removed from dependence on market mechanisms, but since most council housing is produced by private builders its production still retains the commodity form.

State intervention in housing in the early twentieth century was in part a response to the increasing strength of working-class militancy. The Great Depression of 1888-90 saw the first coherent and organised strikes amongst unskilled and casual workers, such as the dockers, gas workers and matchgirls, and the establishment of unions of such workers. At the same time Socialists in the Independent Labour Party and the Social Democratic Federation were winning support and even being elected to Parliament. These are indications of the general increase in working-class strength: the 1915 Glasgow Rent Strike saw this manifested with particular reference to housing, and led to legislation to control rents. However, state intervention in housing cannot be seen as resulting only from working-class pressure. While the timing and form of the 1919 Housing Act was greatly influenced by working-class struggle, it was not a total watershed in the nature of state intervention. While it was the first Act with regard to housebuilding by the state to have a real effect, the foundations for such provision of working-class housing had been laid in the nineteenth century, for example by the 1890 Housing of the Working Classes Act.

The 'housing problem' and state intervention also demonstrate the effect of conflict between fractions of capital. An important aspect of the reproduction of labour power is that it should be adequately housed. As far as the capitalist class in general is concerned the lower the price of adequate housing, the lower wages can be. However, builders and other capitalists involved in the production of housing are less interested in keeping prices low. If there is a situation where the working class cannot afford the price which builders consider gives an adequate return on their capital, then they will find it unprofitable to build housing for the working class. State intervention is in part a product of this conflict of interests, not as a mechanistic response to solve an economic problem, but as an attempt to resolve these contradictions at the political level.

The Case of Oldham

Having discussed the general framework within which the empirical data are analysed, I now turn to look at the case of Oldham. Firstly, the scene in the nineteenth century is set: the nature of property ownership and house-building; this leads on to the discussion of the beginning of local authority housebuilding.

The relationship between the industrial growth and the population growth of the town of Oldham had an important consequence for housing. The growth of both was extensive but steady throughout the nineteenth century, with the result that although the standards of early-nineteenth-century housing were low, by and large the building industry managed to meet the demands of the increasing population, at least for a minimal standard of amenities. The steady growth of the town had an important effect on what was built and how, since there was never the frantic building of very cheap housing to accommodate a rapidly multiplying population.

Even so, Engels wrote that Oldham was one of the worst of the towns in the vicinity of Manchester, towns which were: 'badly and irregularly built with foul courts, lanes and back alleys, reeking of coal smoke, and especially dingy from the originally bright red brick, turned black with time . . . Cellar dwellings are general here' (Engels, 1845, p. 76). The early-nineteenth-century builders were also censured by Alderman Hague, Chairman of Oldham Housing Committee in the 1930s:

> There is no doubt that the local authority at that time allowed
> builders and those who had business ability, and those who had
> capital to invest in property of almost every description, to develop
> without any real idea of town planning, zoning and density . . .
> streets were in many instances run up on every side as fast if not
> faster than tenants could be found. Hence the sudden enlargement
> of the town on every hand, owing to the abode of speculating
> builders, clever lawyers, and money-making bankers, who were, of
> course, anxious to make five per cent of their credit. (Hague, 1934)

However, the early unchecked excesses of bad housing, little sanitation or none, and dirty streets and alleys gave way to better conditions, and during the latter half of the nineteenth century Oldham did not suffer the squalor of tenements which became slums almost as soon as they were built, such as those in Glasgow (Damer, 1976), London or Liverpool (Gauldie, 1974). Wages for skilled workers in the textile industry in Oldham were fairly good in comparison with other trades, except building, and with other textile towns (see Tables 2.1 and 2.2) which meant that people could afford to pay the higher rents which could induce builders and property owners to build better quality housing. There were only two areas of large middle-class houses by the 1890s, near the two parks in Werneth and Glodwick; apart from these the majority of housing consisted of row upon row of terrace houses. In 1891, 1901 and 1911 tenements (which in the Census simply means dwellings) with three or four rooms accounted for about 65 to 70 per cent of Oldham's housing, compared with about 40 to 45 per cent in Lancashire as a whole.

Table 2.1: A Comparison of Wages

	1871	1877	1880	1886	1897/8	1908
Engineering:						
Fitters and Turners	33s	31s — 32s	27s — 29s	31s6d — 31s11d	34s — 36s	32s – 35s
Iron Moulders	32s	34s – 36s	27s6d – 32s	35s7d	40s	
Smiths	30s	32s6d – 35s	28s6d	32s11d – 42s	36s	34s – 36s
Labourers	18s	17s – 18s	16s6d – 18s	17s11d	21s	
Textiles:						
Mule Spinners (coarse)	30s*	27s8d – 29s8d 34s*	28s9d 31s*	33s4d 31s3d*		38s – 46s
Cardoom Grinders	21s*	21s2d – 23s	22s6d	21s5d	1906	29s5d**
Big Piecers	12s*	11s – 13s8d 14s*	12s6d 14s*	13s7d 14s1d*		17s10d**
Building:						
Bricklayers	36s8d	43s6d	40s11d	40s11d	40s9½d	45s5d
Carpenters		39s4½d	39s4½d		40s9½d	40s4½d
Plumbers		33s4d	33s4d		42s2¾d	38s7½d
Painters	36s4d				36s3½d	38s3d

Sources: Bowley, A., 1900: Table facing p. 123: Wages in Engineering in Manchester; Table facing p. 119: Wages in Manchester and District Cotton Trade; Table facing p. 94: London Building Trades Extracts from Trade Union Reports.

* Wood, G.H., 1910: Table 42, p. 131: Estimated Average Weekly Earnings of Various Classes of Cotton Operatives in Lancashire and Cheshire.

** 1906 figures.

1908: Board of trade, 1908.

Table 2.2: A Comparison of Wages in Textile Towns

	1874	1877	1880	1886	1896	1899 - 1900	1905-6
	d	d	d	d	d	d	d
Manchester	177	182½	168	173½			195
Bolton	181	190	181	179	203	213	218
Oldham	201½	209	201½	206	228	240	252
Ashton				195			233
Stockport				167			230
Preston	177½	192	176	183	200	203	222
Blackburn	187	201	183	191	216		248
Clitheroe	188	189	173	176			231
Burnley				214		253	286
Bury and Rochdale				174			234
Scotland	146			147			177

Source: Wood, G.H., 1910: Table 36, p. 116: Estimates of average earnings of cotton factory operatives for an ordinary week's work in the chief centres of the industry.

Back-to-back and single dwelling houses and cellar dwellings comprised only a small percentage of Oldham's housing stock by the late nineteenth century: in 1891, 4,802 out of 27,605 dwellings, 17.3 per cent; by 1919 there were 2,616 back-to-back houses out of a total of about 34,000, 7.7 per cent In 1861 there were 656 cellar dwellings, many of which were closed during the 1870s, leaving 220 by 1894. There were no back-to-back houses built in Oldham after 1881 (Oldham Medical Officer of Health (MOH) Annual Reports, 1886-1974).

The annual MOH reports show that there was, however, official concern about the condition of housing in the town. The main problems were damp and bad ventilation and poor sewerage and drainage, which it was felt, 'must deteriorate the physique, and, therefore, degrade the character of the people' (MOH Report, 1886). The condition of the worst areas, such as Coldhurst and Mumps, however, was to a large extent blamed on their occupants.[5]

The officials were preoccupied with the reasons for Oldham's high death rate and high infant mortality rate; even in comparison with Glasgow Oldham fared worse in the expectation of life after the age of five. There was a particularly high death rate amongst inhabitants of back-to-back houses: 31.3 per 1,000 compared with 7.5 per 1,000 in the whole borough of Oldham in 1894; for children under five the rate was 112.9 per 1,000 for back-to-back houses, but 80.8 per 1,000 in the whole borough. It was thought that this higher death rate might be because back-to-back houses were generally occupied by a lower class of person, even though they were not necessarily overcrowded, since they were usually let whole to one family, while through houses might contain two or three families. In the back-to-back and single houses:

> a general air of hopeless squalor is liable to settle and hang about such houses . . . There can be no doubt of the mischief such a class of house does to health — none whatever — and it is depressing to think that one-seventh of the population is housed in that manner. (MOH Report, 1891)

And yet it was also said:

> in Oldham a considerable number of these dwellings are well built, occupied by respectable working people, and not overcrowded on the land, conditions the reverse of what appears to have existed in the affected areas in Salford. (MOH Report, 1894)

The Oldham local authority initially paid serious attention to its duties under the 1890 Act: the borough had already been divided into several districts, and inspectors appointed under the MOH to survey the housing. In the nine years from 1886 to 1894, 87 houses were closed by order of the Sanitary Committee, and 359 voluntarily closed; in 1895 the figures were 72 and 125 respectively; and from 1896 to 1900 about 70 to 80 houses were closed or demolished annually. After this date, apart from small blocks of houses being cleared, and the declaration of one or two small Insanitary Areas for clearance, the impetus went out of the drive to improve the standard of working-class housing. In the early years of the twentieth century the MOH reported that trade was bad, and that there were many empty houses: according to the 1901 Census about 1,040 houses were habitable but unoccupied, and about 1,400 were uninhabitable. The house-to-house inspection was virtually abandoned after 1902 because of pressure of other work, and from 1898 to 1910 only about 180 houses were closed compulsorily and 250 voluntarily. The Housing and Town Planning Act of 1909 extended the duties of local authorities to inspect all the houses, but in Oldham by 1919 only about a third had been inspected.

Additionally under the 1890 Act local authorities were given two other powers. Firstly, they could provide dwellings to be owned and managed by themselves; thus for the first time the state could directly intervene in the production of houses. The question then is whether the state would employ its own workers to build such houses, and thereby either compete with construction firms or remove the unprofitable sector of housebuilding from them, or whether contracts would be put out to private firms, thereby removing the risk of speculating in building by providing a guaranteed sale. So, one needs to ask whether and to what extent this and subsequent Acts were an attempt by the state to assume responsibility for an area of reproduction of labour power which no longer afforded a sufficient profit for building capital, and to what extent did they aid a group of capitalists, in the construction industry, at the expense of other groups and fractions of capital. Since the majority of council houses have been built by private builders rather than by local authority direct works departments, the result of state intervention has been to fulfil these potential functions simultaneously. This is not to say that the aim of the state was in any sense as clear as this; state intervention rather resulted from an awareness that some state housing provision was necessary to ensure the adequate reproduction of labour power and to counter growing working-class pressure and agitation on the housing issue.

Secondly, local authorities could acquire land. This reflects the level of struggle between industrial capitalists and landowners. The private ownership of land does not constitute a necessary element in capitalist production. But since land is a condition of production, the private ownership and control of land can act as a barrier to the development of industry by the imposition of rent, which has to be paid for out of the surplus value created in production. Similarly, land rent, and in its capitalised form the price of land, will be reflected in the cost of providing housing and consequently in the rents or price of houses. If the value (i.e. the amount of labour time necessary to produce it) of housing is high this increases the value of labour power, and therefore the amount of labour time necessary for the reproduction of labour power, and thus reduces the surplus labour time and the surplus value created. The working class may struggle to increase wages to meet higher housing costs by cutting into the surplus value which would otherwise be appropriated by the industrial capitalists. Thus it is in the interests of industrial capitalists for housing and land rents to be kept at a low level, yet the private ownership of land works against this.

It is thus important to note that in Oldham large areas of land were owned by industrial capitalists, such as Hibbert & Platt the textile machine makers. While there appears to be little or no data on the price at or readiness with which such industrialists disposed of their land, some study of house deeds shows that the land was often leased in small plots to people who then had a few houses built, and maybe lived in one of them. Given that it would be in the industrialists' interests to keep housing costs low for their workers, and since by the nineteenth century they were rarely actually building new housing themselves, it is reasonable to assume that land was made readily available by industrialists in Oldham, at a low price, for others to undertake the job of house building. Being industrialists first and landowners second, they would have been unlikely to try and make profit out of land speculation.

Under the 1890 Act, the local authority in Oldham acquired no land and built no houses, a situation typical of most local authorities at that time. In 1913 a plan was approved but never executed for dual tenements in blocks of six houses containing twelve dwellings, at £125 a dwelling. Certain savings could be made by constructing the floors and staircases out of wood instead of steel joists and concrete stairs, and by dispensing with the hot water installation and bath, to bring the cost down to £100 per dwelling. The original plans made provision for two bedrooms, but the MOH recommended that 'one bedroom to each dwelling would be sufficient for the class of persons who in his opinion would be suitable as tenants' (Memo, 1913). As regards rent, the scheme was not expected to be completely self-supporting and rent would: 'be gauged more by the ability of the persons to pay rather than the exact amount necessary to cover the cost of drainage and street making, as well as the cost of management, collection of rents, repairs, beautifying, etc.' This would mean a rent of about 3s for one-bedroomed and 3s 6d for two-bedroomed dwellings.

By the turn of the century the local authority considered there was very little slum property, and no large area of slums. A less complacent view was taken by people with closer interest in the quality of working-class life. For some years the housing situation had been causing concern in the Trades Council. In contrast to its initial protestations that 'Trades Councils should be Trades Councils, and not made into political institutions for party purposes' (Oldham Trades Council, 1892), within a couple of years, following the strikes and lockouts during the depression of 1893, it was campaigning for representation on the local council.[6] It also began to broaden its sphere of interest from merely dealing with questions of industry and trade to cover issues affecting the everyday life of its members, such as housing and pensions. In the Report of 1900, it was stated that little had been done to solve the housing problem because of the interests of landlords,

house builders' desire for profits, and the apathy of the greatest suffer-
ers. While some people believed that the situation in Oldham presented
no problems, in fact thousands were housed in a manner which was a
disgrace and danger to all. Since private enterprise apparently could
not cope, public bodies should be urged to do their duty. In 1904
delegates were sent to conferences on the land question; the private
ownership of land was seen as an 'iniquitous system', 'the worst and
greatest of all monopolies'. The Lancashire Land Reform Council was
formed in 1904 to educate public opinion and to enlarge people's
rights in the nation's land, a move which was heartily supported by the
Trades Council.

In 1908 its concern over the condition of housing in Oldham led the
Trades Council to enlist the aid of the National Housing Reform
Council, which sent an inspector to Oldham. He reported that there was
a great scarcity of suitable workmen's dwellings and that 10,000 people
lived in a state of overcrowding.[7] Following this, questions were asked
in the House of Commons, and the Ministry of Health sent a medical
officer, Dr. Farrar, to investigate. He was much more complacent,
stating the 'figures do not indicate a grave amount of overcrowding in
Oldham', that 10,000 artisans owned their own houses, and although
undesirable conditions did exist, the situation was not as black as some
reformers had depicted. He did, however, admit: 'In the case of many
houses which have been built for periods of more than twenty years,
the best streets have not been properly made up and remain squalid,
dirty and full of rats' (Bateson, 1949, p. 187). He made various recommendations to the Corporation, for example that they should take over
back passages (which was done), and rigidly enforce regulations governing new streets and buildings.

The Board of Trade Report of 1908 provides a detailed description
of the prevalent type of housing in Oldham at that time. Almost all
two-roomed houses were back-to-back; they were generally occupied by
labourers, at a rent of 2s 9d to 4s per week. Three-roomed houses were
mostly occupied by the labouring population, at a rent of 3s 9d to
5s 3d, 'though some of a better class command higher rents, and are
taken by a better class of tenant'. Four-roomed houses were the most
common type: the rent was between 5s and 6s. There were comparatively few five-roomed houses: they were rented for 5s 6d to 7s 3d a
week, though 'a superior type occupied by the better class artisans,
foremen, etc., is let at rents above this range, up to about 8s 3d per
week'.

The Board of Trade Report largely confirmed the findings of the

National Housing Reform Council inspector with regard to over-crowding: in 1901 there were 1,224 overcrowded tenements, 4.1 per cent of the total, inhabited by 10.191 people, which was 7.4 per cent of Oldham's population. The situation had improved since 1891 when 13,515 people, 10.1 per cent of the population, had been living in over-crowded tenements.

By 1912/13 the MOH reported that the artisan population was generally well housed, especially compared with other manufacturing towns. Any housing defects were largely because of generations of neglect rather than structural defects. There was a problem for small families of the poorer class since the closure of a number of back-to-back and single houses had made it more difficult to find suitable houses to rent: 'The newer houses in the town are of a larger type, and owing to this and the greatly increased cost of building the rents are beyond the means of the poorer class of workers, tending to cause overcrowding' (MOH Report, 1912). This is borne out by the figures, which show that in 1912 there were 40 cases of overcrowding given notice, and 74 in 1913.

The fact that Oldham's housing suffered from less deficiencies than that in some industrial towns reflects the industrial prosperity enjoyed by the town and its residents in the nineteenth century. However, by the turn of the century the inadequate quantity of a certain type of dwelling was becoming apparent. It was soon not only the 'poorer class of worker' who was affected but a large proportion of the working class, as the building of working-class dwellings of any type virtually came to a standstill.

Tenure Patterns and Property Ownership

Having described the housing conditions which were prevalent by the turn of the century, I continue with a discussion of the nature of property ownership and the changing pattern of tenure.

At the beginning of the twentieth century most people still lived in privately rented accommodation. One aspect of my research has been a detailed study from Rate Books in order to discover: the range of house types, based on rateable value; the nature of property ownership, both owner-occupation and landlordism, including the socio-economic structure of property ownership and changing tenure patterns. The sample of streets for which data were collected contained about 500 houses, varying from year to year as houses were built or demolished.[8] The housing was remarkably homogeneous: in 1882 the 18 houses up to £2 10s would mostly be cellar dwellings; the 188 in the range up to

£4 10s would mainly be back-to-back or single houses; the other 243 would be terrace houses, of which 114 were between £5 10s and £6, and only 31 were over £7. These rateable values contrast with figures of about £30 for semi-detached houses and £40 to £60 for detached houses at this period in the few middle-class streets. The four houses built by mill owners and textile machinery manufacturers in Werneth Park had rateable values of £180 and £280.

As Table 2.3 shows, there was a striking change in the nature of landlordism over the period covered. Gauldie says that in the second half of the nineteenth century it became uneconomic for the companies in 'company towns', such as Baxter Bros in Dundee, to continue to build houses for their workers: increased foreign competition forced employers to invest in new machinery and buildings rather than housing, and increasingly profits went into speculative investment, often abroad. It was thus only small scale non-expanding industries which continued to feel the advantages of providing housing. However, this view is disputed by Melling (1976) in his discussion of the housing of workers at the Clydebank shipbuilding yard. His conclusion is that company housing was still important in this expanding industry until as late as 1914 to 1919, and that not only was it calculated still to be economic to provide housing, but also that the question of industrial relations was crucial: on the one hand housing was used as an induce-ment to get the workers to accept changes in the labour process, such as dilution during the First World War, and on the other it was still a means of social control, with the threat of eviction helping to maintain a co-operative workforce. The difference in the conclusions of these two writers indicates that an important issue to consider is not only whether housing was or was not a good economic investment in 'company' towns, but also whether the company was still trying to attract labour.

Although Oldham was not a 'company' town, it was largely a one industry town and as such is comparable to the two studies mentioned above. In this respect it is closer to Gauldie's conclusions than to Melling's. Certainly the importance of mill owners and cotton manu-facturers as house owners declined during the later nineteenth century, while that of the petty bourgeoisie, such as food retailers, owners of small manufacturing enterprises, and of professional people rose, as shown in Table 2.3. The table indicates that there were quite a large number of cases where it was not possible to make a definite identifi-cation of a property owner in the street directories. From general knowledge of the town, however, I believe that those people identified are representative of property owners. In other words, those not definitely identified were probably also petty bourgeoisie.[9]

The provision of working-class housing thus passed from large industrialists, who were interested not only in making a profit from renting houses but also in attracting labour to the town, to the petty bourgeoisie, who saw the ownership of a few houses purely as a means of making small, safe investments.

The only cotton spinning or manufacturing company to maintain its property ownership was Thomas Mellodew & Co., which built and owned the 19 houses in Alexandra Terrace, Moorside, one of the streets in the sample. In fact, this was an unusual case. Until the mid-nineteenth century Moorside was an isolated hamlet, where Thomas Mellowdew went in 1842 to run a mill, after his mill in Royton had been a victim of the 'plug' riots. Because of the distance from the centre of Oldham, Mellowdew began to purchase and erect houses for his workforce, until the whole of Moorside village except for a few houses became his; he also built a school and a church. When he died in 1879 he and his company owned between 300 and 400 dwellings, as well as the surrounding land including two coal-pits, and he had branched out from the spinning of cotton and manufacture of velvets into tile and brick-making as well (Obituary, 17 May 1879).

The building society movement enjoyed wide support in Oldham: by the end of the 1860s there were 66 building societies in Oldham, with a subscribed capital of about £800,000 (Price, 1958, p. 189). And Gauldie (1974, p. 343 and p. 206 says, 'one of the societies most successful in attracting working men, the Oldham society . . .' and 'in Oldham, where genuine working-class membership was very high (mill hands from Platts [*sic*, in fact they were engineering workers] making the majority)'. Under an Act of 1874 building societies as such could not own property, apart from for their own use; but if they were limited companies there were no such restrictions. In the full survey of 1906 they owned 909 houses and houses and shops, or 2.8 per cent. These companies were notable for their ownership of new housing for rental which was why I wished to discover who had been involved in their setting up; whether they were mill owners wishing to diversify their financial interests, builders and contractors, estate agents and brokers, or other professional people, or whether they too represented the increasing fragmentation of property ownership amongst diverse manufacturers and retailers. However, it has proved difficult to do more than speculate from scraps of information about just a few of these companies. From the survey of 1906, the seven largest companies

Table 2.3: Occupations of Property Owners 1841 to 1921

	1841		1854		1864		1882		1896		1906		1916		1921	
	A	B	A	B	A	B	A	B	A	B	A	B	A	B	A	B
	221	108	354	260	473	303	458	265	505	352	491	345	462	297	460	276
Occupation not certain	43.9		26.0		35.5		42.1		30.3		29.7		35.7		39.4	
Name not given	7.2		0.6		0.4										0.7	
Cotton spinning and other textile owners	30.3	62.0	35.6	48.5	21.2	33.0	10.9	18.9	8.3	11.9	7.7	11.0	5.6	8.8	6.3	10.5
Company secretary/Mill manager					0.2	0.3	0.2	0.4	0.6	0.9	1.0	1.4	0.6	1.0	0.7	1.1
Cotton worker							3.5	6.1	2.5	3.7	3.9	5.5	3.9	6.1	3.2	5.4
Machine/metal worker			6.5	8.9			2.2	3.8	1.2	1.7	1.6	2.3	0.4	0.7	0.4	0.7
Blacksmith/millwright/wheelwright					2.8	4.3	3.9	6.8	3.0	4.3	2.9	4.1	3.1	4.7	2.4	4.0
Bobbin/spindle/reed maker	2.7	5.6	3.1	4.2	1.9	3.0	2.4	4.1	3.0	4.3	2.4	3.5	3.1	4.7	2.4	4.0
Engineering worker							1.3	2.3	3.0	4.3	2.6	3.8	2.2	3.4	1.9	3.3
Basket & skip maker/brush maker/saddler/clogger					1.7	2.6	2.6	4.4	1.0	1.4	1.8	2.6	1.5	2.3	1.5	2.5
Hatter/tailor/dressmaker	8.1	16.7	1.1	1.5	3.4	5.3	3.3	5.7					0.2	0.3	0.7	1.1
Food retailer/shopkeeper	5.9	12.0	1.4	1.9	6.1	9.5	2.2	3.8	9.9	14.2	10.0	14.2	7.8	12.2	8.9	14.8
Innkeeper/beer seller/lodging house keeper			1.4	1.9	1.5	2.3	4.6	7.9	0.8	1.1	0.2	0.3	0.6	1.0	0.7	1.1
Brewery							1.3	2.3	2.5	3.7	3.9	5.5	3.1	4.7	3.5	5.8
Salesman/card broker							1.5	2.7	2.0	2.8	1.4	2.0	2.2	3.4	1.5	2.5
Carrier			3.1	4.2	2.5	4.0	0.7	1.1	3.0	4.3	3.1	4.3	2.6	4.0	2.6	4.4
Building trades	0.5	0.9	1.7	2.3	5.9	9.3	2.0	3.4	4.5	6.5	4.3	6.1	4.9	7.7	5.2	8.7
Building club			17.0	23.1	9.1	14.2										
Solicitor/estate agent/architect			2.5	3.5	6.1	9.6	7.4	12.8	9.9	14.2	8.8	12.5	11.0	17.2	8.5	14.1
Teacher/minister/chemist/doctor					0.2	0.3							1.9	3.0	1.7	2.9
Householder							5.5	9.4	12.2	17.6	10.0	14.2	8.7	13.5	7.2	12.0
Miscellaneous (under 3% Column B each)	1.4	2.8			1.5	2.3	2.4	4.1	3.8	5.4	4.7	6.7	1.5	2.3	1.3	2.2

Column A: Total number of dwellings and percentage owned by each occupation.
Column B: Number and percentage of occupations definitely identified.

were: Oldham Estate Co. Ltd: 185 properties; the County Land and Estate Co. Ltd: 140 properties; the Oldham Trust Co. Ltd: 114 properties; Anchor Investment Co.: 58 properties; Queens Building Society: 56 properties; High Lee Property Co.: 48 properties; and the Lancashire Land Co.: 45 properties.

Lawrence Slater, 1870-1942, an accountant and estate agent, and a Conservative, was chairman of the Lancashire Land Co. and on the board of the County Land and Estate Co. Ltd. Another member of the board of the latter company was John Taylor, 1845-1907, originally a gas meter inspector for Oldham Corporation, and later a stock and share broker, with interests in several spinning companies, and a Liberal. Two directors of Oldham Trust Co. Ltd were Edward Stephenson, died 1921, a builder and contractor and director of several spinning companies, and a Liberal; and Joseph Jackson, 1857-1909, a builders' merchant and a Liberal. The Queens Building Society, based in Manchester, was one of the largest in the country; the agent in Oldham was William Jones, a printer. Of the small companies for which any information was found, most seem to have involved estate agents and accountants, stock and share brokers, or insurance agents, who may also have had interests in spinning companies.

It would seem, therefore, that the building and managing of property by property companies was done by professional people or builders as a financial venture in its own right, rather than as an attempt by members of the textile or other industries to house their labour force. The aim of the House & Mill Co. Ltd, which owned 16 properties in 1906, was probably not dissimilar from the aims of the other companies: 'The objects of this company are to afford a safe investment for loans, and the lending of money on mortgage' (Advertisement in Worrall's Directory, 1891).

The fact that it was new housing which was owned by these companies indicates that it must still have been possible to derive a profitable income from rented property, particularly if such property was in sizeable numbers, presumably because overhead costs would be reduced, and the new housing could command higher rents. This is supported by the fact that the County Land and Estate Co. Ltd and the Oldham Estate Co. Ltd both maintained their property ownership throughout the period of the sample, up to 1936, when council housing, owner occupation, and rent restrictions were all beginning to have their effect on the private rental market. The fact that it was companies which were providing a large proportion of the new housing also suggests that it was becoming too expensive for individual investors to consider new housing as a source of profit. One might then ask why companies did not continue to expand their investment in housing in the post-First World War period. One of the main reasons was probably the rise in the cost of building which made housing less attractive as an investment compared with other opportunities.[10]

Despite the interest of building companies, property renting was still largely a matter of private rather than company, whether financial or industrial, initiative. The reasons for this will be discussed in some detail later, but briefly it was because there were few other opportunities for small investors until the late nineteenth century, while the industrial companies, notably mills, were usually still organised on a family concern basis, even if they were legally joint stock companies, and profits were largely ploughed back into the industry or paid as dividends. Additionally, after the middle of the century, as noted, such companies were not concerned with trying to attract labour to the town. What happened when the small investors, too, found other outlets for their investments will also be discussed later.

As regards the relative importance of owner occupation and private renting, Table 2.4 shows the totals from 1841 to 1936.

Table 2.4: Tenure 1841 to 1936

Year	No. of Houses in Sample	Owner Occupied		Rented	
		No.	%	No.	%
1841	221	8	3.6	213	96.4
1854	354	16	4.5	338	95.5
1864	473	46	9.7	427	90.3
1882	458	22	4.8	436	95.2
1896	505	21	4.2	484	95.8
1901	489	24	4.9	465	95.1
1906	491	27	5.5	464	94.5
1906 Total	32,974	2,731	8.3	30,243	91.7
1911	471	23	4.9	448	95.1
1916	462	23	5.0	439	95.0
1921	460	26	5.7	434	94.3
1926	475	65	13.7	410	86.3
1931	500	104	20.8	396	79.2
1936	502	92	18.3	410	81.7

In fact, the full survey of 1906 gave a total of 8.3 per cent owner occupation, compared with 5.5 per cent from the sample. Because of the small number of houses from each ward, the figures for each individual ward are not very accurate, although it is apparent from the 1906 data that some wards had 15 to 17 per cent owner occupation;

but it would seem that the full sample was not unrepresentative of the general pattern throughout Oldham. This detailed survey of owner occupation was carried out because I wished to verify or refute the assertions about the extent of working-class owner occupation, since this has been cited as a reason for working-class conservatism in a town like Oldham. Because of the number of owner occupiers who did not appear in the street directories, or where the name was given at a different address, it was not possible to make a thorough check on the socio-economic characteristics of owner occupiers. However, the indications are that the number of working-class people included among owner-occupiers was very small. Given that the total number of owner occupiers in 1906 was 2,731 out of a total of 32,974 houses, it is clearly invalid to talk of an extensive amount of working-class owner occupation at this period.

Nevertheless, the ideology of thrift and self-help was strong, as evidenced by extensive membership of Friendly Societies and Co-operative Societies. In fact, the two chief institutions for the purchase of houses in Oldham were the Industrial Co-operative Society, in the west of the town, and the Equitable Co-operative Society, in the east. The Board of Trade Report of 1908 states that in 1906 the Building Department of the former Society advanced £21,278 to members on the security of cottage property, and since its commencement had advanced a total of £338,545, enabling 2,144 houses to be bought at an average of £158 per house. The operations of the latter Society were on a smaller scale: during 1906 £10,777 was advanced and 60 members bought houses, bringing the total to 834 since its commencement in 1868; and also during 1906 it drew up a 'houses for sale list' for members wishing to sell or buy houses. These two Co-operative Societies were both formed in 1850, with several cotton operatives among their founder members; even when some of these worked their way up into the middle classes (one became a Poor Law officer, another became manager of Asa Lees, the engineers and textile machine makers) they remained members of the Co-operative Societies.

The Production and Financing of Houses

I return now to the issue of investment in housing raised in the analysis of property ownership. I examine the relationship between investment in industry and investment in housebuilding; why people reduced their investment in new building and where they then invested their money; and what implications this had for the housing of the working class, leading to an explanation of state intervention in the provision of housing.

During the boom years of the nineteenth century the building industry by and large kept pace with the demand for housing. Technological
changes, to increase production in industry or in building, were few.
Industry met the problem of productivity by relying on keeping wage
rates low and using the available labour to the fullest legal extent, and
often finding ways to circumvent the various Factory Acts. This was
particularly the case with regard to the employment of women and
children and shift working. The building industry built smaller, meaner,
houses, crowded into courts and back alleys, despite building regulations and Public Health Acts. It continued to use traditional methods
of construction, and there was a ready supply of cheap building
materials, such as bricks and wood, from small local firms. Even in a
relatively prosperous town such as Oldham, where, as has been noted,
the standard of housing was probably higher than in some other industrial towns, one of the main concerns of the MOH as late as the 1890s
was the number of houses which were not connected to drains and
sewers.

However, by the turn of the century in the textile towns, and
earlier in the more recently industrialised areas, in manufacturing
industry machines were increasingly being developed to take the place
of skilled human labour and to increase production. Similar changes
did not occur in the building industry: it withdrew almost entirely
from the sector which proved least profitable rather than attempt to
find a way of providing working-class housing more cheaply. At the
same time the cost of building materials began to rise rapidly, a situation which was exacerbated by the First World War and the shortage
of supplies in the years following it. The problem was not merely that
the building industry became 'out of step' with developments in other
industries, but that it did not formulate methods to overcome this
uneven development.

In the discussion of building cycles and their relationship to industrial investment, Parry Lewis (1965, p. 87) says that in the mid-nineteenth century, 'The course of housebuilding around Manchester
echoes pretty faithfully the course of investment in the textile industry.' In other words, as the textile towns expanded in cotton production, so housing expanded, rather than investment in industry being to
the detriment of building and vice versa. This was the period when it
was still necessary to attract labour to the towns to man the expanding
industries of cotton and engineering; as Table 2.3 shows, a majority of
houses were then directly owned by mill owners.

The building of all kinds of houses virtually ceased in 1862-3 in Lancashire during the Cotton Famine, when many people emigrated and marriages and births declined. In addition, the cessation of wages forced many families to share their houses; and others had to withdraw their savings from building societies. While nationally the availability of credit and the overall economic climate are reflected in housebuilding figures, regionally there were wide fluctuations because of local events, such as the Cotton Famine. This is also apparent in the type of housing which was built: although the mid-nineteenth-century boom was experienced throughout the country, it took a different form in the industrial towns (where row upon row of cheap terrace housing sprang up to accommodate and facilitate the reproduction of an urban working class) from London and its suburbs (where the middle class was beginning to congregate).

During the textile boom of the 1870s there were even differences between towns within the region. By the early 1880s Oldham and Ashton had developed their use of the self-acting mule, while towns like Burnley and Rochdale continued to use the old throstle spinners, and their different fortunes are reflected in a comparison of building indices, as in Table 2.5.

Table 2.5: Comparison of Building Indices 1901-10 = 100

Year	Oldham	Rochdale
1877	618.1	167.0
1878	217.7	156.7
1879	180.0	136.4
1880	213.9	69.0
1881	160.0	32.2
1882	150.3	33.7
1883	177.1	27.3
1884	251.7	34.3
1885	237.5	40.5
1886	247.6	48.4

Source: Parry Lewis, 1965, pp. 314-15

However, as the sample of streets for Oldham showed, towards the end of the nineteenth century it was houses with a higher rateable value which were being built, in other words, there was less concern to provide housing for the working class but rather a desire to maximise the profits obtainable from housing. In this respect one can compare the cost and profit in building different types of houses, which clearly demonstrate why builders eagerly sought to fulfil the wishes of the growing middle class. The account books of a large Oldham building firm, T. Partington & Son Ltd (Table 2.6), show the magnitude of difference in profit between building blocks of houses, probably for rental, and individual houses for owner occupation. The difference in price cannot be accounted for by inflation in general prices, since the cost of the houses in 1901-2 was higher than in 1909-12.

Table 2.6: Housebuilding Accounts

Date	Buildings	Cost	Price	Profit	Profit as % of Cost
1901-2	12 houses	£2,054 0s 0d	£2,230 0s 0d	£176 0s 0d	8.6
1902-3	10 cottages	£1,368 4s 1d	£1,798 13s 9½d	£430 9s 8½d	31.4
1909	2 houses	£212 10s 0½d	£423 0s 0d	£210 9s 11½d	99.0
1912	1 house	£140 17s 8d	£324 0s 0d	£183 2s 4d	130. 7

The Changing Nature of Investment

As Dyos and Reeder (1973, p. 361) point out: 'The housing of the poor, as of the rich, was an item of real property . . . it was expected to yield profits commensurate with whatever were regarded as the risks of investing in it.' If it did not provide these profits, or was less fruitful than other investments, then builders would cease to build, even if 'demand' for housing, in the form of an increasing population, an increase in households, or deterioration of existing housing conditions, was high. Despite growing aspirations towards owner occupation, the proliferation of building societies, and the ability to pay higher rents, by the early twentieth century new building was rapidly decreasing, as housing became a less profitable area for investment. Table 2.7 shows the number of housing completions in Oldham fell after the turn of the century, yet the population continued to increase and the older housing deteriorated.

Table 2.7: Number of Housing Completions in Oldham

March 1871 to March 1876	2,578	March 1896 to March 1901	2,471
March 1876 to March 1881	3,926	March 1901 to March 1906	1,598
March 1881 to March 1886	3,530	March 1906 to March 1911	1,558
March 1886 to March 1891	2,171	March 1911 to March 1916	1,173
March 1891 to March 1896	1,357	March 1916 to March 1921	50

Why, then, was there this move away from investment in house-building, especially for the working class in the last quarter of the nineteenth century? Parry Lewis writes that, 'the early 1870s saw a mania of co-operative company flotation in and around Oldham' (p. 125); in 1874-5 45 companies were floated in Oldham itself. It is interesting to note that the investors in these companies were not just the big bourgeoisie, as had been the case in the early nineteenth century (Foster, 1974, chapter 6) but all classes of people. Before 1873 it is estimated that at least three-quarters of the shareholders in local spinning companies were wage-earning manual labourers (Farnie, 1953). However, there is no calculation of the size of these shareholdings and such small shareholders probably held only a handful of shares each. Parry Lewis says that the crisis in the textile industry in the mid to late 1870s, and heavy calls on unpaid-up share capital hit workers badly, many of them losing most of their savings, and that by 1885, only 7½ per cent of mill employees were shareholders in cotton spinning companies, having transferred what was left of their savings to savings banks and cottage property (Parry Lewis, 1965, p. 126).

However, Smith (1954) refutes the assertion of such a high level of working-class ownership of shares, in his research on limited liability companies in Oldham. While he found that the promotion of companies in Oldham was indeed largely financed by local capital, and while shares of low denomination (£5 to £10) were common, an examination of several share registers proved shareholding by cotton operatives to be the exception. Thus, the working class cannot have had the influence on investment in industry and housebuilding attributed to them by Parry Lewis.

Nevertheless, whether or not working-class ownership of shares was high, the growth of joint stock companies was one factor in the decline of investment in working-class housing. Oldham was a leading centre of joint stock companies by the 1880s and about 25 per cent of their capital was supplied by shopkeepers (Farnie, 1953). As the sample of streets showed, shopkeepers and food retailers also accounted for a sizeable proportion of property owners, but it would appear that any expansion of their savings was invested in joint stock companies rather than in property, or indeed in anything else: 'The shoemaker, hatter and clothier all alike complain of bad trade. No fashion, they say, will entice the joint stock share-holders in at their doors' (*Co-operative News*, 1874, quoted in Farnie, 1953). Thus while the opportunities for financial investments in Oldham were limited, people invested in housing as a safe place providing a steady income. Since the workforce

was reasonably well paid and since industrialist landowners had prior
interests and therefore were less likely to wish to make profits from
land speculation, but rather to see their workers cheaply but adequately
housed, it is not surprising that much of Oldham's late-nineteenth-
century housing was of a higher standard than in poorer or more
rapidly expanding towns, such as in the North East. It was when these
steady incomes could no longer be guaranteed, because of rising building standards and building materials costs, and with the competition
from other investment opportunities that working-class housing lost its
position as a sure and safe investment for the small investor.

Another reason in Oldham for this decline in housebuilding was
probably the upsurge in the cotton industry up to 1914: Jones (1959)
says that between 1896 and 1914 75 new mills were built in the
Oldham district. It would seem that unlike the mid-nineteenth century,
when investment in industry and housing went hand in hand, in this
case there was an inverse relationship, largely because there was no
longer a need to attract labour into the town. Technological changes in
the textile industry, such as the introduction of the self-acting mule to
replace the hand mule, made the industry less labour intensive in the
last quarter of the nineteenth century; so an expansion in production
capacity such as took place in the early twentieth century was not
accompanied by such an expansion in population.

The Implications for Working-class Housing

Obviously, house building did not cease completely, and there was
even a minor boom around the late 1890s and 1910. However, as has
been said, this was largely of the better type of housing, which illustrates that private industry would no longer build cheap working class
housing. For example, it was in 1906 that the Oldham Garden Suburbs
Ltd was formed. While this was intended to provide houses for the
working class, along the lines of Ebenezer Howard's plans, in fact only
about half the planned 300 houses were ever built, and the rents were
too high for most working-class families.

The housing of the working class thus still remained a problem. It
is clear that what was at issue was the profitability of building certain
types of houses. Where a high rent or a high price could be guaranteed
builders were still as keen to build, but the price that housing for the
working class would have had to command to make it profitable would
also have placed it beyond the reach of the working class. One reason
for this is that working-class housing could no longer consist of single
or back-to-back dwellings or terrace houses of a very low standard: the

imposition of various standards and building regulations in the interests of public health inevitably meant that the difference in cost between working-class and middle-class housing was greatly diminished, yet the working class did not receive a commensurate rise in wages to enable them to pay for these higher standards.

It was, then, partly in response to this problem, which is essentially a problem of the reproduction of labour power, that the state began to intervene in the provision of housing directly.

State Intervention in Housing

While few local authorities used their powers under those sections of the 1890 Act dealing with housebuilding and land acquisition, nevertheless this Act was important in ushering in a new era in the role of the state: an era when its legitimacy to intervene was not seriously questioned. State policy over housing at this time should also be seen in the context of state intervention in social welfare generally at the turn of the century.

A paper by Burgess (1978) discusses the role of Lancashire in the formation of social policy in terms of the measures passed in 1908 by the Liberal Government, measures which he calls: 'an ad hoc package of ameliorative measures that would legitimate private property and a capitalist-market economy' (p. 9). This 'New Liberalism' was based on theories of, for example, T.H. Green and Arnold Toynbee, and advocated state initiatives only when existing institutions had failed, the intention being to complement and support self-help rather than replace it. The aim was for a 'moralised' capitalism where well paid workers would share as citizens in the fruits of capitalism. Lancashire cotton operatives were the model of the 'better sort' of workers: they were comparatively prosperous (with several members of a family working, household incomes were high even if individual wages were not); and they had a long tradition of self-help and thrift through savings banks, Friendly Societies, and Co-operative Societies.

The slowing down of the rate of growth of the cotton industry in the late nineteenth century created tensions between different grades of mill workers as the chances of promotion to the élite of minders and carders were reduced. However, this did not lead to calls for collective provision of services, but rather for a strengthening of existing welfare measures. Burgess says that the leaders of the cotton operatives identified closely with their employers, and with New Liberalism. The tradition of self-help institutions was also important in deflecting the potential for working-class demands for state collective provision of welfare. Furthermore, many cotton mill owners made certain welfare provisions, in a calculating paternalistic style which is still found today. Finally, the cotton operatives' success in using political institutions for limited ends, such as the eight-hour day, encouraged them to work through existing channels rather than adopt a more militant approach.

The context for the introduction of the 1919 Act was thus: the falling profitability of cheap but decent new working-class houses as far as builders and landlords were concerned; a growing concern about the deteriorating standard of health of the working class; the fear of the potential threat from the working class as a result of organised working-class pressure; and the previous introduction of various other social welfare measures, which complemented the ideology of self-help rather than challenged it. The 1919 Housing and Town Planning Act for the first time compelled local authorities directly to provide good quality houses for the working class. It became the local authorities' duty to survey the housing needs of their districts and make provision where existing housing was inadequate. In practice this meant that nearly every local authority embarked on a programme of municipal housebuilding within the next couple of years. The subsidies provided by the central government to assist these programmes were extremely generous. Although the rents were to be a good deal higher than pre-war rents they were still far below an economic rent: houses which had cost £170 to £250 before the First World War cost £700 to £1,000 by 1919-20; also interest rates had risen so that local authorities were likely to be paying about 6 per cent, whereas before the war the rate was about 3½ per cent. The upshot of this was that the loss per house could be £50 to £80 per annum.

The building of these early estates demonstrates the divergence between the needs of the working class and what the state actually provided in terms of housing. It would seem that there was more publicity and rhetoric surrounding the central government's policy towards working-class housing than real commitment, bearing in mind that Bowley (1945, p. 145) estimated that the number of houses required nationally from 1919 to 1923 was 1,074,000 but that the number built was 252,000, making a shortfall of 822,000.

It was first decided to build houses for the working classes in Oldham under the 1919 Act in March 1919, and layouts for two sites, involving 500 houses, were submitted to the Ministry of Health. The consultant architects were Messrs. J. Crouch and W.A. Harvey of Birmingham, with a panel of local architects to draw up the actual plans.

In December 1919 the Ministry of Health and the Housing Commissioner said that 500 houses were inadequate to meet Oldham's needs. They calculated the number of houses needed as in Table 2.8.

Table 2.8: Assessment of Oldham's Housing Needs

Shortage of houses in 1911 at 4.7 persons per house	329
Houses demolished 1911 to 1919	131
Houses required to meet average growth of population during next three years on a calculation based on average growth during the five years preceding the war	1,433
Additional houses required to meet deficiency caused by conversion of 2,640 back-to-back houses into through houses	1,320
	3,213
Deduct houses built 1911 to 1919	1,170
Leaving number of houses required	2,043

This did not include the existing back-to-back houses which would also have to be dealt with.

Following this the Council were required to submit a new scheme, of at least 1,000 houses; this was approved in January 1920. From early in 1920 the high cost of building materials was noted at various council meetings; resolutions from Hull and Worcester urging the Government to institute an enquiry to secure the lowering of prices were adopted in Oldham. A similar resolution from Torquay was adopted in June 1920, and one from Eccles in January 1921. Oldham passed its own resolution in 1923.[11]

The high cost of building was presumably one of the reasons why tenders were slow for the first stage of building: only one tender was received, from the Oldham and District Building Trades Association, of £950 each for 24 parlour and £850 each for 24 non-parlour houses. This tender was approved by the Housing Commissioner in June 1920. In July a similar tender for a further 509 houses on three sites was approved.

Another reason for the lack of tenders was presumably the large amount of commercial work in the district by the time building was started on the council estates: when the Committee expressed dissatisfaction at the slow rate of building, the Oldham and District Building Trades Association said it was because of the difficulty in getting skilled labour, such as brick setters, when they could earn much higher wages in commercial work. But by May 1921 building workers were beginning to suffer a series of wage cuts, as the economic situation worsened.

The slow rate of building was compounded by the increasing intervention of the Housing Commissioner in restricting the type and range
of houses planned. In addition, he intervened in the employment of
ex-soldiers to build streets and sewers. Oldham was reminded that
excess expenditure due to the employment of 'unemployed labour'
would only rank for financial assistance in places where the Ministry
of Labour certified that unemployment was serious. Any plans to use
'unemployed labour' would have to be approved by the Housing
Commissioner first. The Ministry of Health had originally planned for
500,000 ex-servicemen to be absorbed into the building trade, but by
June 1921 this had been cut to 160,000 since commercial work was
practically at a standstill and it was inopportune to employ ex-servicemen when skilled craftsmen were already out of work. From the
beginning of 1921 to June 1922, wages for building craftsmen were
reduced from 2s 4d to 1s 8d per hour, and the number of hours was
reduced from 46½ to 44 per week.

Once Oldham's first estate (Hollins) containing 300 houses was
finished in 1922, work virtually ceased on housing for the working
class. Some road work and sewering had been started on the other
two sites, but in July 1922 the Ministry of Health withdrew its authori-
sation for the erection of further houses, and suggested the Council
should consider disposing of portions of the surplus housing lands
with a view to the erection of houses by private builders. A slight
concession of 50 houses was allowed if Oldham would undertake to
take financial responsibility for a further 150, which was agreed. The
estate of 50 houses (Greenacres) was completed in 1925. Eventually
assistance was received from the Ministry of Health for the other 150
houses, by the use of Public Health legislation for the clearance of an
'Unhealthy Area'. Originally the MOH had recommended that the area
should be cleared and 300 three-storey tenements built to house the
resident population of 1,274 people, since, as he said, they would not
wish to live on the outskirts of the town and many of them were not
suitable tenants for ordinary cottage houses. The residents were in fact
rehoused in the lower standard estates of Barrowshaw and the second
part of Greenacres, between 1925 and 1927. The houses on these estates were smaller than those built under the 1919 Act, and than about
half of those which were built under the 1924 Act; they also had outside lavatories, and they were on the outskirts of the town, right up on
the edge of the moors.

In contrast the 1919 Act houses were much sought after. Even after nearly sixty years the high standards which the subsidy system allowed local authorities to indulge in is apparent. As Oldham's retired Housing Manager commented: 'It was a nice estate, lots of green and trees and grass verges and things, which, apart from the ravages of time and people, still show through. It's one of our better laid-out estates.' This view is echoed by the handful of elderly tenants who have lived on the estate since it was built, though they felt it was not as 'select' as it had been in the early days: 'The other tenants aren't as nice. . . . There was a schoolmaster next door, and one across the back. Everyone was sociable, and they all had their gardens done; it was beautiful. People used to come down from the town to look at them.'

When the estate was built it was bounded by open fields, and several of these tenants reminisced about the walks they used to have over the fields and up to Hartshead Pike. The solid construction of the houses, and their spacious interior design must have been in even more marked contrast to the cramped terrace houses than they appear today; they also had inside bathrooms and lavatories. The cost of building these houses was about £265,000, divided between eight local building firms and the Oldham and District Building Trades Association.

At the end of 1922 in Oldham and the surrounding district the provision of houses in relation to the number approved, and bearing in mind that this itself was far short of the number assessed as required, is shown in Table 2.9. This does not include the further 50 houses built on the Greenacres estate.

Table 2.9: Houses Approved and Erected Under 1919 Act

	No. of Houses Contemplated	No. Erected	No. Abandoned
Oldham	1,000	300	700
Chadderton	300	0	300
Royton	200	52	148
Crompton	200	60	140
Lees	75	0	75
Springhead	50	0	50
	1,825	412	1,413

Judging from the cutbacks in the number of houses provided, Cullingworth appears to be correct in saying that this new involvement of the state in the provision of working-class housing was not meant to be permanent, but merely to alleviate the immediate post-war shortage of houses. He adds that the rapid rise in building costs led to a swift abandonment of the high level of subsidy, and that:

> It was generally held that the subsidised building programme was
> itself responsible for the rise in building costs and, furthermore, that
> this was making it all the more difficult for private enterprise to
> fulfil its traditional role as the main supplier of working-class
> houses. (Cullingworth, 1966, p. 17)

There were no houses built in Oldham under the 1923 Act, but over
1,100 under the 1924 Act, though not until the years 1930 to 1934.
The later houses reflected the reduction in subsidies in that they were
less spacious. In this one can see a concrete example of the subordination
of the needs of the working class to the dictates of the dominant class.
The deterioration in standards reflected the dominant ideology which
virtually said 'once a slum dweller, always a slum dweller'.

While the number of council houses was still minimal compared with
the overall housing shortage, it was thought that the housing standards
of even the poorer working class would be improved, by a 'filtering up'
process. It was obvious by the end of the 1920s that this was not
happening: the poor continued to live in insanitary conditions. In the
early 1920s there are several references in the MOH Reports to the
fact that although many houses were unfit, they were not closed
because of the general housing shortage, a defective roof being better
than no roof at all.

The houses built under the 1930 slum clearance Act, though they
show some improvement on the 1924 houses, did not reach the size of
houses built under the earlier slum clearance order. Oldham's 1930
slum clearance programme covered about 900 houses, most of which
had been demolished by 1940. Yet less than 700 houses were built
during the same period. While council housing subsidies certainly
improved the housing standards of those who were lucky enough to
be rehoused, they exacerbated rather than alleviated the overall housing
problem.

The Implications of State Intervention

The response of the local authority in Oldham to the central government's
Housing Acts was thus greatly constrained by the central government
itself. The general thrust of state intervention in housing in the nineteenth century had been largely negative, with a view to controlling or
destroying insanitary housing, one result being that fewer working-class
houses were built. After the First World War, state intervention can

initially be seen as a real gain for the working class. In the 1919 Act lay a promise of an end to the squalid and overcrowded conditions within and around much working-class housing; an end to sustaining a private landlord's quest for an economic return on his investment.

Yet the corollary of this was that it was also a gain for capital. The state could now not only indirectly regulate the housing of the working class, through the local authority it now became a direct landlord and provider of houses. While it would seem to be an overstatement to see the provision and allocation of council housing as a deliberate attempt by the bourgeoisie, through the state, to divide the working class, nevertheless in the early years the effect was that only the 'cream' of the working class managed to get council tenancies. In Oldham, in the allocation of tenancies official priority was given to ex-soldiers, and, it would seem from interviews with elderly tenants, also to white collar state workers, such as teachers and civil servants. Unofficially it also helped to know someone on the Council: one couple said that they had a relative on the Council who had been instrumental in getting a house allocated to them. But the rents effectively excluded many people. The cost of about 10s plus about 5s for rates per week meant that many working-class families could not even contemplate applying for them.

Not only could the state then control the allocation of a highly prized reward, once tenants were selected their behaviour was, and still is, subject to more stringent restrictions than private tenants'. Council tenants still do not have the same security of tenure as private tenants, and they can be evicted for a wide range of misdemeanours. The list of proscribed actions is long, as is the list of tenants' duties.

On the one hand, then, there is careful vetting of prospective tenants, those being assessed by the Housing Visitors as 'good' having a greater chance of early rehousing, and of being rehoused on the 'better' estates; while on the other hand, once they become council tenants people lose certain rights and may be subject to close scrutiny. The concern of the local authority for protecting and preserving what is seen as a piece of public investment rather than someone's home is apparent.

While the control of housing owned by the state has been removed from the vagaries of 'the market', its construction, the financing of construction costs through loans, and its potential as a commodity to be exchanged have not been so removed. In the provision of council housing the state is usually directly involved in the creation of surplus value, by private builders, and in its appropriation, by landowners, private builders, and finance companies giving loans. Given the large amounts of money involved and the potential value as a commodity it is hardly surprising that the state is concerned with the way this resource, the mass of council housing, is used by tenants.

Virtually regardless of any assessment of 'need', housing, together with other social expenditure, has thus been expanded or cut by the central government in attempts to regulate the national economy:

> The kind of national policy which has constrained local authorities' operations is illustrated by the recurring pattern of cuts in public expenditure. The costs of economic crisis are repeatedly shifted onto the poorly housed with devastating effects. Arising in response to pressures from the Treasury and international financiers and speculators the benefits of such policies go to finance capital. (CDP, 1976, p. 11)

Conclusions

One aspect of the importance of using a Marxist analysis to discuss the evolution of housing policy is its emphasis on the necessity to study the reproduction of capitalist relations of production and of the conditions for capitalist production and accumulation, as well as studying production itself. The needs of the working class have had only little influence on the type of housing which has been provided for them, but rather their subordinate and exploited position within the production process has been mirrored in their housing. Through working-class organisation and agitation local authorities and the central government *have* at times been forced to change their policies, for example, in the cessation of building high rise or deck access blocks, and even their demolition in some cases. But in the meantime it has been the working-class residents who have had to bear the social and economic costs of badly designed and/or badly built housing, in terms of loneliness, vandalism, heating bills, damp destroying furnishings, etc.

Private landlords, once there was no longer a need for mill owners to attract labour to the town, in Oldham were concerned with housing largely as an area for investment, and the extent of their property ownership thus depended on the structure of the finance market and alternative opportunities. The state's housing policies have also been responses to and reinforcements of various structural determinants, even if this has not been recognised to be the case. The state has primarily intervened to try and regulate demand, adjusting the relative importance of different tenure groups, by giving a variety of subsidies. But the fundamental issue has not been resolved, or even, it seems, recognised to be the fundamental issue: the form of production which gives rise to the high value, and therefore cost, of housing. Thus, under capitalism, state housing policies, and local government's interpretation of them, can be little more than palliatives to ameliorate, but not fundamentally change, the worst problems.

The basic contradiction between the low productivity of the building industry and its relative backwardness in technology, and the requirements of capital in general to reduce the value of commodities, including labour power, in order to increase accumulation (see Ball, 1977) was apparent in the late nineteenth century and is still apparent. The basic housing problem, the shortage of good, cheap houses for the working class, still remains a crucial issue, one which policies aimed at 'consumption' cannot hope to solve. It is only through the agitation of the working class that cuts in standards will not continue to be imposed on their housing, and that they will be able to maintain the gains for which they have struggled so long.

Notes

1. I might add here that this applies to Britain in the twentieth century, where local government acts largely only as a result of legislation passed by the central government. It might be that in the nineteenth century (or in other countries) when the centralisation of control of the state was less advanced, and when localities did indeed control their own police, education and other functions, the term 'local state' may have some validity.

2. 'Institutions and apparatuses do not "possess" their own "power", but simply express and crystallise class powers . . . the state is not a mere tool or instrument of the dominant classes to be manipulated at will . . . The task of the state is to maintain the unity and cohesion of a social formation divided into classes, and it focusses and epitomises the class contradictions of the whole social formation in such a way as to sanction and legitimise the interests of the dominant classes and fractions as against the other classes of the formation, in a context of world class contradictions.' (Poulantzas, 1974, pp. 70 and 78)

3. This may be enforced by means of repression as, for example, was the case with anti-trade union legislation and action. Or the means may be more subtle: through the operation of what Althusser calls the Ideological State Apparatuses, such as the church, the education system, and the family, the status quo is largely reproduced and accepted as such.

4. See also M. Ball. 'Bearing in mind that economic crises are founded in the sphere of production, rather than in exchange and distribution, that the primary recuperative force in crises is the restructuring of production capital rather than the pushing down of wages, the state's intervention in crises must be located there.' (Fine & Harris, 1976, p. 170). Yet this has not been the case with regard to housing.

5. 'The district A people [probably Werneth] are better endowed by nature. They come of a stronger stock. They are more intelligent and more keenly alive to the requisites of health. They possess and have exercised the qualities of self-denial and sobriety. Their life is regulated and restrained. They have been able to choose women of good education and physique. Their children would not readily

succumb to disease. If district B were to be inhabited by these particular folk, the damp would disappear from the walls, the dirty ceilings would become white, the houses would be vented artificially, and flowers would make their appearance in the windows. The streets would assume an aspect of cleanliness and brightness, and the neighbourhood would not know itself.' (*MOH Report, 1889*).

6. Oldham had seen an increase in organised working-class militancy. In 1885 the Oldham Provincial Card and Blowing Room and Ring Frame Operatives' Association was formed, which amalgamated a number of small associations, largely of semi-skilled workers and including many women. The growing strength of the Cardroom Workers' Union towards the end of the 1880s led to intensified pressure for an agreed wages list; the first such list was drawn up in 1891. During the years 1892-3 Oldham experienced the most bitter strike in the history of the spinning industry, which lasted for 20 weeks, over a proposed reduction in wages of 5 per cent. The issue was finally settled by the Brooklands Agreement, whereby a compromise reduction of 2.91 per cent in wages was agreed and a somewhat complicated arbitration system was established. However, there seems to have been very little militancy over housing issues.

7. Overcrowding was defined as two persons per room, children under 10 counted as half a person.

8. A full survey of ownership was done for 1906 to check the sample.

9. This is supported by the research of P. Laxton at Liverpool University. In a study of the sale and ownership of plots of land in Bolton between 1851 and 1861 he found out of 44 owners: 6 provision dealers or food retailers; 8 manufacturers of goods or machines; 7 clerical or professional people; 2 building contractors; 2 master cotton spinners; 2 widows; 4 miscellaneous; and 13 unidentified.

10. There was a severe shortage of building materials in the immediate post-war period, with production of bricks, for example, only being a third of the years preceding the war. This was one of the main reasons for the high cost of building: Richardson and Aldcroft (1968) say that in 1920 the average price of all building materials was about three times the pre-war level. The shortage and high price of materials discouraged builders from constructing houses when costs were at their peak. Prices did fall, but in 1923 to 1924 they were still more than double the pre-war level.

11. 'That whereas as a result of reductions made in wages paid to operatives in the Building Industry since May 1921, the labour costs in a house for the working classes are now 100 per cent above 1914 costs, and whereas the prices of materials required in the erection thereof, averaged over the house, are approximately 150 per cent above 1914 prices, and whereas houses are urgently needed by the Nation, the Government be urged to take immediate steps to combat the effect of trade rings at present existing in the Building Material Trade, thereby enabling the housing conditions in Oldham and elsewhere to be materially improved.' Oldham Resolution, March 1923.

References

Ball, M. 'British Housing Policy and the House Building Industry', paper presented at CSE, 'Urban Change and Conflict' Conference (York, Jan. 1977); revised version in *Capital and Class*, no. 4

Bateson, H. 'A centenary History of Oldham' (Oldham County Borough Council, Oldham, 1949)

Board of Trade. 'Cost of Living of the Working Classes: Report of an Enquiry by the Board of Trade into Working Class Rents, Housing and Retail Prices together with the Standard Rates of Wages prevailing in certain occupations in the Principal Industrial Towns of the United Kingdom' (HMSO, 1908)

Bowley, A.L. *Wages in the United Kingdom in the Nineteenth Century* (CUP, Cambridge, 1900)

Bowley, M. *Housing and the State* (George Allen & Unwin, London, 1945)

Castells, M. *The Urban Question: A Marxist Approach* (François Maspero, 1972), English trans. Sheridan, A. (Edward Arnold, London, 1977)

Cockburn, C. *The Local State: Management of Cities and People* (Pluto Press Ltd, London, 1977)

Community Development Project. 'Whatever Happened to Council Housing?' (CDP Information and Intelligence Unit, 1976)

Cullingworth, J.B. *Housing and Local Government in England and Wales* (George Allen & Unwin, London, 1966)

Damer, S. 'Working-Class Housing and Working-Class Incorporation: Glasgow 1860-1919', paper to Political Economy of Housing Workshop (unpublished, Manchester University, 1976)

Dyos, H.J. and Reeder, D.A. 'Slums and Suburbs' in Dyos, H.J. and Wolff, M. (eds) *The Victorian City: Images and Realities* (Routledge & Kegan Paul, London, 1973)

Engels, F. *The Condition of the Working-Class in England* (Leipzig, 1845; English ed. Panther Books Ltd, London, 1969)

Engels, F. *The Origin of the Family, Private Property and the State* (1884), in Feuer, L. *Marx and Engels* (Fontana, London, 1959)

Farnie, D.A. 'The English Cotton Industry 1850-1896' (MA Thesis, Manchester University, 1953)

Fine, B. and Harris, L. 'Controversial Issues in Marxist Economic Theory' in Miliband, R. and Saville, J. (eds), *The Socialist Register 1976* (Merlin Press, London, 1976)

Foster, J. *Class Struggle and the Industrial Revolution* (Weidenfeld & Nicolson, London, 1974)

Gauldie, E. *Cruel Habitations: A History of Working-Class Housing 1780-1918* (George Allen & Unwin, London, 1974)

Hague, Alderman J. 'Housing History in Oldham', in *Oldham Chronicle* (19 and 20 Feb. 1934)

Jones, F. 'The Cotton Spinning Industry in the Oldham District, 1896-1914' (MA Thesis, Manchester University, 1959)

Laxton, P. Unpublished research, Department of Georgraphy, University of Liverpool.

Marx, K. and Engels, F. *The German Ideology* (1845-6; English ed. Lawrence & Wishart, London, 1970)

Marx, K. and Engels, F. *The Communist Manifesto* (1848; English ed. Progress Publishers, Moscow, 1967)

Melling, J. 'Employers and Company Housing 1880-1919: The Case of a Clyde Shipbuilding Yard' (unpublished paper, Glasgow University, 1976)

Memorandum from Borough Surveyor to Housing and Town Planning Committee, Oldham, 24 April 1913

Oldham County Borough, Rate Books 1841-1936

Oldham County Borough, Surveyors and Building Committee, Minutes of Meetings 1919-23

Oldham Medical Officer of Health, Annual Reports, 1886-1974

Oldham Trades Council, Annual Reports, 1892-1913

Parry Lewis, J. *Building Cycles and Britain's Growth* (Macmillan, London, 1965)

Pickvance, C. (ed.), *Urban Sociology: Critical Essays* (Methuen, London, 1976)

Poulantzas, N. *Classes in Contemporary Capitalism* (Editions du Seuil, Paris, 1974); English trans. D. Fernbach (New Left Books, London, 1975)

Price, S.J. *Building Societies: Their Origin and History* (Franey, London, 1958)

Richardson, H.W. and Aldcroft, D.H. *Building in the British Economy Between the Wars* (George Allen & Unwin, London, 1968)

Slaters' Directories of Oldham, 1843, 1895

Smith, R. 'The Lancashire Cotton Industry 1873-1896' (PhD Thesis, Birmingham University, 1954)

Smith, R. 'An Oldham Limited Liability Company 1875-1896' in *Business History*, vol. IV (1961)

Wood, G.H. *The History of Wages in the Cotton Trade During the Past Hundred Years* (Sherratt & Hughes, Altrincham, 1910)

Worralls' Directories of Oldham, 1871, 1875, 1884, 1888-9, 1891

This research was carried out under SSRC Research Grant No. HR 3656/1.

3 STATE, CLASS AND HOUSING: GLASGOW 1885-1919*

Seán Damer

It has also been suggested that the agitation for short lets is only part of a general socialistic programme. We cannot endorse this view. The matter, in our view, has been taken up on its own merits, without ulterior views.

Report of the Departmental Committee on House-Letting in Scotland, Cd. 3715, 1907, p. 4.

Some of those who interest themselves in the tenant's case showed clearly that their interest extended beyond the present situation, their avowed aim being to force the State or the municipality into building workmen's cottages by means of capital provided free of interest.

Report of the Committee Appointed by the Secretary for Scotland to Enquire into the Circumstances Connected with the Alleged Recent Increase in the Rental of Small Dwelling-houses in the Industrial Districts of Scotland, Cd. 8154, 1916, p. 7.

1 Introduction

The importance of studying the relations between (apparently) local struggles and the introduction of 'social policy' at the level of the state seems to me to be in its possibilities for illuminating the workings of capitalism. It is the contention of this article that a study of housing militancy on Clydeside shows that it is an historical process which dialectically relates the levels of 'community' and 'state'. But as 'community', or the 'locality', is always an arbitrary spatial enclave, there is a problem in making this relationship to the state, which can be reified by being equally arbitrarily 'photographed' in time. But the

*I should like to acknowledge my very real indebtedness to Mrs M. Manchester of the Baillie's Library, Glasgow, and Mr Eddie Frow of the Working Class Movement Library, Manchester. Their encyclopaedic knowledge of local history and sources, and their unfailing courtesy and willingness to assist, have been crucial to the research on which this article is based. I also wish to acknowledge both helpful comments on, and masterly editing of, an earlier draft of this article by Andy Pollak.

effort must be made as the events of Red Clydeside, and particularly the housing struggle, *did* have important effects upon the state, and more particularly, between 1914 and 1918, upon a British state at war.

While this is not the place to enter into an extended discussion of Marxist theories of the state, it is germane to the analysis offered here to indicate briefly my position. This is a Leninist one, which argues, *contra* Poulantzas,[1] that the state has no autonomy from classes. It has an *apparent* autonomy, which is to do with the fact that it does not have a one-to-one relationship with the dominant fraction(s) of capital. Indeed, the state cannot have such a relationship, as it is the instrument of domination of the proletariat by the *whole* of the bourgeoisie. The question of how the apparatuses of the state are shared out amongst the fractions of the bourgeoisie is a subordinate question compared to the question of how the state divides the working class. (This is not to deny the inevitable contradictions of capitalist development, or the tensions which occur from time to time between different fractions of capital: it is merely to stress that the state is an absolutist *bourgeois* state.)

The class struggle, the battle of the bourgeoisie to continue its domination and exploitation of the proletariat, is continuously being fought out at all levels of the state and its apparatuses: every innovation of capital is contested between capital and labour. The state is the cockpit of class struggle as well as the instrument of class domination: its forms are the outcome, the expression, of class struggle. Clearly, then, according to specific historical conditions, different balances of class forces and patterns of class alliances will characterise different periods of the social formation, and will be reflected in the apparatuses of the state, both ideological and repressive. This means that whereas under capital, state power is always in the hands of the bourgeois *class*, the proletariat can, has done, and will continue to win significant tactical victories at all instances of the social formation. It should also alert us to the fact that historically, under capital, the masses can suddenly act at a time and in ways which no one could have predicted — they are ahead of the revolution briefly, so to speak. Thus from a Marxist point of view, the internal relationship of the state to the proletariat at a time of sudden mass movement — as at the epoch of the 'Red Clydeside' — with all its subsequent 'social policy' connotations, urgently needs theorising.

John Foster has said, in locating the theoretical importance of social change under capital:[2]

Most of those who concern themselves with this (and they start with

Marx) would see capitalism's social development as being determined by people's response to it as a *class* system. It is the struggle against its class nature that helps drive the system forward and (on occasion) over-throws it. It is the response to the alienation that also (on occasion) helps sustain it. And it is finally the interplay of both with the underlying dimension of economic change which produces the system's characteristic pattern of development. The way in which this takes place provides − in its detailed working − much of the perspective we are looking for.

This is the perspective this chapter seeks to find − and in so doing, also seeks to explain why there should be such a marked shift in the class struggle over Glasgow housing in the mere nine years between the two reports quoted at the head of this chapter.

In summary, this chapter argues that the 1915 Rent Strikes in Glasgow, and the subsequent 1915 Rents and Mortgage Restrictions Act, constituted a gain − a class victory − for organised labour. Further, it argues that this act was a *sine qua non* of the 1919 Housing and Town Planning Act. It does *not* argue that these gains were the result of the struggles of Clydeside men and women alone, but does argue that the events of 1915 in Glasgow were the culmination of a *national* class struggle over housing whose origins go back to at least 1885. It rejects arguments among bourgeois social scientists that these were *not* gains, or were only partial gains, or were gains which did not cost anybody anything.[3] It rejects notions that this was a 'social', 'community', or any other kind of sociological 'movement'.[4] This is not to say that outlandish claims are being made for the Rent Strikers: it is not argued that theirs was a 'revolutionary struggle'. Glasgow in 1915 was not Petersburg in 1917 − although Glasgow in 1919 was probably the nearest that any British city ever came to it. But what *is* argued is that the rent strike was located in a *mass* movement which transcended, albeit briefly, the typical splits of skill, sex and religion, in the working class; that its leaders were socialists of both the reformist and revolutionary traditions, who *all* theorised the rents struggle in *class* terms; and that the leadership and the masses fused in a militant, oppositional and thoroughly *political* struggle which was successful.

2 The Class Struggle over Working-Class Housing, 1885-1914

Perhaps the most notable fact about the class struggle over working-class housing in the earlier part of this period is that there was not one − or so all the conventional histories of housing development say. Enid

Gauldie, who has produced the most comprehensive survey to date, states that in the nineteenth century, there were no secret societies or riots about housing as such.[5] She argues that the government of the day randomly produced housing legislation 'as a sop to quieten agitation on other matters'.[6]

A preliminary examination of readily available data suggests that this was indeed the case. The year 1885 is taken as the starting point of the period under discussion precisely because there was a Royal Commission on the Housing of the Working Classes in that year, and the Minutes of Evidence to this Commission contain an impressive range of evidence on such housing — from people who generally did not live in it.[7] There was a clear comprehension in mid-Victorian Britain that there *was* a working-class housing problem, although there was considerable dis-agreement about its constitution. One fact was already established, however: that it was the task of private enterprise to supply houses for the workers. There was a blind faith in the infallibility of 'market forces'. Even some labour leaders evinced a thoroughly reactionary attitude to any idea of forces other than private enterprise constructing houses for the working people. The President of Edinburgh Trades Council gave the following evidence to the Royal Commission:[8]

> *Q.* Do you desire that the municipality should take public money for the purpose of building houses for the working classes? *A.* No, I should not approve of, say, the Town Council of Edinburgh becoming responsible for the housing of the people. If an impression of that description were to get abroad, if every family in the city believed that the Town Council were responsible for a proper housing, I am afraid that it would strike at that industry and enterprise that lies at the very root of our national existence.

When asked about the role of the state, the president replied that he thought that the state should lend money cheaply, and should permit authorities to purchase compulsorily land adjacent to the city, and that was all.[9] This worker simply reproduced contemporary bourgeois ideology.

But under the apparent hegemony of interests amongst the witnesses to the commission lurked real problems. The existing housing legisla-tion was essentially to do with slum clearance — and that on a piecemeal basis. There was no real compulsion on local authorities to rehouse those slum-dwellers rendered homeless by clearance operations, and it was common knowledge throughout the country — as witness after

witness to the commission made clear — that such policies only resulted
in the compounded overcrowding of adjacent areas.[10] Yet the orthodox
'filtering-up' thesis was also trotted out as the way in which this particular problem would be resolved. This notion held that with the
construction of new artisan dwellings, the 'better class' of tenants
would move into them, leaving a vacuum behind which would spon-
taneously be filled by a species of upwards ripple which would eventually suck even the dreaded 'residuum' out of its rookeries into the next
best thing, whatever that was. (That this was a particularly pernicious
ideology has been demonstrated by Stedman Jones in his study of
Victorian London.)[11]

Yet the contradictions between the sheer scale of the slum housing
problem, and the pathetic attempts at its solution, made arguments
about municipal housing inevitable, as the following evidence to the
1885 Commission from the Lord Provost of Glasgow makes clear:[12]

Q. But it is a point which I noted down to ask you, whether at
municipal elections it formed one of the questions that were put
to you? *A.* Yes, it always does. *Q.* The idea, you say, is abroad in
Glasgow that it would be right for the municipality to undertake
the housing of the poor upon a large scale? *A.* I will not say that
the idea is abroad; it is one of the questions that are, or were (it is
not so much so now) put to candidates asking to be returned upon
the town council — whether they were in favour of erecting houses
for the working classes.

So while the working people of Glasgow had, on the face of it, made
housing into a municipal issue as early as 1885, they, and their brothers
and sisters all round the country were not very militant about it at this
stage.[13] Their docility is caught by another witness to the Royal
Commission, a clergyman who represented the Edinburgh Social and
Sanitary Society:[14]

Q. Do you happen to know the feelings of some of the lowest
grades? *A.* I think I do.
Q. Is there any great feeling of resentment about the places they are
obliged to live in? *A.* No, they accept them, because they cannot
help themselves.
Q. But there has been no agitation, has there, amongst the people
themselves on that score? *A.* No, we have a class of people to deal
with that require to be urged on to do a thing of that kind, other-

wise they are satisfied. I think their feeling is that they cannot help themselves.

Q. There is no feeling of resentment amongst themselves, is there?
A. No, I have never heard any complaints at all. I think a great many of them might live in better houses if they were as they ought to be; if they kept more sober.

If the poor lived in slums, then the state could be reassured that they were too drunk to revolt.

But the material living conditions of the mass of the working class were too awful for a situation of pacificity to persist. Additionally, the events of the 1880s and 1890s had led to an upsurge in the trades unionisation of the semi- and unskilled workers. It was quite clear by the last decade of the nineteenth century that private enterprise could or would not solve the problem of the housing of the working class. While it is apparent from a variety of sources that there were many localised struggles over housing by 1900, perhaps the most important phenomenon to emerge for the purposes of this argument was the Workmen's National Housing Council. It is important because not only did the Council articulate if not orchestrate the national struggle over workers' housing, its effects were felt in Glasgow.[15] What follows is the briefest of summaries of its activities, and I am happy to acknowledge that it is totally derived from the first-rate thesis of Dave Englander on the Council.[16]

Three compositors founded the Workmen's National Housing Council in 1898 as a result of despair over their continuing problems with high rents. It is of critical importance to note that all three were members of the SDF, their leader being Fred Knee, a man who devoted so much energy to the struggle for working-class housing that he eventually died of exhaustion. Again, it is important to note that *Justice*, the SDF newspaper, had been agitating for non-profit-making municipal housing from as early as 1885.[17] Indeed, *every* liberal and left-wing group including trades councils all over the country, had the municipalisation of housing as a central issue throughout the last decade of the nineteenth century, and right up to the outbreak of the First World War.

The council campaigned on the municipalisation issue through its own organ, *The Housing Journal*; through the organisation of both local and national conferences; by sending specialist speakers all round the country; by lobbying Parliament; by getting sympathetic MPs to ask questions in the House and, in 1890, forcing a bill, with TUC backing,

on reluctant members. While Knee and his comrades, as Marxists, saw
that the housing question was a *political* one,[18] and one that could only
be solved eventually by the working class itself,[19] they were obliged
under the circumstances of the time to take to reformist routes for
their strategy — even if they themselves had no illusions about their
efficacy.

What is important to note is threefold: firstly, that essentially it was
the efforts of the Workmen's National Housing Council which forced
the state to begin even to consider subventing housing finance in the
years before the First World War;[20] the second is the *political* context
of the Council's struggle; the third is that in parallel with these activities in England, the *Scottish* Housing Council was founded after the
Glasgow Trades Council held public meetings in 1899 and 1900.[21]
This became the (Scottish) National Labour Housing Council in 1918.

The point is: by the start of the First World War, the issue of state
financing of working-class housing was abroad in the working class of
this country. More than that, the vigour with which the working class
had pursued the issue, through the Workmen's National Housing
Council, and other forms of agitation, had forced upon a reluctant
state, the realisation that it was going to have to foot the bill eventually. So while Gauldie may be right there were no secret societies or
riots over housing in the nineteenth century, what is equally right is
that there was a strong working-class organisation around the housing
issue, albeit pursued in a reformist, parliamentarian tradition.

Before going to Glasgow, a word of caution. It would be incorrect
to argue that it was the action of the working class *alone* which pushed
the state into this realisation. Rather it was the changes in the material
base of British capitalism at the time of its imperialist adventures in
Southern Africa (culminating in the Boer Wars) which gave rise to the
working class's ability to conceptualise and tackle the housing problem. These changes also produced a shift of ideology in the bourgeoisie
such that *it* began to seek for new practices and new rationalisations as
regards working-class housing, as regards the politics of *reproduction*.
An important factor in this slight shift away from the entrenched
laissez-faire attitudes of earlier decades was the disastrous physical
condition of the urban working class exposed by the Boer Wars. The
sheer *scale* of the health problem reported upon by the Inter-Departmental Committee on Physical Deterioration[22] posed problems for
British capital not just in winning South Africa's vast natural resources
for plunder, but also in terms of the reproduction of labour power at
home — at a time of increasing tension with Germany, and the begin-

nings of an accelerated arms race. Thus at the level of the state, there
was a contradiction: that between the need for accelerated capital
accumulation, and static or deteriorating facilities for the reproduction
of labour power. The working class nationally was able to take advantage of this contradiction and construct a social practice which not only
involved increasing industrial militancy, but also the organisation of the
campaign for better housing for its members, under its control.

3 Glasgow Housing and the Local Housing Struggle, 1885-1914

The empirical facts about Glasgow's stock of housing around 1885 are
reasonably well known, and are discussed in a variety of sources.[23]
Suffice it to say that in 1881 some 25 per cent of the city's population
lived in 'single-ends' – one-roomed houses, while upwards of 50 per
cent lived in 'rooms-and-kitchens' – two-roomed houses. While the
slum-clearance programme of the City Improvement Trust since 1866
had cleared some of the worst areas, particularly in the old city area,
Glasgow, like most other British cities, had simply not used the existing legislation to rehouse the dispossessed. The iron law of the market
was supposed to swing into operation to supply their housing demand.
So, again as elsewhere, those wretches flooded into the neighbourhoods
adjacent to the clearance areas, only to exacerbate the already bad
problem of overcrowding. On top of this, the city's population was
growing by 'natural increase', by immigration from the Highlands and
Ireland, and by the steady incorporation of surrounding burghs. The
net result of all this was a housing problem of staggering dimensions,
the critical part of which was overcrowding, although there still remained a stock of technically unfit older buildings which were in fact
inhabited. In 1901, the population within the municipal boundaries
was 776,967; the house accommodation was as follows:[24]

1	apt. houses:	36,422
2	apt. houses:	72,099
3	apt. houses:	27,695
3+	apt. houses:	24,630

The proportion of the population living in each size of house was as
follows:

		Old City	Extended City*
1	apt. houses:	15.89	14.050
2	apt. houses:	49.95	47.054
3	apt. houses:	20.49	20.476
3+	apt. houses:	13.67	18.420

However one does ones accounting, the facts of the matter are that at the turn of the century, nearly 70 per cent of the city's housing stock consisted of houses of not more than two rooms, in which lived somewhat more than 60 per cent of the city's population. Now on top of this accommodation, all privately rented, was a plethora of lodging- and rooming-houses: houses-let-in-lodgings; farmed-out houses; made-down houses, as they were variously known. These were the doss-houses, flop-joints and brothels of the city, the depair of the sanitary and policy authorities, the cesspools of iniquity.

The economics of this situation prove interesting to excavate. Jim Treble, in an important article, has shown that as a substantial proportion of the Glasgow labour force in late Victorian times was affected by seasonal factors, many unskilled and semi-skilled labourers had a constant battle to stay above the poverty line.[25] This was dramatically illustrated by a witness to the 1892 Glasgow Presbytery Commission on the Housing of the Poor, a member of the Socialist League, in what constitutes perhaps the first formal report of a comment on the political context of housing in Glasgow.[26] This witness stressed the poverty of many Glasgow workers, and gave detailed evidence of the incomes of various occupational groups. He estimated that there were some 50,000 people in the city on no more than 18s per week. About this time, the rent of a single-end averaged 2s 6d per week, and that of a room-and-kitchen was 4s.[27] The Presbytery Commission noted that the weekly rent of a *bed* in a rooming house was around 4s,[28] while the other sources suggest that in the shadier refuges, the nightly rent was between 8d and 1s.[29] The profits to be made out of ownership and/or management of these slum properties was colossal, as I have noted elsewhere.[30] The Socialist League witness to the 1892 Commission summed it up tersely:[31]

thus you have the fact that thousands of honest and industrious men have to support families on less than is allowed for the maintenance

* This means the old city plus the recently incorporated burghs. The figures in the second column are given to three decimal places in the census

of families of paupers in our poorhouses and families of convicted criminals in our prisons.

The state of many — but not all — of these houses was atrocious. The Presbytery Commission notes that a single privy in the back-court for a whole close was common, and cites cases where one served 22 families,[32] and another, 40.[33] This commonly led to the sink — if one existed — being used as the toilet.[34] The overcrowding was so great that it was not uncommon to keep a corpse in the house for a day or two, even to the extent of having it in bed with the living.[35]

How was this appalling housing situation dealt with, firstly by the landlords, and secondly, by the tenants themselves? How did the class struggle over housing express itself? The landlords of Glasgow were a powerful and organised cartel, that much is plain from the literature. Their interests were powerfully represented on the corporation. Their rapaciousness was startling, even among a class not noted for its munificence. They used every trick from physical force to ideological terror to repress their working-class tenants. To exemplify: as I have discussed in detail elsewhere, there was the phenomenon of 'ticketing' houses.[36] These ticketed houses were subject to unannounced raids in the middle of the night — after midnight — by sanitary inspectors who had the powers to bring surplus occupants to court. A point to stress here is that these inspectors were police, the sanitary police. In the latter half of the century, there were some 85,500 Glaswegians living in 23,288 ticketed houses, who were subject to a form of interference and control which seems unthinkable now. It was made fairly clear that these midnight raids were as much to do with repression as with the control of disease, as the Report of the 1904 Glasgow Municipal Commission on the Housing of the Poor makes clear:[37]

> In practice, 'ticketing' is only resorted to when, from the character of the property and of the tenants, it is considered desirable to inspect houses for overcrowding during the night. It may be taken for granted, therefore, that there are many houses which, from their size, might legally be ticketed which escape owing to the character of the tenant, or from some other circumstance.

In other words, under the guise of medical mission the practice of ticketing and raiding was really one of the many attempts made by the state during the Victorian years to penetrate, comprehend and destabilise the collective organisation of the poor in their slums.[38]

The class hatred of the rentiers of Glasgow was also clearly expressed in other aspects of their behaviour. The only ordinary worker to appear before the 1904 Municipal Commission relates how after complaining about lack of repairs in a leaking roof in his room in a farmed-out house, he was evicted, and found it impossible to find other accommodation.[39] Even although he was working and could pay a deposit, he could not find accommodation as (i) he came from a farmed-out house, and (ii) he did not have a factor's 'line', or reference. Thus, compelled to live in a room in a farmed-out house by exigency, this worker complained about lack of repairs, did not get satisfaction, withheld his rent and was evicted. The fact that he did not have a 'line' indicated that he was a trouble-maker of some kind, and he would be forced into the worst kind of accommodation. The irony was bitterly compounded for this poor man in that it is quite clear that the Commissioners did not believe his story, as they kept at the man asking how many times he had tried to find a new house and so on. This man even had references from work, and from a mission. But this was useless against the Glasgow factors' cartel, which, it is clear from all the official enquiries, was notorious in pre-war Glasgow.

For the factors themselves, of course, the poor were where they were because of lack of moral fibre. A witness from the Glasgow Factors' Association told the Presbytery Commission that:[40] 'the contention of the Association (is) that the root of the evil in the housing of the poor is the thriftlessness, intemperance and want of self-respect of a considerable class among tenant occupants.' The kind of Calvinistic cant which could inspire the discussion of housing for the working class in Glasgow is best summed-up in a lecture given by the then Professor of Political Economy at Glasgow University in 1902, ending with a plea for a Municipal Commission into the Housing of the Poor[41] (which was the one of 1904 cited above). He argued that rather than give in to increasing labour demand for municipalised housing — and worst of all come into competition with private enterprise — it is necessary to figure out a way of 'solving the housing problem' which will appease all and cost little. After all, as the professor has it:[42]

There is no centre of moral deterioration and infection worse than a bad home. The slum dwellers, as a rule, are the rats who carry the plague, and there is not even the compensation that the rats grow fat. They grow diseased and lean, and, unhappily, they become the parents of more diseased and yet leaner rats.

So, something has to be done. It is true, there is an absolute shortage of
housing in the city – but, there can be no question of municipal
housing programme interfering with private enterprise building, for the
municipality has to cater for *all* citizens, equally. Thus a municipal
housing programme for the respectable working class would, of course,
confer benefits and privileges upon it which would be undemocratic.
The Professor makes no bones about his position:[43]

> Now I must put it distinctly that my argument – my concession to
> the housing policy – is not based in the least on the advisability of
> what is called 'housing the working classes'. It is based on the
> possibilities of getting rid of a deep seed-bed of evil.

This evil is, of course, the now-familiar 'dissolute poor', and the argument
is that this class has to be hived-off from the respectable poor. The
market will then look after the latter:[44]

> In the absence of special circumstances, it is no part of the work of a
> municipality to build houses at all. But the undoubted duty of every
> municipality is to provide police and sanitary control ... This inab-
> ility to provide police and sanitary control because of the failure of
> private effort to build cheap houses, is the 'special circumstance'
> which justifies and demands corporate action ... It is, then, for the
> improvident and destructive, but not criminal, class that I ask the
> Corporation to build.

The professor must have been surprised at the vehemence with
which so many labour representatives at the subsequent 1904 Municipal
Commission rejected his plea: they wanted municipal housing, for the
decent poor, for themselves!

Around the turn of the century the situation had polarised: the
working class, through its organs and institutions, was maintaining a
steadily increasing agitation for some form of municipalisation and also
for fair rents. By 1898, the ILP had ten members on the Town Council
who were known as the 'Stalwarts' for the relentless manner in which
they pursued municipalisation policies. The central political importance of the housing issue in Glasgow in these years is evidenced by the
very fact that there *were* two local commissions, and a Municipal
Conference (1901) into the housing of the poor, a unique phenomenon
in British urban history. And in parallel with similar activities going on
elsewhere in the country, Glasgow Trades Council took the initiative,

after a series of meetings in 1899 and 1900, in forming a Scottish
Housing Association which made a clear call for state provision of
housing in 1908.[45] The significance of this struggle is that it is an
indicator of how the Glasgow working class was breaking out of the
confines of orthodox Liberal and Tory Party politics, and was beginning to fight a *class* struggle along socialist lines, however primitive and
even incorrect these may seem with the wisdom of hindsight. The
Glasgow bourgeoisie's own defence organisation, the Citizens' Union,
did all it could to sabotage any efforts on the part of the City Improvement Trust to *build* new workers' housing to replace the thousands it
had demolished. A contemporary labour candidate summed it all up
rather well:[46]

> The 'Citizens' Union' consists of men educated in the wrong direc-
> tion; good business men and very likely most of them kind hearted
> and disposed to be charitable; but it is the application of sound prin-
> ciples, not charity, this (housing) problem requires, and I have not
> seen the sign of these in any of their utterances. They are just the
> ordinary bourgeoisie, holding that Labour is a commodity to be
> bought by a competition wage which hunger will compel men to take
> whether it will pay the rent of a decent house or not. They have not
> heard the voice of history calling down the ages.

The voice of history was not long in calling.

What the call was was 'long lets'. This referred to the system by
which houses were let in urban Scotland for long, fixed periods, with
the rent required well in advance. (It was unknown in England, where
lets of houses were practically universally of one week.) This system of
long lets was detested in the west of Scotland: there were conferences
on the topic in Glasgow in 1886, 1894, 1899, 1900 and 1904, the last
three being called by the Glasgow Trades Council.[47] There were liter-
ally dozens of mass meetings, there were resolutions passed by both the
STUC and the TUC, and there was a deputation of Scottish MPs to
Lord Dunedin, the Lord Advocate, in 1904, and a memorial from
three-quarters of the Scottish MPs to the Secretary for Scotland in
1906.[48] Tenant's defence associations sprang up all over Glasgow and
the surrounding burghs: there was general uproar. Nine parliamentary
bills on the issue were presented between 1890 and 1907. The protest
was so strong that the state established an inquiry into it. The report
of this departmental committee was known as the 'Guthrie Report'
after Lord Guthrie, its chairman.[49]

The report itself said:[50]

The grievances complained of by the tenants of workmen's dwellings
are mainly, *first*, the Scotch system of letting by missives for yearly
tacks — i.e. the practice of letting all but the poorest of working
men's houses for a whole year to tenants whose occupation requires
them to shift their residences frequently throughout the year, as
opposed with the weekly or monthly lets of similar houses to similar
tenants in England; *second*, the practice of calling upon the occupants of working men's dwellings to contract for such yearly houses
four months before the term of entry; and *third*, the demand made
upon working men to pay their rates, both municipal and parish
council, in one sum, in winter, when work is scarcest, and when
household expenses are highest.

In 1907, just under half the houses in Glasgow rented at £10 per
annum or more.[51] The system of letting these houses was that practically all houses over £10 rental were leased annually; houses between
£5 and £10 were frequently rented annually, or more usually, quarterly;
the cheaper houses, those below £5, were usually rented monthly or less
usually, weekly; while, as we have seen, rooms in lodging houses were
let daily or weekly. In the first instance, that of the annual lets, rent
was paid quarterly in arrears, generally speaking; in the second case,
rent was quarterly or monthly, in arrears; while for the cheaper houses,
rent was paid monthly or weekly, and in this case, between 50 per cent
and 70 per cent was paid in advance.[52] In the rooming-houses, the rent
was nightly or weekly in advance.

Now all these houses (excluding rooms in lodging-houses) were let
at Whitsun, towards the end of May. But the landlords required to know
if the tenant was renewing his/her lease by the beginning of February,
hence the tenant was committing him/herself to sixteen months'
tenure. A worker, a member of the Paisley Tenants' Protection
Association, put it this way in evidence to the committee:[53]

Q. What in your view is the most substantial grievance? *A*. The
principal one is that although we are paid weekly and fortnightly
wages, we have to sign for an article four months before we take
possession of it; we are bound down to sixteen months, while we
can be dismissed from our work at a week's notice — some can be
dismissed on the spot.

The next trap the tenant found him/herself in was the 'Law of Urban Hypothec', which was even more detested than being forced into long lets. This law actually said that[54] tenants' 'furniture, furnishings, and tools are liable to sequestration by a landlord immediately after they enter on possession of a house as security for rent not then accrued, due, or payable'. The practice seemed to be that if the tenant did not pay his/her rent for the full year, either by falling into arrears or by abandoning the tenancy before the full year was up, the landlord had the right to seize his/her goods under the law of hypothec. These seizures, and subsequent sales of goods, were as squalid an example of insatiable appetite of capitalism then as they are now. They even turned the stomach of John Mann Jnr, one of the most powerful men in the landlord/factor axis of Glasgow, and a steadfast opponent of shorter lets and municipalisation:[55]

> *Q.* I note that in your précis of evidence that you use these words — 'The enforce of hypothec in a small house is the enactment of a tragedy'. Explain what you mean by these words? *A.* It is a pretty graphic expression this, but I remember once, perhaps a quarter of a century ago, when I was not so experienced as I am now, being very much dissatisfied with a small tenant and resolving, as an example to the other tenants, to enforce the law to the utmost, that I carried out the action, sale and all, in that house, and I made a mental vow that I would never do it again. It really was barbarous and absolutely unproductive.
> *Q.* What is the reason of that? *A.* Well, the whole household goods are so restricted and small, and they are everything to the people. You feel that you are taking away their life's blood.

(In a lovely gesture of solidarity, it appears from the report that the neighbours of sequestrated tenants often had a whip-round to buy their effects and give them right back.)[56]

The whole rents issue was exacerbated by another, related, grievance, that of rates. In brief, in Glasgow, gas rates were collected three or four times per year, and the poor rate once per year. On top of these were water and police rates. (Houses on a very low rental — £4 or less — were exempt.) This meant that weekly- or fortnightly-paid workers had to save up on a separate account to pay their rates. Further, the factors collected the money to pay the gas rate — essentially for stair-lighting — but they passed it on to the municipality less 20 per cent rebate for the alleged difficulties of collection.[57] Again, the

tenants were infuriated about this. Consequently, one of the tenants'
demands was for 'compounding' of the rates, that is, adding them all
together in one annual account, then dividing that total by 12 or 52
and paying the rates with their monthly or weekly rents.[58] And, in
respect of these rates, there was yet another dimension in which the
tenants were at the mercy of the factors – and as should be becoming
clear, the latter were merciless. The report states it clearly:[59]

> When returns are given in annually to the assessor for the purpose of
> making up the Valuation Roll, the name of the tenant who happens
> to be at the time in occupation is returned without any statement
> as to the duration of his tenure. He is then liable for the whole
> taxes of the year, even although he is only a monthly tenant; and
> he remains liable, even if, in the course of the year, he removes to
> another house.

Further, as the rates were collected along with the rent, and it was
never clear precisely what the different charges were for, the tenants
suspected the factors of fiddling. Needless to say, the factors were
generally opposed to compounding, although they were prepared to
accept some compromise in this direction given that they could charge
yet another commission for such collection![60] (It should be stressed
that compounding was normal in England at this time, and did not seem
to present any problems to either the factors or the rates collectors.)
    The effects of all this were startling. In this first instance, it meant
constant 'moonlight flits', as the poor fled to avoid paying the rates,
and less often their rents.[61] The report suggests that in 1906, some
15,000 people were involved in such flits,[62] while in the same year,
14,501 rate-payers in Glasgow were disenfranchised for failing to pay
the poor rate.[63] There was constant harassment of the poor by the
factors to get arrears of rent: in 1904, in the burgh court – which
dealt only with *monthly* rentals, meaning smaller, cheaper houses –
there were 9,917 warrants for ejectment, or eviction.[64] But the poor
fought back to the best of their ability; they lodged notice of intent
to defend themselves, which meant an automatic delay of the action
– 7,736 out of the 9,917 proceeded against in 1904 did this.[65]
    Further, strong evidence was given to the committee by the represen-
tatives of the Lanarkshire Miners' Union, one of whom was the
secretary of the Scottish Miners' Federation. (It should be remembered
that the Lanarkshire miners were represented on Glasgow Trades
Council.) They made a powerful case against their situation of tied

cottages, with attendant summary eviction during strikes.[66] (Indeed, the housing situation of the miners was so atrocious, and their struggle so intense, that a Royal Commission was to be appointed to look into the whole matter in 1912 — but that is getting ahead of the argument.)

To conclude the discussion of the important and strangely neglected Guthrie Report, it really did crystallise the contradictions which the authorities in Glasgow faced over working-class housing. Because of the implacable stance of the landlords, Glasgow Corporation could not collect 26 per cent of its annual rates.[67] Further, and more importantly in terms of heightening class tension, there were 16,000 empty houses in the city in 1907.[68] Now while some of this very large number is to be explained in terms of over-building, not all of it is by a long shot. It is to be noted that building in the city had to all intents and purposes stopped a year or two before the committee. Then, there was the repressive nature of the lettings system which clearly drove some people into cheaper rooming-houses and slums where lets were short and nobody asked any questions. Given that it was a time for declining real wages and uncertain employment, this is all the more probable. And further, contrary to received opinion, Glasgow rents were higher — for worse accommodation — than their equivalent in England, as various witnesses forcefully pointed out.[69]

At the end of the day, the committee's report failed totally to address itself itself to the major issues, presenting two minority reports. The first came from Thomas Binnie, a tough, experienced, 'rational' member of Glasgow's property-owning bourgeoisie, asking for a tougher line on evictions, etc. The second came from two commissioners, Mr Howden (Secretary of Glasgow & District Unemployed Workers' Committee) and Mr Dobbie, pointing out that the key problems have not been resolved, and in general supporting the workers' case. Thus for the third time in fifteen years, no action was forthcoming from an official enquiry into working-class housing in Glasgow.

Agitation on the rents issues continued, and in 1911 the state was forced to react to this pressure by passing the House Letting and Rating Act. Basically, this resulted in monthly lets for houses with an annual rental of under £21, thus overturning the recommendation of the Guthrie Report that annual rents should continue, but with only one month's notice being necessary on either side. But this led to renewed trouble, as landlords seized on the opportunities offered by monthly lets to increase the rents gradually. It also meant more accusations of fiddling-the-rates, now collected with monthly rents.

The working-class offensive started in 1911 with the foundation of

a radical and centralised City Labour Party with housing as a central
plank, and an official policy of the erection of cottages instead of
tenements.[70] It continued in 1913 when John Wheatley, then in the
ILP, and a Glasgow Town Councillor, published his celebrated
pamphlet: *£8 Cottages for Glasgow Citizens*. With typical cogency,
Wheatley went straight to the root of the problem:[71]

> poverty alone is universally associated with bad housing. Mere
> tinkering with the contributory causes, while ignoring the main one,
> is idle futility. The brimming river which is bearing the people to
> destruction will continue to carry them on its deadly course even
> though here and there you may dam a rivulet.

This proposal for £8 cottages for the workers, to be subsidised from the
considerable profits made by the corporation from its municipalised
tramways, produced a furore. It was violently opposed by the
bourgeoisie who saw it as directly attacking their interests, which
indeed it did. Perhaps what caused the greatest agitation was the militant strategy adopted by Wheatley and his comrades in the town council
meetings, where they filibustered, disrupted, and in general railroaded a
debate on the proposal.[72] Further, Wheatly wrecked the Tory group's
proposal to solve the city's housing problem by building new single-
ends.[73]

The housing situation was also being propagandised by Glasgow's
revolutionaries in the SDP with John MacLean speaking and writing on
the subject. His own branch, Pollockshaws, had organised a housing
council in the city and this kept up a steady pressure on landlords while
agitating on the issue of council houses.[74] In 1913, the SDP organised a
Scottish Federation of Tenants' Associations in the context of increasing agitation about rents increases.[75]

Further, Glasgow Trades Council, with its regular meetings of four
hundred plus delegates, also agitated on the issue and according to
Shinwell, was involved in legal action against landlords' rent increases
before the First World War.[76]

So a summary of the working-class housing situation in Glasgow on
the eve of the outbreak of the First World War goes like this: there were
in fact some 13,000 empty houses in the city.[77] This demonstrated that
there was a discrepancy between the rental of these houses and the
ability of workers to pay it. As a consequence, many of them were
forced to live in grotesquely overcrowded conditions in one- or two-
roomed houses many of which did not even have the elementary sani-

tary facilities considered reasonable in these days — i.e. an inside toilet. The majority of these workers lived on or near the poverty line. They were pinned down in the housing market by the absolute hegemony over it enjoyed by the landlords and factors of the city. For the unemployed or those who could not work for whatever reason, the housing situation was desperate. Without the ability to pay the regular rent demanded in a decent house, on monthly or longer lets, and especially without a factor's line, the poorest were driven downwards in a spiral which ended in some filthy, ill-lit ticketed house in a backland.[78] Even for the best paid worker living in a newly constructed two-roomed house, there still remained the anger of knowing that the factor was screwing every last farthing out of him. The arrogance and the greed of Glasgow's rentiers, having their tenants in a near-monopoly situation, had produced an anger amongst the working people of Glasgow which expressed itself in *class* organisation through all the organisations of labour.

4 The War and the Rent Strike

As there is now a considerable literature on the Rent Strike of 1915, and its context of the Clyde Workers' Committee and the wartime events of 'Red Clyde',[79] what is offered here is more by way of a schematic account of main events rather than an attempt to provide a 'definitive' historical account.[80]

The First World War brought the Munitions Industry to Glasgow; it also brought about 16,000 munitions workers into the city and 4,000 more to the surrounding areas. This precipitated the struggle over dilution, and the formation of the 'Labour Withholding Committee', later the Clyde Workers' Committee. It is important to realise, as several writers have stressed,[81] that the engineers involved in this committee were old-fashioned craft unionists, élitist to a degree, and somewhat full of themselves. Further, the Engineers' Union, the Amalgamated Society of Engineers (later AEU) was organised on a locality basis, which, as we shall argue later, was to have an impact on the rent strike. In any event, in a situation of near monopoly, the Glasgow landlords put up their rent, and there was a concerted roar of protest. This started in 1914 when an official corporation inquiry into rent increases investigated 2,000 complaints, and found a clustering of over-charging in the heavily industrial areas of Govan and Partick, where the housing stock was under severe pressure.

In the same year, Andrew McBride, a close comrade of Wheatley's in the ILP Housing Committee, in conjunction with the Women's Labour

League, set up the Glasgow Women's Housing Association, which was
to play a critical role in subsequent events. Helen Crawfurd, one of the
principal forces in this association, describes it thus:[82]

> The housing conditions in Glasgow in 1914 were appalling and the
> Labour Party before the War initiated a Glasgow Women's Housing
> Association. The two strongest sections of this Association were in
> Govan and Partick (the principal industrial areas of the city). Mrs
> Mary Barbour, afterwards a Councillor, and Magistrate in Glasgow,
> was the leading woman in Govan, while Mrs Ferguson was the
> leader in Partick . . . John Wheatley . . . Mr McBride and other
> labour men advised and assisted behind the scenes . . . The Glasgow
> Women's Housing Association took up this issue (rents' increases),
> and in the working class districts, committees were formed to resist
> these increases in rent. Cards, oblong in shape, were printed with the
> words: RENT STRIKE. WE ARE NOT REMOVING, and placed in
> the windows of the houses where rent increases were demanded . . .

In January 1915, 450 delegates attended an ILP Housing Conference;
they supported the £8 scheme. Thereafter, again at the behest of
Wheatley and McBride, a Glasgow Labour Party Housing Committee
was founded in February 1915, with official links with Glasgow Trades
Council; its main aims were to organise tenants against increased rents,
and to support municipalised housing to be paid for by the tramway
surplus and state grants.[83]

Thus the centralised City Labour Party had rent control and municipalisation as central planks, as did the ILP and the SDF. It is interesting
in passing to note that Maclean's demands were explicitly for *state*
provision of housing while the reformist Wheatley was still somewhat
obsessed with £8 cottages from the tramway surplus. In any event, the
'official' labour movement was intimately involved with the creation of
grass-roots organisation among Glasgow women.

There were further grass-roots organisations which played a critical
role in mobilising support for the rents strike, as Iain McLean has
demonstrated:[84] these were the ward committees; the labour representation committees; and the tenants' defence and protective societies.
The importance of those various committees is that they were democratic, collective organisations located directly within the working class
in their own neighbourhood; they had a capacity for mass mobilisation
which the official parties did not. And again, as Melling has documented,
these organisations incessantly lobbied the corporation, and undertook

agitprop in their localities.[85]

The eviction of a soldier's family in Govan in April 1915 produced a popular uproar, and again Melling is correct in stressing the patriotic indignation which was one of the phenomenal forms the anger took. This can be seen from the slogans on the banners carried by protesters in contemporary photographs.[86] Willie Gallagher describes the conse-quent organisation in Govan:[87]

> In Govan, Mrs Barbour, a typical working class housewife, became the leader of a movement such as had never been seen before, or since for that matter. Street meetings, back-court meetings, drums, bells, trumpets − every method was used to bring the women out and organise them for the struggle. Notices were printed by the thousand and put up in the windows: wherever you went you could see them. In street after street, scarcely a window without one: WE ARE NOT PAYING INCREASED RENT.

In early summer, there was a huge demonstration on Glasgow Green where again the workers stated their refusal to pay increased rent.[88] By this time, the rent strike had spread from Govan to Partick where a local factor, Nicholson, had carried the offensive to the workers by both raising rents and prosecuting rent strikers. By August of 1915, there were rent strikes all over Glasgow: in their article, Ann and Vincent Flynn state that they have evidence of strikes in Govan, Partick, Parkhead, Pollokshaws, Pollok, Cowcaddens, Kelvingrove, Ibrox, Govanhill, St Rollox, Townhead, Springburn, Maryhill, Fairfield, Blackfriars (Gorbals) and Woodside.[89] What is interesting to note about these areas of the city is that they are mark-edly different: heavily industrial areas, more respectable artisanal areas, and also slum areas. What is also important is the *mass* char-acter of this movement. The excitement and tension of the period strikes the reader in all the contemporary accounts − Gallagher again:[90]

> 'Will we let them get away with this?' was the new war-cry resound-ing in every street. 'Never!' thundered the reply from the women. All day long in the streets, in the halls, in the houses, meetings were held. Kitchen meetings, street meetings, mass meetings, meetings of every kind. No halt, no rest for anyone, all in preparation for the sitting of the court when the test case came on. As in the streets, so in the factories. 'Will we allow the factors to attack our wages?'

'Never!' Every factory was keyed up and ready.

In October 1915, 15,000 Glaswegians were on rent strike, including five Labour councillors.[91] By this time, the women were assaulting the factors and bailiffs, pelting them with rubbish, flour, etc. A Govan man recalls a contemporary attempt at eviction:[92]

> On this particular occasion there was one very popular person, she was being evicted. She was a widow and had four or five children and the neighbours decided that she was not going to be evicted. So, the women hid themselves on the stair and when the Sheriff Officers came along one of them was pounced on by the women, and mind you, when women 'jump' you, you are being jumped! He was quite a big powerful man but he finished up in the midden, and the police came round of course, but nobody saw anything, and the poor man went away in one helluva mess.

And always in the forefront of the propagandising and organising were John Maclean and his lieutenant, James McDougall. They spoke incessantly throughout 1915 at factory and shipyard gates, and at mass meetings. When Maclean was eventually arraigned on 27 October for two offences against DORA, he was released on bail, after giving a pledge that he would not speak publicly on the war issue. However, he made it plain that he had every intention of continuing to speak on the rents issue.[93] Every Sunday night, Maclean addressed a huge meeting in Bath Street and urged the case for revolutionary socialism.[94] His Marxism night class, originally started in 1906, at this time averaged 493 – the cream of the shop-stewards movement.[95] The effect of this revolutionary leadership on rank-and-file workers must have been incalulable, particularly in Govan where as a local teacher (until dismissal), Maclean was both well known and popular.

Other forms of more orthodox, reformist agitation also increased. After a series of public meetings in Parkhead, Partick, South Govan and Ibrox,[96] the corporation received a deputation of tenants demanding that the corporation petition the government to prevent rent increases during the war.[97] The corporation not surprisingly voted against this. A Labour councillor promptly laid down a motion demanding that the corporation set up a special committee to look into the whole question of land, rent and new housing.[98] Within days, Labour councillors were again pressing the corporation to petition the government to hold rents to the pre-war levels: this time it was passed.[99] At the same time, the corporation was considering a letter from Davie Kirkwood of the Clyde Workers' Committee on the poor housing conditions in his area, a clear indication that the housing issue was (at least) *known* in that committee.[100] Throughout this period, there is a running series of petitions and deputations to the corporation demanding, variously, that rents be pegged at pre-war levels; that the eviction of soldiers' dependants be declared illegal; that a government commission be set up to investigate the issue; that fair rents courts be set up; and that the corporation take the initiative in building tenements as private enterprise is not interested.[101]

Elsewhere in the country's munitions areas, particularly in Sheffield, there was similar if less intense unrest. But in Glasgow, by November 1915, 20,000 people were on strike,[102] and the action was heating up. The violent agitation over the sacking of the Fairfields shipwrights and their imprisonment for refusing to pay their fines led the state to institute very rapidly a 'Commission of Enquiry into Industrial Unrest'.[103] On the streets, there were increasingly militant confrontations with the factors. Helen Crawfurd describes one in Govan in her autobiography:[104]

In Govan ... where a woman had been persuaded by the House Factor to pay the increase, having been told that the other tenants had paid, Mrs Barbour got the men from the shipyards in Govan to come out on the street where the House Factor's office was, and then went up with the woman and demanded a return of the money. On the Factor being shown the thousands of black-faced workers* crowding the street, he handed it over.

In October, there was a mass march to St Enoch's Square, and again the importance of women in this struggle is evidenced by the contemporary photographs.[105] There was yet another deputation to the corporation. The city was in a ferment. Tension heightened even more when some of the munitions workers involved in the Partick rent strike were taken to the small debts court by the intractable Nicholson.[106] This was a cause of particular bitterness amongst the working class as a conviction there meant that the rent arrears could be docked-off the workers' wages, and the whole context of this kind of move fairly pulsated with historically-derived class hatred, as has been demonstrated. However, and wisely, their case was suspended as they were munitions workers. The next move came when McKinnon

* The workers' faces were black from conditions of work in the yards and the sheds.

Wood, the Secretary for Scotland, was dispatched by the state to talk
with Andrew McBride and James Stewart, another leader of the strikers.

Now it should be remembered that throughout the First World War,
the state's intelligence services had been busily reporting on the
Glasgow situation, where the Chief Constable, James Verdier Stevenson,
had had his education in repression in the Royal Irish Constabulary.[107]
One of Basil Thompson's 'Fortnightly Reports on Revolutionary
Organisations at Home and Morale Abroad' was to describe Scottish
industrial workers as 'of a deeper red than most red-flaggers'.[108] The
Ministry of Munitions also had regular reports from its own 'Intelligence Officer' in Glasgow. And further, the state had used convicted
criminals as spies and agents provocateurs in the city.[109] So it was in
the context of considerable trepidation at the level of the state that
McKinnon Wood set up an official enquiry into the rents issue on
Clydeside — and elsewhere in Scotland — in October. This enquiry was
conducted by Lord Hunter, a judge, and Professor Scott, who held the
Chair of Political Economy at Glasgow University. (Ironically, Hunter
had been Liberal MP for Govan from 1910-11, before being made a
judge.) Of them, Labour Councillor Paddy Dollan remarked:[110]

> Please note that neither of the two gentlemen is a representative of
> Labour, so that the working classes who are worst affected by the
> increases of rent are unrepresented on the committee of inquiry.
> Watch!

They reported very quickly.[111]

In this Report — the 'Hunter Report' — the ubiquitous Thomas
Binnie reappears, this time making out a case for increased rents
because of the increased burden of taxation, and the increased cost of
repairs, which the poor landlords have to cover.[112] However, the real
issue soon appears, when witnesses start discussing interest rates and
the profitability — or lack of it — in housing bonds as opposed to
government stock.[113] Andrew McBride appears, in his capacity as member of the Glasgow Labour Party Housing Committee, and in a hard-
hitting testimony makes it clear that he and the committee are not
interested in the ability of the landlords or bond-holders to make
profits:[114]

> (McBride): *A.* What I suggest here is that the primary object of our
>   Committee is to secure better conditions for the people. We argue
>   that the rents are too high. It does not matter what causes bring

about high rents. We say that they can be changed, so that, therefore, if the system cannot be worked by private enterprise, then they must go by the board and bring the houses within the reach of the working classes.

Q. How are you to determine, according to your view, what is the fair rental of all houses? *A.* There can be no fair rental with private enterprise meeting the needs of the people . . .

Q. . . . Looking at it from the point of view of private enterprise, if the owner has to meet the increasing costs of materials and the increased cost of living, is it not somewhat hard on him that he should not get any further return from his property? *A.* I think it is admitted that property-owners live very comfortably under any circumstances . . .

Q. . . . You have admitted throughout that you are not in favour of private enterprise? *A.* I think anybody who has studied the question admits that nobody but the Corporation or Government can build houses in future.

The message is rammed home by the next witness, Baillie James Stewart, another member of the committee:[115]

Have you, any more than Mr McBride, considered the question as to what sum of money would be involved in the municipal enterprise which you desire to see? — Millions.

Have you formed any opinion as to where they are to come from? — Yes.

Where? — From the State.

So far as the case against the private owner is concerned —? — The private owner does not build a house for me to live in; he builds a house to make a profit out of me. The primary reason is profit, the same as he builds a factory to make munitions of war, etc.

He goes on to argue that rents increases are in fact not necessary as Parliament could legislate that (i) bondholders could not lift their bonds for the duration of the war, and (ii) interest could be frozen at pre-war rates.[116] Wheatley then appears and with customary clarity pins down the opportunism of bond-holders as the key to the rents issue.[117] He points out that capitalists take advantage of the soaring interest rate during wartime and that this should be controlled by the state, which should pin the rate of profit at what it was on average for the three years before the war started.[118] Lord Hunter comments:[119]

> *Q*. I am afraid that that is a pretty difficult undertaking for the Government? *A*. It is only difficult to the Government so long as they are prepared to pay more attention to the privileges of the people who are living on the wealth produced by others than to the safety of the State. Immediately the Government gets over that and pays no attention to class interests or privileges the difficulty will disappear.

If this is not an argument conducted in class terms, it is hard to know what is.

Lloyd George decided upon an enquiry, but on 15 October, rents were raised again in Glasgow, probably in an effort to force the enquiry into accepting half the increase.[120] The areas of Kinning Park and Whiteinch had joined in the strike. Working-class defence organisation was now articulated throughout all sections of the population. It was towards the end of October that the famous assault on the sheriff officers out to evict 'a widow' from her house in Merryland Street, Govan, took place. The local women attacked the officers 'and their assistants with pease meal, flour and whiting. A woman was arrested on a charge of assaulting one of the officers'.[121] The women forced the release of their arrested sister.[122]

Again, Maclean was still agitating at a furious pace, and it seems that he was most persistent in his efforts in Govan and Partick, which were both centres of rent strike resistance, and also heavily industrial areas, immediately adjacent to the shipyards and docks along the banks of the Clyde. There was certainly co-operation between Govan and Partick tenants: on 13 November, there was a mass march to Thornwood Park in Partick, where the speakers included Helen Crawfurd and Mrs Ferguson, one of the Partick strikers' leaders.[123]

But the flash point came on 17 November, when eighteen rent striking munitions workers were due for trial in the Small Debts Court in front of Sheriff Lee. Thousands of men and women marched on the court. The contemporary accounts give some idea of the drama of the occasion — Helen Crawfurd:[124]

> I will never forget the sight and sound of those marching men with black faces. Thousands of them marched through the principal streets down to the Sheriff Court and the surrounding streets were

packed. John Maclean, MA, afterwards imprisoned for his anti-war activity, and first consul for the USSR in Glasgow, was one of the speakers, who from barrels and upturned boxes, addressed the crowds.

Willie Gallagher:[125]

Into the streets around the Sheriff's court the workers marched from all sides. All the streets were packed. Traffic was completely stopped. Right in front of the Court, John Maclean was on a platform addressing the crowd as far as his voice could reach. In other streets near the court others of us were at it. Our platforms were unique. Long poster boards had been picked up from the front of newspaper shops. These were placed on the shoulders of half a dozen husky well-matched workers and the speaker was lifted on to them. It was a great experience, speaking from a yielding platform and keeping a measure of balance while flaying the factors and the war-makers. Roar after roar of rage went up as incidents were related showing the robbery of mothers and wives whose sons and husbands were at the front. Roar followed roar as we pictured what would happen if we allowed the attack on our wages.

Inside the court, there was a great deal of tension as a deputation of workers from Dalmuir told the sheriff that they would be out on strike if the rent strikers were convicted. One of that deputation remembers that day:[126]

I was appointed a member of a deputation to interview the Sheriff from the Dalmuir shipyards, representing 60 patternmakers and about eight joiners . . . we met the Sheriff inside in a private room prior to his taking the case, and after some talk, in which he was wanting to continue the case, I had the good fortune to be able to say: 'Mr Sheriff, with all due respect to your position as a legal luminary, we did not come here to negotiate. We have come here as messengers from the shipyards and from the engineering shops to tell you that any continuation of this case will be taken as action against the tenants. We workers at all times believe that a bird in the hand is worth two in the bush, and I have to advise you that we cannot send these men back to work. There are thousands more prepared to come out, and if the case is continued, I want to assure you that instead of the thousands you see here today, there will be over

100,000 out tomorrow . . .'

They were followed by further deputations of industrial workers.

At the demonstration of between 10,000 and 15,000 workers outside the sheriff court, John Maclean had been instructed to telegram the prime minister, Asquith, as follows:[128]

That this meeting of Clyde munitions workers requests the Government to state, not later than Saturday first, that it forbids any increase of rent during the period of the war; and that, this failing, a general strike will be declared on 22 November.

After considerable discussion, the sheriff managed to get the petitioner to drop the case against the rent strikers. When the news came outside, there was massive rejoicing. As Gallagher said:[129] 'All night long the celebration of the victory went on.'

On the same day, McKinnon Wood put a memo to the Cabinet asking that a bill to freeze rents at the pre-war level be introduced to Parliament.[130] (McKinnon Wood must also have had some personal experience of what was going on in Glasgow as he was MP for the heavily industrial constituency of St Rollox in Springburn, where as has been seen, there was a rent strike in progress.) McKinnon Wood added to this memo:[131]

The (Hunter) Committee was not directed to make any proposals for legislation, but . . . I find that both members are impressed, as a result of their enquiry, with the necessity of action being taken to stop increases in rent. I understand that the Minister of Munitions attaches considerable importance to the agitation as contributing to the unrest which exists throughout the Clyde districts, where . . . labour difficulties have caused him much anxiety.

And finally:[132]

The agitation is growing, and I think it is necessary that a prompt decision should be taken by the Government, otherwise there are signs that demands for interference will become more clamant and will expand in scope and character.

The next day, there was a formal announcement that a Rent Restrictions Bill would be introduced in the House of Commons. On 25 November, eight days after the demonstration, Walter Long of the Local Government Board introduced the Rents and Mortgage Interest (War Restrictions) Bill: it applied to all houses under £30 annual rental in Scotland. It became law in four weeks flat, receiving the Royal Assent on 25 December. This was a famous victory.

5 Interpretation

The immediate and long term effects of the act were considerable. It was obviously a massive gain for the rent strikers everywhere, and a sickening blow for the landlords. It was a great morale booster for the labour movement. Trades councils all over the country found themselves heavily involved in producing literature explaining the act to workers, running meetings and either defending tenants or prosecuting landlords in court.[133]

But its ramifications in terms of the state's housing policies were profound. It sparked off a series of crises which the state had not theorised and for which it had no articulated policies. These crises were essentially to do *both* with the reproduction of labour-power, *and* of the relations of production. In other words, it was a period of crisis of *re*production. Before the rent strikes, housing was seen by capital as more or less irrelevant to problems of repressing and controlling the working class — so long as it could continue to burst up the rookeries and other hideaways of the lumpenproletariat. In terms of the reproduction of labour power, the Victorian state had only a glimmering of the awful human costs of poor housing, and with the exception of a handful of its intellectuals, had certainly not grasped the centrality of housing in the reproduction process. The events of the war in general, and rent strikes in particular, changed all that.

Consider three contemporary events. Firstly, as I have stressed earlier, the Glasgow rents struggle was not unique, although it was certainly the most dramatic. As Alan Clinton has shown, agitation on the rents issue took place all over the country, and indeed, after the Rents Restriction Act was passed, both Camberwell and Woolwich Trades Councils claimed that it was they who were responsible.[134] Manchester Trades Council issued a pamphlet in 1915 on rent increases for its members, set up a Tenants' Defence Association, and followed the matter very closely.[135] Thus while it was Glasgow's rent strikes and blockade of the court which forced the state to act, this action detonated what was a long-term smouldering issue in the working class, heated-up to flash-point by the events of the war.

Secondly, the Commission of Enquiry into Industrial Unrest reported

in 1917, and it had sat in Glasgow throughout the events of 1915.[136]
The report stated that in the eight Scottish areas investigated, seven
had mentioned housing as a major source of unrest. The Commissioners for Scotland noted the appalling state of Scottish housing,
particularly on Clydeside, and explicitly observed that the government
was going to have to do something about this source of unrest and
dissatisfaction:[137]

> In Scotland there is an immediate need for about 100,000 workers'
> houses . . . The industrial unrest attributable to this cause, it is
> strongly represented, can only be allayed by the Government taking
> steps with a problem that appears to have grown too great for
> private enterprise now to meet.

Precisely what Wheatley, McBride, *et. al.*, had told the Hunter Committee, and what witnesses had told the 1904 Municipal Commission in
Glasgow. Working-class militancy which united the workplace and the
home, the points of production *and* reproduction, was volatile —
something the state could no longer ignore.

Thirdly, the Royal Commission into Scottish working-class housing
which had been started in 1912, had continued during the war after a
temporary halt, and reported in 1918.[138] As is well known, the Report of
the Royal Commission stated in absolutely unequivocal terms that (i)
the overall picture of housing for the working class of Scotland was
atrocious; (ii) that the scale of the problem was so massive that only
state intervention could solve it; (iii) that the costs to Scottish workers
in terms of health and morale was disastrous; (iv) and that Scottish
workers were very bitter about this situation.

The state was still hesitant. Individuals like Addison, the Minister
of Health, had spent the last two years of the war urging the government to *compel* local authorities to do something about working-class
housing, but he was in a position of isolation.[139] The Rents Restriction Act was meant to be only a temporary measure, but in spite of
subsequent trimming, it remained a permanent feature which broke the
stranglehold of the rentiers, the 'urban bourgeoisie', over the development and reproduction of capital at the local level. The insistent pressure over housing from a now-aroused and no longer deferential and
jingoist but class-conscious proletariat which was totally alienated from
the apparatuses of the state by the end of the war, was what *compelled*
Lloyd George to establish the Cabinet Committee on Housing Policy in
1918, and make his canting 'homes fit for heroes' speech at the end of

the year. The state was *compelled* to produce the 1919 Housing and Town Planning Act out of thin air, as it had absolutely no *worked out* policy for the systematic provision of working-class housing.[140] And the provisions of this act were truly radical: the state *compelled* local authorities to survey and report upon, with plans for the construction of, working-class housing in their area. The state was pledged to meet all costs above what was realisable from a penny rate. It does not matter that this act also was meant to be a temporary affair, that its provisions were too generous, or that it was sabotaged by finance capital. What it established as an indestructible fact was that workers would be housed by the state as of right. Working-class demands had been articulated to a level where the state *had* to intervene to accommodate them. It is my contention that without the 1915 Rent Strike in Glasgow, there would have been no 1915 Rents and Mortgage Restrictions Act, and without the 1915 Act there would have been no 1919 Housing and Town Planning Act in the form in which we know it. So although she may have not been aware of it at the time, when Mrs Barbour and her sisters in Govan were throwing whiting at the sheriff officers, they were making history.

There remains a final question about the rents strike. Why was it so spectacularly successful? This question has not yet been properly addressed and these concluding remarks attempt to make a political assessment of this struggle.

Clearly a number of factors were at work in wartime Glasgow. Firstly, and a point of which not enough is made in the literature, there are the historical traditions of the Glasgow working class. It is often remarked that this class is essentially composed of immigrants from Ireland, on the one hand, and the Highlands of Scotland, on the other. But what is to be remembered about such a population was the hatred they bore with them of the property-owning classes. The savage depopulation of rural Ireland and Scotland was a dramatic instance in British history of the necessary costs of capital's insatiable need to expand. The point is that the working class of Glasgow had a historically-derived propensity to militant anti-landlord action, given the right situation, and the right leadership. It should not be forgotten that Harry McShane's father was Irish, Willie Gallagher's father was Irish and mother Highland, and both John Maclean's parents were also Highlanders, victims of the clearances.

Secondly, there was the role of the women involved. We are just beginning to learn in detail of their importance in the rents strike, but some of what we do know casts new light on the events of the strike.

Some of the women leaders were suffragettes and had experiences of direct action. For example, Helen Crawfurd had been in jail three times before the start of the war for militant action, including smashing the windows of the Minister of Education in London, and the army recruiting office in Glasgow.[141] The Glasgow suffragettes had a tradition of militancy which included blowing up all the telegraph and telephone cables, and cutting the wires, around the city.[142] Further, being excluded from skilled jobs at the point of production, and thus being largely ignorant of the 'parliamentary road' followed by trade union procedure, when women took collective action, it was frequently direct and to the point. Further, and relative to the first point above, when there was resistance to clearance in the Highlands, it was the *women* who did the fighting — as in the Battle of the Braes in Skye. It is not unreasonable to suppose that this tradition would have carried over among Glasgow's working-class women of Highland origin. (Interestingly enough, the area of Partick, where the Rents Strike was highly organised, was and is a substantially Highland area.) With experienced leaders like Helen Crawfurd, the Glasgow women became a force to be reckoned with, as the factors and landlords found out to their literal cost. It is worth noting, from the quotation on p. 95, that Helen Crawfurd says that it was the *women* who got the *men* out from the shipyards. This is suggested in other accounts and memoirs. Thus Tom Bell says:[143] 'The women marched in a body to the shipyard and got the men to leave work and join them in a demonstration to the Court.' Clearly, the role of the Glasgow Women's Housing Association in this struggle was critical, and their active intervention decisive.

Thirdly, there were the changes in the relations of production brought about by the exigencies of wartime. The units of production on Clydeside were huge: the Parkhead Forge, Harland & Wolff's, etc. Traditionally, these had been the preserve of craft-conscious engineers and the like, and in some, Protestants only were employed. And because of the sheer scale of these units, and the nature and intensity of the pre-war class struggle, these plants were heavily unionised: even before the start of the war, Beardmore's Parkhead Forge had 60 shop-stewards,[144] while Barr & Stroud's, Weir's in Cathcart and the Albion Motor Works in Clydebank also had a militant shop-stewards' organisation before 1914.[145] It must be remembered that this shop-stewards' organisation was absolutely without parallel elsewhere in the country. But with the rapidly expanding nature of the munitions industry, dilution broke down the craft-based occupational culture of the engineers, as the semi-skilled and unskilled workers, including women,

poured into the sheds and yards. With the departure of the old
defensive, and somewhat élitist, culture of the engineers, the ground was
ripe for new forms of political organisation to appear. Further, as was
noted earlier, the ASE union branches were organised on a locality basis,
thus issues which were of importance in the neighbourhood could be
discussed in these branches. It seems totally plausible that the rents
issue would be formally discussed at branch meetings, especially in areas
like Govan and Partick. It is totally implausible that the issue was not
discussed at work.

Fourthly, there was the nature of the leadership of the Clydeside
movement. What is important to understand about this leadership was
its compact nature: Wheatley, Maxton, Maclean, Kirkwood, Crawfurd,
Barbour, Ferguson, McBride, McDougall, Gallagher, McShane and all the
rest constituted a readily identifiable cadre, a tangible vanguard. They
all knew each other, even if they had political differences. Their political education and experience was unrivalled in Britain. They worked,
politicised, socialised and talked endlessly with each other. Helen
Crawfurd, for example, discusses in her memoir how she was a personal friend of Agnes Dollan and Jean Barbour of Govan and Mrs
Fergusion of Partick, and also Willie Gallagher, Tom Bell and Arthur
McManus.[146] Wheatley and Kirkwood were the first office-bearers of
the Scottish Labour Housing Association and John Maclean took over
from Davie Kirkwood in 1916. All the memoirs of the period point to
concerted discussion and action. And they also point to the fact that
these leaders were well known, and were in demand as speakers and
organisers. These leaders were in the main directly from the working
class themselves and so to that extent were trusted, thus when the
Clydeside mobilisation came, it came from within the working class
itself, with its own leadership. (This again is not to say that these
leaders were in total agreement: there was clearly a tension in this
leadership between the reformists and the revolutionaries. It is ironic
to note that Wheatley's successful co-option of Kirkwood into the
reformist camp had the objective outcome of smashing the 40 Hours
Strike, as the latter was the man who sold out first.)

Finally, there is the question of the political strategy of this leadership. What they did was not only correct, but was to have far-reaching
effects on Scottish political culture in the working class. They — or
more correctly the revolutionaries among them — hammered away at
the lunacy of the war. They organised workers' self-defence against the
Munitions of War Act and DORA. They struggled to maintain some
control of the labour process in rapidly changing industries. They

organised at the point of production and in the neighbourhood. They
helped turn a jingoist local working class of 1914* into a class-conscious
mass in 1915. Their analyses were consistently offered to the mass in
class terms. The fact that in 1915 the Glasgow working class came
together on the issue of rents did not make the Rents Strike a 'mere
tenants' struggle'. It was a *class* struggle. Lenin has said of classes:[147]

> Classes are large groups of people differing from each other by the
> place they occupy in a historically determined system of social
> production, by their relation (in most cases fixed and formulated
> in law) to the means of production, by their role in the social
> organisation of labour, and consequently, by the dimensions of the
> share of social wealth of which they dispose and the mode of
> acquiring it. Classes are groups of people one of which can appro-
> priate the labour of another owing to the different places they
> occupy in a definite system of social economy.

Crucially, the Clydeside leaders saw this: they taught and organised on
the basis of a struggle against *capitalism as a system*. They tied the war,
conscription, dilution, the rising cost of living, rent increases, and
general human misery into a picture which was the inevitable result of
capitalist production. Their success was startling. The mass movement
in Glasgow transcended the classic splits in the working class: skill,
religion and sex — albeit briefly. Men and women, Catholic and Protes-
tant, engineer and labourer, fought against the rent increases. They
fought in the face of an attack on their standard of living. They saw a
chance for success, went for it in an effective offensive and achieved a
visible defeat of a class enemy, thus helping to lay the basis for a mass
party of the labour movement. They understood what John Maclean
meant when he said:[148] 'Property has made fiends of men. But moralising
is a waste of time.'

* On the Cenotaph in George Square in Glasgow, it notes that of some 8,654,465
men and women from this country participating in the Services in the First World
War, Glasgow supplied over 200,000 — i.e. between a fifth and a sixth of the city's
population.

Notes

1. Cf. N. Poulantzas, 'The Capitalist State: A Reply to Miliband and Laclau in *NLR*, 95; *Political Power and Social Classes* (NLB, London, 1973); and *Classes in Contemporary Capitalism* (NLB, London, 1976).

2. John Foster, *Class Struggle and Industrial Revolution* (Weidenfeld & Nicolson, London, 1974), pp. 3-4.

3. Cf. Peter Dickens, *Social Change, Housing and the State*, CES Conference Paper (York, 1977). Also Paul Wilding, 'The Housing & Town Planning Act 1919 – A Study in the Making of Social Policy', *JNL Soc. Policy*, 2, 4 (1974).

4. Cf. Joe Melling, *The Glasgow Rent Strike and Clydeside Labour 1914-15: The Rise of a Social Movement* (Mimeo, Department of Economic History, University of Glasgow, 1978). Also Joe Melling, 'Comment on the Clyde Rent Strike, 1915' in *Journal of the Scottish Labour History Society*, no. 13 (1979); also Iain McLean, 'Popular Protest and Public Order – Red Clydeside, 1915-1919', J. Stevenson & R. Quinault (eds), *Popular Protest and Public Order* (Allen & Unwin, London, 1974).

5. Enid Gauldie, *Cruel Habitations* (Allen & Unwin, London, 1974), p. 17.

6. Ibid., p. 17.

7. *Royal Commission on the Housing of the Working Classes*, C. 4409, 1885: Report and Minutes of Evidence, vols I-V. Hereafter *RC*, 1885.

8. Ibid., vol. V, *Minutes of Evidence for Scotland*, para 19, 188.

9. Ibid., para 19, 199. See also paras 19, 262-3.

10. Cf. Gauldie, *Cruel Habitations*, *passim*.

11. Gareth Stedman Jones, *Outcast London* (Peregrine, Stevenage, 1975).

12. *RC*, 1885, vol. V, para 19, 719-20.

13. A point about research arises here. It would be very interesting to study elections in Glasgow to find out if working-class people brought pressure on voters to elect candidates who supported – verbally at any rate – municipal housing. The obvious parallel is with the 'selective dealing' strategy as described by Foster.

14. *RC*, 1885, vol. V, paras 13, 291-4.

15. Which brings me to my second research point. The detailed links between the Workmen's National Housing Council, and the Scottish Housing Council still need to be investigated. There are some elementary if important questions to be answered, such as: did Scotland/Glasgow send any delegates to the National Council? Did any Scots delegates attend the Council's many conferences, including the National Conference in 1913? Did any National Council delegates attend the 1902 demonstration in Glasgow called by the Scottish Council?

16. David Englander, *The Workmen's National Housing Council* (MA Thesis, University of Warwick, 1973). I am grateful to Mr Englander for permission to cite his thesis.

17. Ibid., p. 35.

18. Cf. Englander, *The Workmen's National Housing Council*, *passim*.

19. Ibid., p. 33 ff.

20. Ibid., *passim*.

21. Harry McShane, *Glasgow District Trades Council Centenary Brochure, 1858-1958: A Hundred Years of Progress* (GDTC, Glasgow, 1958), p. 19.

22. *Report of the Inter-Departmental Committee on Physical Deterioration*, Cd. 2175, P.P. 1904.

23. See, for example: Charles Allan, 'The Genesis of British Urban Redevelopment: The Glasgow Case' in *Econ. Hist. Review*, vol. XVIII (1965). Geoffrey Best, 'The Scottish Victorian City' in *Victorian Studies*, vol. II, no. 3 (March, 1968). John Butt, 'Working-Class Housing in Glasgow' in S.D. Chapman (ed.), *The History of Working Class Housing* (David & Charles, Newton Abbot, 1971).

Seán Damer, *Property Relations and Class Relations in Victorian Glasgow* (University of Glasgow Discussion Paper in Social Research, no. 16, 1976).

24. Cf. 1901 Census of the City of Glasgow.

25. J.H. Treble, 'The Seasonal Demand for Adult Labour in Glasgow, 1890-1914', *Soc. Hist.*, vol. 3, no. 1 (January 1978).

26. *Glasgow Presbytery Commission on the Housing of the Poor, 1892,* hereafter *1892 Comm.*

27. Ibid., p. 178 ff.

28. Ibid., p. 41.

29. Cf. A.K. Chalmers (ed.), *Public Health Administration in Glasgow: A Memorial Volume of the Writings of James Burn Russell.* (Jas. MacLehose & Sons, Glasgow, 1905).

30. Cf. Damer *Property Relations*, pp. 22-3.

31. *1892 Comm.*, p. 179.

32. *1892 Comm.*, p. 122. A word for our English readers: a 'close' is the common entrance stair of a tenement.

33. Ibid., p. 134.

34. Ibid., p. 124

35. Ibid., p. 174. Interestingly enough, this particular horror struck many explorers in the Glasgow slums, and it is also reported in the 1904 Municipal Commission. It was also noted in London, cf. A.S. Wohl, *The Eternal Slum* (Edward Arnold, London, 1977).

36. Cf. Damer, *Property Relations.* Also Seán Damer, 'Wine Alley – The Sociology of a Dreadful Enclosure', *Soc. Rev.*, vol. 22, no. 2 (May 1974).

37. *Glasgow Municipal Commission on the Housing of the Poor, 1904*, p. 2. Hereafter *1904 Comm.*

38. Cf. R.D. Storch, 'The Policeman as Domestic Missionary: Urban Discipline and Popular Culture in Northern England 1850-1880', in *The Journal of Social History.*

39. *1904 Comm.*, evidence of A– B–.

40. *1892 Comm.*, p. 129.

41. William Smart, *The Housing Problem and the Municipality* (University of Glasgow, Free Lectures, Glasgow, 1902).

42. Smart, *The Housing Problem*, p. 10.

43. Ibid., p. 12.

44. Ibid., pp. 22-3.

45. Cf. McShane, *Glasgow District Brochure.*

46. John Ferguson, *An Address to the Citizens of the 25 Wards*, 2nd ed. (Glasgow, 1902), p. 4.

47. Cf. Clinton, *passim;* McShane, *passim;* also, *Glasgow Herald*, especially 26 Feb. 1904.

48. Cf. *Guthrie Report,* paras 8751-8811.

49. *Report of the Departmental Committee on House-Letting in Scotland,* vol. 1 – Report, Cd. 3715, 1907; vol. II – Minutes of Evidence, Cd. 3792, 1908. Hereafter *Guthrie Report* or *Guthrie Mins.*

50. Ibid., p. 2.

51. At this time (1907), the size of house by average rent went like this (p. 3 of the *Guthrie Report):*

> Up to £ 7 (per annum) – 1-roomed house
> Up to £12 (per annum) – 2-roomed house
> Up to £18 (per annum) – 3-roomed house
> Up to £25 (per annum) – 4-roomed house

while the total number of houses in Glasgow by rental was as follows:

At and under £4	:	2,045
£4 1s to £10	:	92,132
£10 1s to £15	:	33,844
£15 1s to £20	:	20,808
Above £20 1s	:	26,449
		175,278

53. *Guthrie Mins,* para 1820 ff., and *passim.*

53. *Guthrie Mins,* para 565.

54. Ibid., para 769.

55. Ibid., paras 5083/4.

56. In the course of writing this article, Miss Anne-Marie Narloch, formerly of Townhead and now of Ruchill told me that this practice is happily still in existence in Glasgow. When warrant sales are on neighbours buy up the goods and return them, and Miss Narloch tells me that in Ruchill, strangers are driven away with knives! It is clear that research on the impact of the detested factor and sheriff officer on working-class life in Victorian Scotland is urgently needed.

57. *Guthrie Mins,* para 1078 ff.

58. Ibid., para 678 ff.

59. *Guthrie Report,* p. 5.

60. Ibid., p. 25, where Thomas Binnie wants 15 per cent commission!

61. Ibid., p. 10.

62. *Guthrie Mins,* para 1269.

63. *Guthrie Report,* p. 12.

64. *Guthrie Mins,* para 998.

65. Ibid.

66. Ibid., para 4823.

67. Ibid., para 1196.

68. *Guthrie Report,* p. 3.

69. *Guthrie Minutes,* para 1617; 4494 ff. Research is still urgently required on the connection between the feuing system and rent-levels, as it is clear that the differences between Scottish and English rent-levels depend on their different land-tenure systems and the different laws enshrining these.

70. Cf. Samuel Cooper, *John Wheatley, A Study in Labour Biography* (Ph.D Thesis, University of Glasgow, 1971), p. 64. I am grateful to Dr Cooper for permission to cite his thesis.

71. John Wheatley, *£8 Cottages for Glasgow Citizens* (Glasgow, 1913), p. 5. This pamphlet is among a collection of Wheatley's papers in the National Library of Scotland.

72. Cooper, *John Wheatley,* p. 66 ff.

73. Ibid.

74. Cf. Nan Milton, *John Maclean* (Pluto Press, London, 1973), p. 46.

75. Ibid., p. 69.

76. Emanuel Shinwell, *Conflict Without Malice* (Odhams, Feltham, 1955), p. 39.

77. *Report of the Glasgow Medical Officer of Health,* 1914.

78. A backland was another tenement run-up in the backcourt formed by the rectangle of four existing tenements. These backlands generally contained back-to-back flats, and lacked lighting, sanitation and water.

79. Cf. John Broom, *John Maclean* (McDonald, Loanhead, Midlothian, 1973); Ann and Vincent Flynn, 'We Shall Not Be Removed' in Laurie Flynn (ed.), *We Shall Be All* (Bookmarx, London, 1978); Willie Gallagher, *Revolt on the Clyde* (Lawrence & Wishart, London, 4th ed., 1978); James Hinton, *The First Shop Stewards' Movement* (Allen & Unwin, London, 1973); Bob Horne, '1915: The Great Rents Victory', *Scottish Marxist,* no. 2 (winter, 1972); Walter Kendall,

The Revolutionary Movement in Britain 1900-1921 (Weidenfeld & Nicolson, London, 1968); John McHugh, 'The Clyde Rent Strike, 1915', *Journal of the Scottish Labour History Society*, no. 12 (February, 1978); Harry McShane & Joan Smith, *No Mean Fighter* (Pluto Press, London, 1978); Joe Melling, *The Glasgow Rent Strike*; Joe Melling – article in this volume; Joe Melling, 'Comment on the Clyde Rent Strike'; Nan Milton, Letter in *Scottish Marxist*, no. 3 (Jan/March 1973); Nan Milton, *John Maclean;* Nan Milton, *John Maclean – In the Rapids of Revolution* (Allison & Busby, London, 1978).

McHugh's article was published when this paper was in advanced draft form, so I have not re-written it to take account of his analysis. Rather, this paper should be seen as expanding on, as well as challenging, some of his statements.

80. In terms of the minutiae of the actual rent strike, it relies considerably – but not totally – on Joe Melling's paper; which empirically is easily the best so far, but, I suspect, not the last. While I believe that Melling is to be congratulated on some original empirical research in this paper, I also believe that there is a lot more work to be done on the rents strike and its period, and have raised some research issues in these footnotes. It should also be apparent that I disagree with Melling's conclusions, as well as some of his detail.

81. Cf. Kendall, *The Revolutionary Movement,* and Hinton, *The First Shop Stewards' Movement.*

82. Helen Crawfurd, Typescript autobiography, n.d., p. 114. This typescript is held in the Marx Memorial Library in London. ('Crawfurd' appears in the literature spelt with both an 'o' and a 'u'. I have used the latter as it appears the more common). Hereinafter referred to as 'Crawfurd mss.'.

83. Cited in Iain McLean, *The Labour Movement on Clydeside 1914-1921* (Ph.D. thesis, University of Oxford, 1970), p. 25. I am grateful to Dr McLean for permission to quote his thesis.

84. McLean, *The Labour Movement, passim.*

85. Melling, *The Glasgow Rent Strike, passim.*

86. Cf. the photographs in Flynn (ed.), *We Shall Be All.*

87. Gallagher, *Revolt on the Clyde,* pp. 52-3.

88. Melling, *The Glasgow Rent Strike, passim.*

89. Ann & Vincent Flynn in Flynn (ed.), *We Shall Be All*, p. 33. In a personal communication, the Flynns tell me that they derive their evidence from a systematic combing of, *inter alia, The Glasgow Herald* and *The History of the Ministry of Munitions.* In terms of the Glasgow Rent Strike, this is clearly the most important area for further research. For example, Springburn was a tightly-knit locomotive-building neighbourhood, with many of the houses being in company-owned tenements. What happened there?

90. Gallagher, *Revolt on the Clyde*, p. 54.

91. *Forward* (30 Oct. 1915).

92. From oral history of Mr N. Foulger taped by the author.

93. *Govan Press* (29 Oct. 1915).

94. Nan Milton *John Maclean, passim.*

95. Ibid., p. 11.

96. Cf. *Glasgow Corporation Minutes,* Print 2392, no. 26, 23 Sept. 1915. Hereafter *Glas. Corp. Mins.*

97. *Glas. Corp. Mins.,* 2474, no. 27, 7 October, 1915.

98. Ibid., 2477, no. 27, 7 October 1915.

99. Ibid., 2484, no. 27. 14 October 1915.

100. Cf. David Kirkwood, *My Life of Revolt* (Harrap, London, 1935), p. 120 ff.

101. *Glas. Corp. Mins,* prints 1711, 1718, 1722, 2393, 2476; all 1915.

102. *Forward* (13 Nov. 1915).

103. Cf. also *Commission of Enquiry into Industrial Unrest,* Cd. 8669.

Hereafter *1917 Comm.*

104. Crawfurd mss., p. 145.

105. See footnote 86 above.

106. Melling, *The Glasgow Rent Strike, passim.*

107. Cf. Harry McShane (ed.), *Glasgow 1919 – The Story of the 40 Hours Strike* The Molendiar Press, Glasgow, n.d.

108. *Fortnightly Report on Revolutionary Organisations at Home and Morale Abroad*, Cab. 24/71, Gt 6425, 2 Dec. 1918, p. 4.

109. Cf. Raymond Challinor, *The Origins of British Bolshevism* (Croom Helm, London, 1977), pp. 41-2.

110. Cf. *Forward* (23 Oct. 1915).

111. *Report of the Committee Appointed by the Secretary for Scotland to Enquire into the Circumstances Connected with the Alleged Increases in the Rental of Small Dwelling Houses in the Industrial Districts of Scotland*, Cd. 8111, 1915 – The 'Hunter Report'. Also Minutes of Evidence to above Committee, Cd. 8154, 1916. Both in P.P. 1916-1918. Hereafter *Hunter Report* and *Hunter Mins* respectively.

112. *Hunter Mins.*, para 150 ff.

113. Ibid., cf. evidence of Gillies, para 223 ff.

114. Ibid., cf. evidence of McBride, para 581 ff.

115. Ibid., cf. evidence of Stewart, para 720 ff.

116. Ibid., para 744 ff.

117. Ibid., cf. evidence of Wheatley, para 931 ff.

118. Ibid.

119. Ibid., para 945.

120. Melling, *The Glasgow Rent Strike, passim.*

121. *Glasgow Herald* (29 October 1915).

122. An interesting footnote to history occurs here: the subsequent issues of both the *Glasgow Herald* and *The Govan Press* carried a letter from the factor responsible for the property, pointing out that there was no widow in it. The tenant was alleged to be a wilful defaulter – and the demonstrators were alleged to be 'outsiders' – presumably Jean Barbour & Co. In any event, it was a successful *ruse de guerre!*

123. Cf. *The Govan Press* (15 Oct. 1915).

124. Crawfurd mss., p. 146.

125. Gallagher, *Revolt on the Clyde* pp. 55-6.

126. Retirement speech of Bro. George 'Jock' Strain, in *Report of the 6th Annual Delegate Conference of the Amalgamated Society of Woodworkers, Blackpool* (June 1952). I am most grateful to Eddie Frow for bringing this most interesting reference to my attention.

127. Melling, *The Glasgow Rent Strike*, pp. 48-9.

128. Nan Milton, *John Maclean*, p. 103.

129. Gallagher, *Revolt on the Clyde*, p. 57.

130. Iain McLean, *The Labour Movement on Clydeside*, p. 27.

131. Quoted in ibid., p. 29.

132. Ibid.

133. Cf. Clinton (1970), p. 229.

134. Ibid.

135. Ibid; see also, *Annual Report of Manchester & Salford Trades and Labour Council, 1915.*

136. *1917 Comm.*

137. Ibid, *No. 8 Division: Scotland; Report of the Commissioners for Scotland*, para 8.

138. *Royal Commission on the Housing of the Industrial Population of*

Scotland, Rural and Urban, Cd. 8371, pp. 1917-18.

139. Bentley B. Gilbert, *British Social Policy, 1914-1939* (Batsford, London, 1970) p. 140.

140. Ibid. See also: Marion Bowley, *Housing and the State* (Allen & Unwin, London, 1945).

141. Crawfurd mss., p. 88 ff.

142. Ibid., p. 112

143. Tom Bell, *Pioneering Days* (Lawrence & Wishart, London, 1941), p. 110.

144. Challinor *The Origins of British Bolshevism,* p. 105.

145. Bell, *Pioneering Days*, p. 108.

146. Crawfurd mss., p. 112.

147. V.I. Lenin, 'A Great Beginning' in *Lenin — Selected works* (Moscow, Progress Publishers, 1977), pp. 481-2.

148. Nan Milton (1978), p. 192.

4 HOUSING POLICY IN LEEDS BETWEEN THE WARS

Robert Finnigan

In the twenty years between the two world wars some 53,000 houses
were built in Leeds, and of these 20,000 were provided by the municipality; in fact Leeds was one of five provincial cities which together
accounted for 20 per cent of all local authority house building in
England and Wales between 1919 and 1939.[1] The process which led to
the local authorities becoming landlords on such a large scale in these
years has a history dating from the early decades of the nineteenth
century and the growing concern about the environmental consequences of industrialisation. During the second half of the century
these anxieties focused on housing conditions, with the result that the
traditional belief in the ability of market forces alone to adequately
meet the housing needs of an urban industrial society came under
increasing attack. Thus the passing of the Housing and Town Planning
Act in 1919 can be viewed not only in the context of post-war reconstruction policies, but also as the culmination of protracted campaigning
for intervention by the state in the housing market.[2]

Addison's Housing Act was foreshadowed in 1915 by the introduction of rent controls on working-class houses as a response to the
potential for social and political instability arising out of the war-time
housing shortage. State intervention in housing and the denial of profit-
making from scarcity rents led property-owners in Leeds to complain
that 'houses are not being regarded as a commodity the same as
provisions supplied at advanced prices by the grocer'.[3] Indeed, political
expediency dictated that for the present housing could no longer be
regarded as an economic commodity subject to the vagaries of market
forces. Any hopes that this development could be reversed after the war
withered away in the face of the housing crisis which existed in Britain
in 1918-19. This crisis comprised two different elements; on the one
hand there was the perennial problem of how to accommodate the
urban poor in conditions which could be regarded as being of an acceptable minimum standard; on the other there was a general shortfall in
the supply of houses. Of particular significance was the housing shortage
experienced by the middle classes and more prosperous groups in the
working class, who in 'normal times' had been able to afford better

quality housing. This situation was a new phenomenon created by the virtual cessation of house building during the First World War (following several years of declining activity in many areas), continued population growth, and an increasing rate of household formation in the immediate post-war period. The problem was compounded by the accepted fact that in the short term at least private enterprise would be unable to provide houses for these groups in sufficient numbers or at rents they could afford, given the rise in building costs and the disincentives to commercial investment in housing.[4] The Addison Act, therefore, was another political response to further dislocation in the housing market.

Within the context of this and subsequent legislation in the 1920s the local authorities emerged as major suppliers of new houses. The experience in Leeds suggests that they did so in response to housing demand rather than housing need; the crucial difference between these was summed up by a local Labour councillor in 1920 when he noted that 'the need for a house does not constitute a demand unless accompanied with the willingness and ability to pay the rent fixed for that house'.[5] As a result of policy decisions made at both national and local level, housing subsidies in the 1920s effectively served to stimulate the demand for new houses from what E.D. Simon called the 'Clerk-artisan' class – those in white-collar jobs or skilled trades, earning more than £3 a week, and able to afford at least 10s in rent when the majority of the working class paid substantially less.[6] Demand for low-priced housing meant a continuing market for low quality housing, located in the main in the very areas where living conditions had been a major factor in the pressure for housing reform before 1914.

The slum areas of cities like Leeds were still a cause for concern in the 1920s but their continued existence was tolerated for being better than no accommodation at all for the poor, since neither the state nor private enterprise found themselves able to provide new houses to let at anything like the rents they could have afforded. The realisation that council housing did not represent an effective answer to the needs of those living in overcrowded and sub-standard housing fostered the belief that it could do so by adding to the total housing stock and thus allowing poorer families to 'filter-up' into houses vacated by those who took up residence on the new suburban estates. By the late 1920s it could be seen that this faith had been misplaced, given that many council tenants were young married couples, in effect 'new families' who had previously lived with relatives and therefore did not release accommodation for use by others; moreover, after 1923 house rents were decontrolled on change of tenancy with the result that the market for vacated property was further restricted. The passing of the Greenwood Act in 1930 testified to the growing awareness of the failure of housing policy since 1919 to alter the basis of housing provision, and provided the local authorities with the means to tackle the slum problem head-on. Ironically, it took the financial crisis of the following year to realise the potential of Greenwood's initiative. The concentration of subsidies on slum clearance rehousing in 1933, therefore, marks the point at which housing policy began to deal with the underlying housing problems which had been a feature of urban life in Britain for over a hundred years.

The study which follows[8] examines the application of housing policies in Leeds between the wars, and the factors which determined the character of these policies. Collectively the local authorities acted within a framework of national housing legislation, but the way they did so individually represented a reaction to pressures emanating from various sources, both within the locality and beyond.[9] Thus, although there were two distinct chronological phases of municipal housing activity in Leeds, either side of 1933, which have already been identified at national level, this divide also reflected important local factors which led to a marked politicisation of housing matters in the city during the 1930s. The first part of the essay, therefore, comprises a brief survey of housing policy in Leeds between 1919 and 1930, and is followed by a more detailed examination of the controversial policies which made the city 'the Mecca of all housing reformers'.[10]

I

In his Annual Report for 1933 the Leeds Medical Officer of Health reviewed the progress made on housing in the city since the end of the First World War and found that 'for all the thousands of new houses erected the slum population has not diminished by so much as one family nor have the conditions of the poorest wage earners been ameliorated in the slightest degree'.[11] In fact over 25,000 houses had been built in Leeds since 1919, including nearly 11,000 provided by the City Council. There were two main reasons why this provision had failed to affect the underlying housing problem in the city, which replicated the shortcomings of local authority housebuilding nationally: in short it was too little and too expensive.

Under the Addison Act Leeds achieved a higher rate of building than any other major provincial city, completing 7.3 houses per thousand of its 1921 population, compared to an average of 4.0 for all county boroughs in England and Wales.[12] In all 3,329 houses were built, out of

an original programme for 5,800, the estimated number required to
make good the post-war housing deficit in the city. The local scheme
was beset by the difficulties common to the majority carried out under
the Addison Act — cost inflation, shortages of labour and materials,
and delays. The schemes made slow progress largely as a result of the
close supervision exercised by the Ministry of Health in an attempt to
minimise the Treasury's financial liability, given rising costs and the
open-ended nature of the penny rate subsidy.[13] Thus by June 1921
when the axe fell on the Addison scheme only 225 houses had been
completed and occupied in Leeds.[14] The political implications of the
continuing housing shortage meant that the corollary to the end of the
Addison scheme was the development of an alternative policy to provide houses on a more 'economic' basis.[15]

The 1923 Housing Act was devised amidst calls from the local
authorities for a housing scheme based on fixed subsidies and greater
freedom from central interference. The government for its part was
only too ready to agree, given the financial trauma it suffered as a result
of open-ended Treasury subsidies and detailed supervision of local
schemes. The financial arrangements introduced in the Chamberlain
Act, together with its explicit denial of a permanent role for local
authorities as housebuilders reflected the general Conservative approach
to the housing question.[16] Indeed, in Leeds the ethos of the government's policy was anticipated in December 1922 with the announcement
that municipally owned building plots valued at £48 would be sold to
builders for £5 each on condition they erected 'artisans' houses for sale
to owner-occupiers.[17] The enthusiasm for owner-occupation was based
on political as well as economic considerations, in that it presented the
'best and surest safeguard against the follies of Socialism';[18] or as Ald.
Sir Charles Wilson, leader of the Conservative party in Leeds in the
1920s, told Labour councillors, 'It is a good thing for the people to buy
their houses. They turn Tory directly. We shall go on making Tories and
you will be wiped out.'[19]

It is not surprising, therefore, that in May 1924 Leeds was reported to
be among those local authorities 'far from being in sympathy' with the
new Labour Government's approach to housing policy.[20] The Wheatley
Act was based on two principles: firstly, that there was to be a permanent place for local authorities in the housing market, and secondly,
that subsidies were to be used to stimulate the demand for housing
both for its own sake and to enable the planned expansion of capacity
in the housebuilding industry.[21] Conservative opposition to municipal
housebuilding was already manifest, and when it was announced that

the scheme would provide Leeds with 30,000 new houses by 1940 the Chairman of the Improvements Committee, Ald. Lupton, predicted 'a rapid rise in the price of houses if such a large programme were attempted';[22] for the *Yorkshire Post* the use of subsidies artificially to create housing demand was simply 'a dole disguised'.[23]

The lukewarm response to the Wheatley Act in Leeds did much to determine the pattern of local authority housebuilding in the city between the wars, as illustrated in Table 4.1:

Table 4.1: Contributions of Inter-war Housing Acts to Local Authority Housebuilding (%)

	Addison	Chamberlain & Wheatley	Greenwood and subsequent Acts
England & Wales	15	52	33
Leeds	17	31	52

Sources: (i) M. Bowley, 'Housing and the State' (1944, App. 2.
(ii) Leeds City Council, Annual Reports: Improvements Committee (1919-33), Housing Committee (1933-9).

The combined total of Chamberlain and Wheatley houses built by the City Council was just under 6,200, equivalent to 12.8 per thousand of Leeds' 1931 population; this was a poor record, especially when compared to that of nearby authorities such as Bradford, with a figure of 19.6, York 29.0, and Wakefield 50.2.[24] The consequences could be clearly felt by those in search of a house; in the year ending March 1926, for example, the council received 3,000 new tenancy applications but let only 87 new houses in the same period.[25] Against this background Labour had regularly charged its opponents with deliberately restricting the supply of new houses to protect local property interests, and warned that the result would be an explosion in rents when decontrol was introduced.[26] For its part the party did attempt to improve the rate of building to the extent that out of 5,700 houses built in Leeds under the Wheatley Act between 1924 and 1933, 38 per cent were contracted for in the two years from November 1928 when the council was under Labour control.[27]

The Leeds experience, therefore, tends to undermine the assertion that it was the Wheatley Act which 'established the provision of adequate housing as a social service'.[28] Local factors determined that although council housing went some way towards meeting housing demand in Leeds in the late 1920s, it failed to tackle the problem of housing need — measured by the deficiencies in both the size and quality of the existing housing stock. Between 1921 and 1931 the city's population increased by 4.2 per cent to 483,000, and the number of households by 16.8 per cent to 129,000; the number of occupied dwellings rose in the same period by 16.1 per cent. As a result the number of families per dwelling rose from 1.015 to 1.021.[29] (This increase in housing density was a general trend, for out of the five leading provincial cities only Birmingham, which built over 40,000 council houses in the 1920s, improved its ratio.)[30]

The problem of overcrowding was interrelated with that of the slum areas, since both testified to the effect of poverty on housing standards. The cause for concern in Leeds was the number and condition of back-to-back houses in the city. In 1930 there were nearly 128,500 houses in Leeds and of these over 75,000 were of this type.[31] As one observer noted, 'They are not scattered timidly about the place as in Birmingham, Liverpool and Manchester. Leeds is a town of back-to-backs.'[32] Not all of them were slums but almost 50 per cent were single or two roomed dwellings, often built in long unbroken rows or enclosed yards, and dating from the first half of the nineteenth century; in effect they were a localised version of the *laissez-faire* response to the housing needs of the first generations of urban industrial workers. It was this group, comprising nearly 34,000 houses, which formed the slum problem in Leeds in the inter-war years. In 1921 the report of Neville Chamberlain's committee on the unhealthy areas commented that 'owing to the enormous number of back-to-back houses' Leeds was 'confronted with the most difficult problem to be found in any of the provincial towns'; it concluded that in respect of the oldest it was 'difficult to suggest any method of dealing with them short of complete clearance'.[33] The committee's findings were based on evidence from the MOH and the City Engineer, who pointed out that the crux of the slum problem was the question of rehousing: 'the inhabitants of the unhealthy areas lived in low rented and overcrowded houses, and to rehouse them in new dwellings so long as the present level of building costs was maintained, was economically impossible'.[34]

With the rise in building costs in the immediate post-war period, together with the level of government subsidy, it soon became apparent that in Leeds this would mean gross rents (including rates) of 13s to 20s per week for the new Addison houses. This compared with earlier hopes that the council 'would be able to erect quite a nice house at a sum in the vicinity of 7s 6d a week',[35] and with all-in rents of well under 10s, and often no more than 5s, for the pre-war back-to-backs. Thus, at an early stage it had to be recognised that building by the council did not represent a direct attack on the problems raised by overcrowded and insanitary houses, now compounded by the overall housing shortage. In June 1919 Sir Charles Wilson expressed the hope that 'people in small houses would move into new houses and leave smaller houses for those badly in need of them . . . this was the only way to deal with the problem of the poorest of inhabitants who could not afford the rents of the municipal houses.'[36]

The rent problem was reinforced by the lower level of subsidy provided by the Wheatley Act which meant that the rents of houses built under the act were initially higher than those of the Addison houses. Moreover, the various council estates enjoyed suburban locations several miles distant from the main industrial and commercial areas in the centre of the city, and tenants were saddled with the cost of daily travel to and from their workplaces. Labour councillors argued that these factors placed council houses beyond the means of working-class families. They received support in the MOH's report for 1928 when he commented that with 5,800 council houses completed since the war, and 6,200 built by private enterprise, 'the needs of the better paid artisan and skilled worker have been fairly well met', but at the same time there remained

the problem of the poorer paid worker, the man with an income of 35s to 40s a week (which) has not been touched. He occupies the worst type of house because the rental is low. For him a house on one of the new housing estates would be an economic impossibility, he could not pay the rent. What he wants is a house with a rental including rates not exceeding 6s or 7s, but houses of this type are hard to get and there are none being built.[37]

Labour had long maintained that to produce such houses building costs would have to be reduced and that this could be achieved by employing direct labour.[38] From November 1928 the party's first overall majority on the council afforded the chance to test the claims made for direct labour, but the political need to establish its credibility as a municipal administration dictated that the threat, rather than the actuality, of direct labour was used to encourage lower prices in housing tenders.[39] The Conservative approach was to pursue a policy, advocated by the Ministry of Health,[40] of effectively building down to the means of the poorer tenant. They introduced the 'cottage flat', built in blocks of four, with rents of 5s and 6s for two and three bedrooms respectively, and which eventually accounted for 25 per cent of the dwellings built in Leeds under the Wheatley Act.[41] In addition the council built a new, smaller type of house on sites closer to the city centre which, with the aid of cheaper money and building costs, could be let at 7s to 7s 6d including rates in the early 1930s; in 1933 the Minister of Health, Hilton-Young, called them 'among the best type of municipal house I have seen'.[42]

The 1930 Housing Act introduced by the second Labour Government forced local authorities to face up to the problems inherent in large-scale slum clearance. When Greenwood asked local authorities to prepare five-year clearance and rehousing schemes Leeds City Council had reverted to Conservative control. The advice of the MOH that 3,000 houses should be demolished under the local scheme was rejected, and a programme drawn up for 2,000 demolitions and the 'reconditioning' of a further 9,000 houses; 1,800 new houses were to be provided under the Greenwood Act (for rehousing), and another 3,200 with the Wheatley subsidy, to meet general needs.[43] According to the Conservatives' leader the proposals amounted to what they thought 'would be the amount the ratepayers of Leeds could carry as an additional burden'.[44] This view was not shared by the Labour opposition, and in particular by Cllr the Rev. Charles Jenkinson. He had come to Leeds in 1927 at the age of 40 to take up a living in Holbeck, a parish which contained some of the city's worst slums, and from where he was elected to the council in November 1930; Jenkinson, at least, was determined that the Conservatives' proposals were not to be taken as a *'fait accompli'*.[45]

II

Marian Bowley characterised British housing policy in the inter-war years as a 'series of partially thought out and partially understood experiments'.[46] This charge certainly could not be levelled at the coherent housing policy possessed by the Labour Party in Leeds when it came to power in November 1933. The policy itself had been formulated over the previous two and a half years almost single-handedly by C. Jenkinson, and indeed Labour's victory was the culmination of a vigorous political campaign on the housing issue which he had masterminded. This began at the council meeting of March 1931 when Jenkinson, in his maiden speech, launched a wide-ranging attack on the inadequacy of the Conservatives' housing scheme in relation to the city's needs. When he called for the council to undertake a survey of the existing housing situation and future needs (which he knew would speak for itself) the Conservatives' leader Ald. R.C. Davies declared he would not be influenced by the 'sentimentality' inherent in Jenkinson's arguments, and, moreover, that such a survey would raise 'very difficult and complicated matters of policy'.[47] Jenkinson responded by publishing 20,000 copies of his speech under the title 'Sentimentality or Common-sense', and initiating the first stage in his campaign: the organisation of public opinion behind the call for a review of housing policy. It culminated in a decision by the Conservatives to agree to set up a special all-party sub-committee to carry out such a survey.

During the following twelve months the committee met nine times and took evidence from various organisations in the city, including the churches, trade unions and the local branch of the RIBA. When the MOH was invited to attend he obliged by telling the committee just what Jenkinson wanted to hear: there were over 128,000 houses in the city and some 75,000 of these were back-to-backs, including 33,000 which had been built before 1872; in an echo of Chamberlain's words ten years previously he told the committee that in relation to this latter group 'a small proportion may be amenable to a process of recondition-ing but only at a cost which would make the experiment a doubtful proposition, and at best would be a palliative and not a cure . . . there remains only one alternative – complete demolition'.[48]

It was obvious, from an early date, that the committee would be unable to produce an agreed report because of the divergence between Labour and Conservatives on the slum clearance issue. In February 1932 Davies had said he could see little prospect of Leeds entering upon an expensive slum clearance scheme. Thus the Majority Report issued by the Conservative members in November of the same year, while accepting the need to demolish the infamous '33,000' warned that this was unlikely to be achieved within the next 25 years; on rehousing they proposed to continue with the policy of building houses with rents and locations suited to the means of poor and slum clearance families.[49] By the time Jenkinson and his Labour colleagues published their Minority Report in February 1933 national housing policy had been set on a new course by the withdrawal of the Wheatley subsidy and the Ministry of Health's initiation of the 'slum clearance drive' which called on local authorities to deal with all slums needing clearance by the end of 1938. The Labour document, therefore, proposed the demolition of 3,000 houses annually for five years, and of a further 30,000 in the period 1938-48; the corollary was to be a massive scheme to rehouse over a quarter of the city's population.[50]

The Minority Report became Labour Party policy in August 1933 in advance of the municipal elections, at which Labour secured control of the city council, for only the second time in its history. Two years

before Leeds had been one of the few cities where Labour escaped the
worst of the whirlwind created by the fall of MacDonald's government;
in 1932, there was a 12.5 per cent swing to Labour in Leeds which laid
the basis for victory in the following year, one of the best ever in municipal terms, for the party nationally.[51] Thus the 1933 elections left
Labour with a four seat majority in the council and a virtual guarantee
of power for the following two years,[52] giving Jenkinson and his
colleagues the opportunity they needed to set the housing policy in
motion. From this date, until the Munich crisis, housing was the central
issue in the city's politics. This was inevitable given the size of the
scheme and the conscious attempt to turn council housing into a comprehensive social service.

The need to clear 30,000 slum houses was the *raison d'être* of the
Labour housing programme and the basis from which Jenkinson had
developed his ideas on housing policy. The slum clearance programme
itself was the first of three distinct but interdependent components in
that policy which generated their own intense political conflicts. In
July 1933, under pressure from the Ministry of Health the council had
adopted the proposal for 3,000 demolitions annually for five years at a
cost of over £4 millions. Once in power the Labour Party accelerated
the clearance programme to include 30,000 houses by 1939[53] – equal
to more than 11 per cent of the total number which were to be demolished in England and Wales under the government's slum clearance
drive.[54] The first year of Labour control saw the membership of the
Leeds and District Property Owners and Ratepayers Association increase
by over 50 per cent to 4,580[55] as it became the main vehicle for articu-
lating the landlords' quarrel with both the size of the city's slum
clearance scheme and the 'injustice' of the existing rules governing
compensation for property included in such schemes. The association
had previously denied that it opposed slum clearance *per se* and claimed
its objections were to what it saw as blanket condemnation of back-to-
backs, and the financial losses incurred by landlords in the process of
removing the slums.[56]

But, given that in the prevailing climate of popular opinion, there
was nothing to be gained, and a good deal to be lost, by appearing to
defend slum housing, the landlords' campaign focussed on the compensation issue. The provisions in the 1930 Housing Act for compensating
dispossessed property owners were a re-enactment of those originally
devised in 1919. These had already played their part in delaying slum
clearance in Leeds during the 1920s, but generally the amount of
demolition before 1933 was such that they were of no real political

significance.[57] In September 1934, however, Ald. Davies pointed out that the speed and scope of the present clearance schemes were 'beyond the contemplation' of those who had devised the compensation rules;[58] he had already admitted that the whole question was 'causing a real dif-ficulty among those who were supporters of the Conservative party'.[59] Locally there was a strong alliance between the property owners and the party; builders, accountants, solicitors and others closely associated with property interests in the city accounted for a large number of Conservative councillors,[60] and Conservative lawyers were prominent in their advocacy of the landlords' claims at the slum clearance inquiries. The power to remedy their grievances, however, lay not with the council but with a government which was Conservative in all but name.

The Leeds Association's campaign resolved into two main demands. They wanted increased rates of compensation and greater differentia-tion made between the position of 'speculative' purchasers and that of owner-occupiers and 'general investors' who were allegedly being pauperised by the existing system. Additionally they sought to change the method of sanctioning slum clearance schemes, under which areas 'represented' for demolition by the MOH and subsequently approved by the local authority were the subject of inquiries conducted by inspectors appointed by the Minister of Health, with whom the power of final approval rested. The Association pressed for slum clearance inquiries to be conducted by 'independent tribunals', and the right to appeal against their findings in the courts.

On both these counts the Association had the full support of the Conservative Party in Leeds. Ald. Davies, in particular, was vigorous in pressing the landlords' case, but his campaign encountered the apathy of Conservatives at national level; he complained bitterly that while he received 'sympathy, but no satisfaction' from the party's headquarters, the Minister of Health had offered 'neither sympathy, satisfaction, nor consideration'.[61] The property owners themselves were forced to con-cede that they were 'not in a position, like the great vested interests to force their views on Parliament'.[62] Clearly the power of small property owners, although their numbers were large, to influence Conservative governments had declined in recent years, and increasingly their own financial well-being was being sacrificed for the sake of political con-sensus. The Leeds property owners were embittered by the lack of response from the government, and warned the Conservative leadership that they ran the risk of alienating thousands who hitherto had been among the party's staunchest supporters. In 1935 the Leeds Association floated the idea of nominating its own candidates to embarrass the

Conservatives at the forthcoming general election when, according to
their president, the only issue would be 'who shall administer Socialism
— the people who invented it and have advocated it for years, or the
people who have recently adopted it'.[63]

As the Labour council pressed on with its slum clearance programme
the Ministry of Health's local inquiries into the various schemes became
an important arena for publicising the landlords' grievances. The level
of compensation for houses being taken in slum clearance was alleged
to cause widespread hardship to widows, aged spinsters and retired
people who had previously depended on them for income and were
being driven into the workhouse; much was made of the plight of
owner-occupiers, many of them working-class, who lost their homes
as well as their investment, largely as a consequence of what the Association deemed to be the MOH's extreme feelings against the back-to-back
house.[64] The evidence suggests, however, that the number of such cases
was small; in one clearance area, it was found that out of 1,060 houses
only ten were owner-occupied.[65] The Association's own figures, cover-
ing thirteen clearance areas, showed that the average ownership was
over eight houses.[66] At the time the inspectors repeatedly made the
point that the inquiries were not the arena for arguing against the
administration of slum clearance, their business was to assess the condition of houses scheduled for demolition by the MOH who, it was
pointed out could 'hardly differentiate between different properties in
similar condition according to whether they belong to an individual
who can afford the loss and one who cannot'.[67] These losses, however,
could be substantial, especially for those left with outstanding mortgage
debts. The case of a block of houses being taken for demolition with
£590 compensation only months after being assessed at a value of
£2,545 for death duties[68] was typical of many quoted by the Property
Owners Association.

Important though the slum clearance inquiries were for publicising
the landlords' case locally they provided no real substitute for direct
pressure on central government for legislative changes. At the Conservative Party conference at Bristol in 1934 Davies moved a resolution
calling for an 'equitable basis of compensation for dispossessed owners
of property which has been maintained in a state of habitable repair'.[69]
The debate which followed convinced Hilton-Young, the Minister of
Health, of the political necessity of dealing with the compensation
issue;[70] Baldwin promised that the party's grievances would be considered by the Cabinet. In the following year during the second reading
of the Housing Bill a deputation from the Leeds Association presented

a 25,000 signature petition demanding amendments to the 'confiscation clauses' in housing legislation; several of the city's MPs, no doubt mindful of the forthcoming election, were active in putting pressure on the Ministry. Within the Ministry of Health, however, it was argued that to make material concessions on the compensation issue and the demand for independent tribunals would mean the end of the government's five-year slum-clearance campaign.[71] Thus the 1935 Housing Act failed to meet the property owners' claims; it did prevent 'good' houses in bad neighbourhoods being taken at site value, and special payments were introduced for 'well maintained' houses which were nonetheless taken in slum clearance schemes.[72] Their inability to secure radical changes from the government redoubled the Leeds Associations' efforts to ensure a local régime which would mitigate the worst effects of national policy.

In every sense Labour's rehousing programme was designed as the corollary to the city's slum clearance drive. Before November 1933 it had been council policy to provide rehousing on the basis of dividing the population of clearance areas by five (or sometimes six) and building the resulting number of three-bedroom houses.[73] The Labour aim was to provide, over seven and a half years, sufficient accommodation for every family or individual made homeless by demolition; moreover, the composition of this new housing stock was to be directly related to the demography of the clearance areas as determined in council surveys; dwellings would be built in the following proportions: 30 per cent aged persons' flats, 10 per cent two-bedroom, 50 per cent three- and 10 per cent four-bedroom houses or flats, and of the total number built 5 per cent were to be designed for housing families which included TB victims. Additionally the houses themselves would be of an improved standard, and built on estates with more sophisticated layouts and amenities than previous developments.[74]

Shortly after Labour's victory Leeds completed its 10,000th council house. In December 1933 R.A.H. Livett was appointed the city's first housing director, with the brief to carry out the programme for an additional 30,000 houses by 1941, at an estimated cost of £14.6 millions.[75] Jenkinson imported Livett from Manchester Corporation, whose housing administration had been the model for his own plans. At the time Livett was Manchester's deputy housing director and had been responsible for designing the first stage of the Wythenshawe estate and the city's first block of flats built during the inter-war years. His appointment was opposed by the Conservatives who foresaw, rightly, the introduction of a powerful new influence on the determination of housing policy; they were opposed also to the programme he was being employed to execute, arguing that its effect on the rates would deter new industrial and commercial development in the city. When the specifics of the rehousing programme were announced in January 1934 the inclusion of plans for 'a great block of flats on the continental model' at Quarry Hill testified to the influence of the new housing director. Moves towards building flats near city centres, encouraged by the higher rate of subsidy which such schemes attracted, were enthusiastically supported by Livett. Although Jenkinson himself was sympathetic towards the long-standing local dislike for flats,[76] he was also an admirer of those built in Vienna under socialist administrations during the 1920s; he was finally converted by Livett's claim that by using a French method of prefabricated construction the Leeds flats could become 'an architectural ornament to the city', and economies could be made which would allow the plans to include amenities hitherto unknown in such developments in Britain.[77]

While Quarry Hill became the symbol of the Leeds housing policy in the 1930s it was, paradoxically, Labour's attempt to pursue a more traditional path which provoked the controversy. The development of new suburban estates dominated the rehousing programme. An estate of 3,500 houses was to be built at Gipton in the north-east of the city, and a 'satellite town' of 40,000 people was planned at Seacroft, which would be the largest local authority housing scheme in the provinces after Wythenshawe.[78] It was around a much smaller scheme, however, that a political storm grew up. In February 1934 plans were announced for what Jenkinson later described as 'probably the most magnificent housing estate we shall ever be able to build in this city'.[79] It was to house 10,000 people on a 500-acre site at Moortown, one of Leeds' most exclusive residential areas, bordering on open countryside along the northern edge of the city. The Conservatives were enraged; this was an area where houses sold for over £3,000 and they warned that building the estate would drive the kind of ratepayer who lived in them out of the city. When the scheme came up for council approval in July 1935 the Conservatives' spokesman forecast that the proposed development 'would cause at one the depreciation of all residential property in the neighbourhood'[80] — remarks greeted with applause from the Labour benches. The Conservatives argued that the working class would not want to live at Moortown since the estate would be about six miles from the nearest factory of any size; if it was built they held out the spectre of public transport having to be subsidised out of the rates.[81]

For some the siting of council estates near better-class property was part of an 'unfortunate sequence of events' whereby many of the owners of such property 'being those whose savings, invested in cottages condemned as slums, have been taken away . . . are in addition required through their rate or tax payments to assist in the payment of the rents of those very properties which have caused the depreciation in the value of their own houses'.[82] Such was the opposition to the Moortown estate that the Ministry of Health ordered a local inquiry into the scheme. The town clerk told the inspector that whenever the council sought to develop estates beyond the four miles from the city centre they would face the same sort of protests.[83] Indeed opposition was already growing to the Seacroft plans although this was, the Conservatives assured, 'not because of the people who would live there but because of the effect it would have on the rates of existing property there'.[84] Such opposition to the siting of council housing was no new phenomenon. In 1925 the Ministry of Health upheld the complaints of local residents against the council's plans for a small estate of 460 houses 'of a superior and more commodious type' near the famous Roundhay Park, despite Ald. Lupton's contention that 'great social advantages are to be gained by erecting houses for working-class people in what were formerly regarded as the residential districts of the better to do';[85] given fixed land costs, the Ministry's decision to reduce the number of houses by 100 ensured that the prices, and the eventual rents, of the remainder were increased.[86] In 1935 the resolve of opponents to such schemes was strengthened by the knowledge that council housing was now reserved for emigrants from the slum areas. At the municipal elections that year the promise to abandon the Moortown scheme was a major plank in the Conservative platform.

Throughout the nineteenth century and into the 1920s one of the major obstacles to the wholesale clearance of slum housing had been the limited rent-paying capacity of many working-class families, and the rehousing problems raised by this. Jenkinson was acutely aware of this fact, and thus he conceived as the key to his policy a system of differential rents. Differential rents were a common feature of local housing policies in the 1930s, but the Leeds scheme was hailed as 'the largest and most thorough going . . . put into operation'.[87] As a result its implications were profound and it became the most politically contentious element in the Labour programme. Its basis lay in a simple idea born out of the growing awareness of the failure of housing policies since 1919 to meet housing need, and also, to an extent, out of the search for economies in public expenditure. As advocated in the Greenwood Act and subsequent Ministry of Health circulars the scheme effectively

withdrew housing subsidies from the dwellings themselves, and transferred them to the tenants amongst whom they would be redistributed
according to need. Jenkinson summed it up thus: 'Houses may be
reduced in size and amenity with a view to cheapness, every possible
expedient may be tried to fit houses to means, but the problem of the
housing of the poorest families will remain unsolved simply because no
rent that can be reached, with the aid of an averaged subsidy, will be
within their economic capacity.'[88]

The Leeds rent scheme operated by withdrawing the Exchequer and
rate subsidies from the houses built under the Housing Acts of 1923 to
1930, into a pool which would finance rent rebates. By removing the
subsidies the council had to devise 'economic rents' for each house
type, based on capital cost and annual charges; against these economic
rents tenants would be granted relief according to their circumstances.
The economic rents introduced in April 1934 were generally 70 to 100
per cent higher than the existing subsidised rents. A family's entitlement
to rebates on these rents depended on its size and age structure, for
which allowances were made on a subsistence scale originally devised by
the BMA. The extent to which family income exceeded the subsistence
level determined the amount of rent relief (if any) to be granted. What
made the Leeds scheme unique was the provision which exempted
tenants from paying any rent at all where their income fell below the
given subsistence level;[89] as Jenkinson said, 'we shall not begin to talk
about rent until there is sufficient money in the household to provide
that family with the necessities of life'.[90] The logic of the scheme
derived from his concept of council housing as a social service, and its
failure to fulfil this role hitherto: 'A housing policy must first provide
decent houses and secondly provide that they be decently inhabited.
Housing policy since the war had failed in that families had not been
provided with the conditions of decent living.'[91] Leeds served as an
example of this failure; prior to November 1933 it had been council
policy that no family dependent on public assistance should be granted
the tenancy of a council dwelling larger than a two bedroom flat, i.e.
the lowest rented council property; thus many of those in greatest need
of rehousing, including cases recommended by the MOH on health
grounds, were denied accommodation.[92]

Within the Labour Party there were those who had doubts about the
implications of the rents scheme. To the accusation that he was 'tackling
the problem from the wrong end', and that the solution lay in raising
incomes to a point where requirements such as housing could be had at
market prices, Jenkinson retorted that such a remedy was 'difficult and

in all possibility somewhat distant' while the problems were 'insistent, and the palliative present and potent'.[93] He also rejected the view that subsidies of the kind he was employing tended to keep down wage levels; for Jenkinson differential renting was simply 'the key which alone will open the door of decent dwellings to thousands of families who apart from its use will never enter those doors'.[94] Others argued that the Leeds rent scheme had a major flaw; unlike the tax system it did not redistribute income between rich and poor, but, in a situation more analagous to what happened under the Unemployment Insurance Acts (which compelled those in secure jobs to pay towards the cost of maintaining those more likely to be made unemployed) the rent scheme redistributed income among a group which was already less well off, rather than the community as a whole.[95] Theoretical arguments about the legitimacy of the rent scheme subsided, however, in the face of the inter-party conflict which surrounded its operation.

Given the social composition of council estates in the early 1930s,[96] before slum clearance was in full swing, it was inevitable that a scheme which provided for certain tenants to live rent free, and in effect extended a means test to households not applying for public assistance but merely seeking to avoid higher rents, would alienate both the tenants and public opinion in general. This situation was vigorously exploited by Labour's opponents for political ends. Six months before Labour came to power the Property Owners Association, worried about 'unfair competition' from subsidised rents, had called for council houses then under construction to be let 'at an economic rent, and that any assistance which it is found necessary to give to those who cannot afford to pay an economic rent should be given after enquiry into their circumstances and should be subject to revision as those circumstances change'.[97] Two months later, in July 1933, the Association reported that in answer to the suggestion that 'it would be preferable to fix one uniform rent and to make needed rebates according to circumstances from a pool of the Government subsidy and the local rate charge' the Conservative chairman of the Improvements Committee had remarked that 'they were practically pursuing that course already'.[98] This was a reference to a decision taken in December 1932 to adopt a system of differential rents for the council's first batch of Greenwood houses. Under this scheme two methods were used to determine the rent to be paid: with the first rent could not exceed more than a certain proportion of income (varying from a third for a single person to an eighth for a family of four to six people); by the second method a subsistence allowance was deducted from total income and rent was not to exceed the remainder. Whichever of these was more favourable to the individual tenant formed the basis of his rent relief.[99] Despite this development the Conservatives, allied with three of the city's four daily papers,[100] mounted a vehement attack on the Labour rent scheme, in both principle and practice.

Essentially the Differential Rent Scheme was a mechanism for distributing a basic human requirement (i.e. adequate housing) on the basis of need, and for which payment was to be made according to means. Thus the scheme was inevitably associated with the means test, public assistance and the spectre of the poor law. Labour found it difficult to counter effectively the charge of hypocrisy on the means test, which they had opposed for public assistance but were now extending into a new field of social policy. Thus 'guilt by association' condemned the scheme to many on the estates. That the scheme 'would mean one tenant would be paying for his next door neighbour's visit to the pictures or for his cigarettes'[101] was a widely held view, undermining 'neighbourly contentment' among council tenants; the Conservatives predicted 'something like civil war on the estates'[102] as tenants tried to ensure no one evaded their dues. The symbol of the rents test became the notorious 'Grey Book', the rent book in which tenants had to record their income week by week. The Conservatives argued that the scheme was public assistance under another name and introduced 'a perpetual and periodical means test which would ultimately turn a large portion of the city into a pauper settlement'.[103] Jenkinson, characteristically, replied that indeed it was a scheme of public assistance, as was 'every other form of public subsidy, and the sooner people recognize the fact the better'.[104]

As Jenkinson himself acknowledged[105] the ability to introduce such a comprehensive differential rents scheme was largely a result of the relative prosperity enjoyed in Leeds during the mid-1930s. The size of the local tailoring industry, supported by a bouyant home market, and the growing importance of Leeds as a regional centre during this period meant that some two-thirds of the city's labour force were sheltered from the full effects of the depression,[106] and ensured that enough families could pay economic rents in order to keep the scheme solvent. This particular resolution of the conflict between poverty and good housing was not, therefore, suitable for universal application; in a letter of support to Ald. Dobbs, the Labour leader in Leeds, Jean Mann, the Convenor of Housing on Glasgow Corporation, pointed out that it would be impossible to adopt such a scheme in Glasgow, where over 200,000 people (nearly half the total population of Leeds) depended on public assistance.[107] In Leeds, Jenkinson's opponents accused him of exploiting the city's economic situation, and that political motives lay behind the introduction of the rent scheme. For the Conservatives the corollary to the 'pauperisation' of council tenants, at the expense of independence and thrift, was the creation of 'a body of subsidized and financially interested voters';[108] the property owners felt 'the erection of unlimited number of corporation almshouses to let at sub-sidised rents or no rents at all to such tenants as meet with the approval of the Socialist party constitutes a danger which threatens the entire economic and political structure of the city'.[109] To Jenkinson the implications of the scheme were clear enough; by 1941 the council would own some 50,000 houses, giving it virtual control of rents in the city as a whole, and it was this fact which lay behind the property owners' attacks.[110]

When the rent scheme was first introduced there were predictions of a widespread rent strike by council tenants in the city, but in the event their grievances were channelled by the Tenants' Association into a legal battle against the scheme, rather than mass action. The secretary of the association, whose own rent had risen from 5s 6d to 10s a week because of differential renting, fought a test case against the city council on the legality of the scheme. Eventually the case went to the court of appeal which upheld an earlier judgement in the council's favour.[111] It was against this background that Labour mounted an extensive public rela-tions exercise to bridge the gap between the party and popular opinion in the city. A series of exhibitions, pamphlets and public meetings, however, did little to counter the concerted opposition of the local press towards what was seen as the attempt to create a 'Socialist' city state. At the 1935 municipal elections the electorate was told that the city was in the grip of a 'dictatorship' by 'extreme Socialism', and that the Conservatives would 'leave the people free agents, as they has been in the past, to live like reasonable people and not to be treated like schoolchildren'.[112] Amidst the rhetoric there were promises to kill the Moortown scheme, and a commitment to end differential rents, and with them the 'Grey Book'. The Conservatives went on to gain four seats and after two years in power Labour lost control of the council. But, as Jenkinson and his colleagues had intended, their activities during this period had ensured that it was virtually impossible for their succes-sors to depart radically from the main lines of the policy they had laid down.

In April 1936 the new Conservative council introduced a new rent scheme, but in truth it was a modified version of its predecessor. The scheme divided council tenants into two groups: voluntary tenants (i.e.

those who had moved into council housing of their own volition), who paid a standard, subsidised rent, varying according to the size and type of house; and compulsory tenants (those rehoused as a result of slum clearance). The latter group received a greater share of the subsidy, and were granted additional relief against the standard rent on the basis of the subsistence scales originally drawn up by Labour. All tenants, however, had to pay a minimum rent, equal to a quarter of their standard rent; those unable to pay even this amount were 'obviously cases for Public Assistance through the proper channels'.[113]

In February 1936, when the Labour scheme was still in operation, housing returns showed that out of a total of 11,238 council tenants, 4,398 were paying an economic rent, 5,727 were receiving partial rent relief, and 1,113 lived rent free; two months previously the subsidy pool had been £10,000 in surplus.[114] Jenkinson argued that distributing the subsidy amongst all tenants irrespective of need was wasteful and financially unsound. When a deficit on the pool was revealed in 1937, and the subsistence allowances made less generous to compensate for it, his predictions appeared justified. In part the loss had resulted from the need to reclassify over 1,000 tenants as 'voluntary tenants treated as if they were compulsory tenants'.[115] This new group comprised families who had taken up houses during Labour's period of office and then found the Conservative rents beyond their means. Thus the Conservatives were forced by circumstances into retaining differential rents. The need for them was further reinforced, as Labour had predicted, by the 1935 Overcrowding Act which involved local authorities in rehousing families according to their space requirements, regardless of income. Between 1936 and 1939 the council's tenants pressed for a rent scheme agreed by all parties in the city. They now wanted a scheme based on standard rents for each house type and differential rents for all tenants. Labour supported the proposals but they came to nought because of the Conservatives' refusal to extend differential rent relief to all council tenants on the ground that this was unfair to people in privately rented accommodation.[116]

The other elements in the Leeds housing policy were similarly subjected to revision by the Conservative council elected in 1935, and which remained in power until the Second World War. In February 1936 the Conservatives reverted to the policy of clearing 3,000 houses a year.[117] The backlog of demolition work to be carried out formed the basis for a slowing down in the representation of property for slum clearance; after two years in office the Conservatives had scheduled 1,400 houses for demolition, compared to the 8,000 under Labour between 1933 and 1935.[118] Nevertheless by the middle of 1938 nearly 10,000 back-to-backs in the city had been demolished or confirmed for clearance in the previous four years; the Property Owners Association estimated that while these houses had a market value of almost £900,000, only £120,000 had been awarded in compensation.[119] Thus its failure in 1935 to secure major concessions from the government resulted in serious losses for the property interest. In other areas of policy, where there was greater local discretion, it had more influence to force changes. The Conservatives cancelled the Moortown project, and concentrated further development in extensions to existing estates, or in new ones located in areas of the city where the social geography precluded serious opposition.[120] Cuts in the size of the building programme mirrored the less ambitious slum clearance targets, and the rise in building costs in the late 1930s. In the two years up to October 1937 contracts were let for less than 2,000 dwellings, compared with over 9,000 in the period 1933 to 1935.[121]

Conclusion

The growth of council housing in Leeds between 1919 and 1939 is but one facet of the impact of government social policies on urban development in Britain in the twentieth century.[122] During these years the physical and social environment in this and other cities was transformed as a result of the housing policies adopted by the local authorities. As we have seen these changes were the product of two distinct chronological phases in inter-war housing policy.

After 1933 housing policy in effect reverted to its nineteenth-century character and abandoned the concern of the previous decade with the supply of additional houses to meet the housing shortage, in favour of the enforcement of minimum housing standards. During the 1930s, therefore, the net additions to the national housing stock made by the local authorities were negligible; between 1930 and 1939 they built 273,000 houses but demolished 242,000.[123] The pattern in Leeds was almost identical: by March 1939 the city council had provided 12,429 new houses and cleared 11,482 in the previous ten years.[124] But herein lies the crucial difference between housing policy in the 1930s and that pursued in previous eras. The concentration of subsidies on slum-clearance rehousing represented a belated attempt to tackle the 'conundrum' of the nineteenth-century housing problem — the fact that the clearance of areas of unfit and overcrowded housing in the absence of an effective rehousing policy suited to the needs and means of the urban poor only served to exacerbate the problem, spreading it

into adjoining districts and 'making what had hitherto existed in an
intensive form less concentrated but more extensive'.[125] Thus by the
mid-1930s it can be said that 'Rehousing had been joined to traditional
nuisance removal in public housing policy',[126] with the result that for
the first time housing policy assumed the role of a social service.

The implications of this policy for urban development were profound. The slum clearance drive of the 1930s marked the initial phase
in the renewal of the Victorian industrial city. In Leeds this entailed the
clearance of practically the whole of the 'inner ring' of the city and of
nearly a quarter of the local housing stock. In this way social policy
emerged as a major force in the reshaping of the built environment,
although the process was temporarily halted by the outbreak of war in
1939. Nevertheless by that date 38 per cent of the 153,000 houses in
Leeds had been built since the First World War.[127] Physically they comprised a new element in the urban landscape: the low-density housing
estate. This new phenomenon, however, was of two types; on the one
hand there were the estates of owner-occupied houses developed on a
speculative basis by private builders, and on the other the planned
council estate, 'one of the standard visual symbols of twentieth-century
Britain'.[128]

These two forms of inter-war housing development can in fact be
seen as both the symbol and reality of important social changes which
were taking place during these years as a result of the interaction of
social policy and market forces in housing. As one recent study commented: 'the most important social trend which became apparent during
this period was the decline of the private rented sector and the beginning of its replacement by a society polarised between owner occupiers
and council tenants'.[129] However, this should not be taken as a simple
cleavage along class lines, but as evidence of developments within the
social structure. Given the economic circumstances of the mid-1930s,
one of the consequences of the change in housing policy was the emergence of private enterprise as a supplier of homes to a wider social
spectrum than had been the case in the recent past; in effect it was the
private sector which provided houses for that part of the market served
by the local authorities in the previous decade.[130] In Leeds, for example,
between 1930 and 1939 11.3 per cent of house purchases were made
by people employed in working-class occupations — more than four
times the figure for 1920 to 1929, and only 1 per cent less than that
for the 1960s.[131] Thus the political controversies surrounding the operation of housing policy in these years testified to fundamental changes
in the housing market, whose social and political implications were to

have a profound effect on urban society in modern Britain.[132]

Notes

1. J.B. Cullingworth, *Housing and Local Government in England and Wales* (Geo. Allen & Unwin, London, 1966), p.28. The other cities were Birmingham, Liverpool, Manchester and Sheffield. By September 1939 Leeds had completed 20,970 council houses since 1919, including 3,447 under the Addison Act, 454 under the 1923 Act, 5,733 under the 1924 Act and 8,588 under the 1930 Act (Leeds City Council, Housing Committee minutes, 15.9.39).

2. For the origins, both long-term and immediate, of the Addison Act see O. & S. Checkland, 'Housing Policy: The Formative Years', *Town Planning Review*, vol. 46 (1975), no.3; E. Gauldie, *Cruel Habitations* (Geo. Allen & Unwin, London, 1974); L.F. Orbach, *Homes For Heroes: A Study of the Evolution of British Public Housing 1915-1921* (Seeley Service, London, 1977); J.N. Tarn, *Five Per Cent Philanthropy* (Cambridge UP, Cambridge, 1973); P.R. Wilding, (i) 'Towards Exchequer Subsidies for Housing 1906-1914', *Social and Economic Administration* vol. 6 (1972), no.1; (ii) 'The Housing and Town Planning Act 1919 – A Study in the Making of Social Policy', *Journal of Social Policy*, vol. 2 (1973), no.4; A.S. Wohl, *The Eternal Slum: Housing and Social Policy in Victorian London* (Edward Arnold, London, 1977).

3. *Yorkshire Post* (*YP*), 27.11.15.

4. M. Bowley, *Housing and the State* (George Allen & Unwin, London, 1944), ch.1.

5. *Leeds Weekly Citizen* (*LWC*), 16.7.20.

6. E.D. Simon, *How to Abolish the Slums* (Longman, London, 1929), pp.1-34.

7. Between 1923 and 1931 about 12.5 per cent of the country's working-class houses were decontrolled; decontrolled rents rose to between 85 and 90 per cent above pre-war levels while controlled rents remained about 50 per cent higher (P.R. Wilding, 'Government and Housing . . . 1906-1939', PhD, Manchester, 1970. pp.447-8).

8. This is based on research into housing in Leeds between 1919 and 1939 carried out for an M. Phil. thesis at the University of Bradford.

9. The influence of central government on local-authority housing policies is discussed at length in Dr Jennifer Dale's chapter in this volume.

10. A remark made by Lewis Silkin in 1935, quoted in R. Lloyd, *The Church of England in the Twentieth Century*, vol.2 (Longman, London, 1950), p.131.

11. Leeds City Council, Annual Report of the Medical Officer of Health, 1933, p.240.

12. J.H. Jennings, 'Geographical Implications of the Municipal Housing Programme in England and Wales', *Urban Studies*, vol.8 (1971), pp.121-38.

13. Cf. P.R. Wilding, 'The Administrative Aspects of the 1919 Housing Scheme', *Public Administration*, vol.51 (1973), pp.307-26.

14. *Yorkshire Post* (*YP*), 6.7.21.

15. Wilding, 'Government and Housing', pp. 196-213.

16. Ibid.

17. *YP*, 21.12.22.

18. *YP*, 17.12.24.

19. *YP*, 7.10.26.

20. *YP*, 23.5.25.

21. Wilding, 'Government and Housing', pp. 214-39.

22. *Yorkshire Evening Post (YEP)*, 1.4.24. The Improvements Committee was the one responsible for housing affairs in Leeds until 1933.

23. *YP*, 17.12.24.

24. J.H. Jennings, 'Geographical Implications of . . . Municipal Housing', *Urban Studies* (1971).

25. Leeds City Council, Improvements Committee Annual Report, 1925-6, p.11.

26. *LWC*, 21.5.20; 27.10.22.

27. *YP*, 22.10.22.

28. A. Murie *et al.*, 'Housing Policy Between the Wars: Northern Ireland, England and Wales', *Social and Economic Administration*, vol.5 (1971) no.4, p.263.

29. Registrar-General, Census of England and Wales, 1931: Yorkshire (West Riding) County Report (HMSO, 1932).

30. C. Jenkinson *et al.*, *The Minority Report (Leeds Weekly Citizen*, Leeds, 1933), p.3.

31. MOH Annual Report (1930), p.265.

32. H.V. Morton, *What I Saw in the Slums* (London, 1933), p.37. How this situation came about is examined in M.W. Beresford, 'The Back-to-Back House in Leeds 1787-1937' in S.D. Chapman (ed.), *The History of Working-Class Housing* (David & Charles, Newton Abbot, 1971), pp.93-132.

33. Ministry of Health, *Second and Final Report of the Committee appointed by the Minister of Health to consider and advise on the principles to be followed in dealing with Unhealthy Areas* (HMSO, London, 1921), p. 6.

34. *Yorkshire Observer (YO)*, 3.6.23.

35. *Yorkshire Evening News (YEN)*, 3.2.19.

36. *YP*, 8.6.19.

37. MOH Annual Report (1928), p.221.

38. Direct labour had been Labour's answer to high costs under the Addison Scheme; the Conservatives however favoured the use of non-traditional building methods, and of Leeds' 3,329 Addison houses 1,690 were built by various pre-fabricated means of construction. (Leeds City Council, *A Short History of Civic Housing* (1954) p.19.)

39. *LWC*, 25.10.29.

40. Bowley, *Housing and the State*, p. 45.

41. Leeds City Council, *A Short History of Civic Housing*, p. 23.

42. *YP*, 22.9.33.

43. *YP*, 5.3.31.

44. Ibid.

45. The story of how a clergyman from London's East End came to have a profound influence on the development of twentieth-century Leeds is told in H.J. Hammerton, *This Turbulent Priest* (Lutterworth Press, London, 1952).

46. Bowley, *Housing and the State*, p.3.

47. *YP*, 2.4.31.

48. Leeds City Council, *A Short History of Civic Housing* (1954), p.27.

49. Leeds City Council, 'Report of the Sub-Improvements (Housing) Committee on the Present Position and Future Policy of Housing in the City of Leeds' (1932).

50. Jenkinson *et al.*, *The Minority Report*

51. C. Cook, 'Liberals, Labour and Local Elections' in C. Cook and G. Peele (eds), *The Politics of Reappraisal, 1919-1939* (Macmillan, London, 1975), pp.169-76.

52. Lloyd, *The Church of England in the Twentieth Century*, vol. 2, p.134.

53. Leeds City Council, Housing Committee Minutes, 19.1.34.

54. Bowley, *Housing and the State*, p.154.

55. *Journal of the Leeds and District Property Owners and Ratepayers Association* (Feb. 1936), p.12.

56. Ibid. (May 1930), p.9.

57. Wilding, 'Government and Housing', p. 366. During the 1920s slum-clearance schemes in Leeds were postponed 'in anticipation of legislation dealing with the terms for the acquisition of property'; only when it became clear there was no prospect of this did the City Council proceed. (Letter from Deputy Town Clerk of Leeds to Ministry of Health, dated 28.8.27: PRO/H.LG./47/371.)

58. *YP*, 24.9.34.

59. *YP*, 2.7.34.

60. The professions were the second largest occupational group on Leeds City Council between the wars; although 'managers, businessmen and manufacturers' remained the largest group their numbers were in decline relative to members of the professions. (B.M. Powell, 'A Study of Changes in the Social Composition, Political Affiliations and Length of Service of Members of the Leeds City Council, 1888-1953' (MA, Leeds, 1953), p.138.)

61. *YP*, 24.9.34.

62. *Journal of the Leeds Property Owners* (May 1934), p.19.

63. *YP*, 9.5.35.

64. *Journal of the Leeds Property Owners* (July 1934), p.11.

65. *YP*, 17.2.34.

66. *YEN*, 18.5.34.

67. *YP*, 5.7.34.

68. *Journal of the Leeds Property Owners* (July 1934), p.17.

69. *The Times*, 5.10.34.

70. Wilding, 'Government and Housing', p. 370.

71. Ibid., p.374.

72. Ibid., p.376.

73. C. Jenkinson, *The Leeds Housing Policy* (Leeds, 1934), p.21.

74. Ibid., pp.23-5.

75. The *Architect's Journal* estimated that Leeds needed 70,000 new houses to replace all its slums and reduce overcrowding to an average of no more than 1½ persons per room (*YEN*, 6.10.33).

76. Hammerton, *This Turbulent Priest*, p. 125.

77. For the history of Quarry Hill Flats see A. Ravetz, *Model Estate: Planned Housing at Quarry Hill, Leeds* (Croom Helm, London, 1974).

78. Cf. R.A.H. Livett, 'Housing and Slum Clearance in Leeds', *Journal of the RIBA* (June 1937).

79. *YP*, 4.7.35.

80. Ibid.

81. *YP*, 9.10.35.

82. Bramham & Gale (Estate Agents) Ltd, *The Property Market* (Leeds, 1933).

83. *YP*, 9.10.35.

84. *YP*, 3.10.35.

85. *Leeds and Its History* (*Yorkshire Post*, Leeds, 1926), p.101.

86. *YP*, 21.7.25.

87. G. Wilson, *Rent Rebates* (Victor Gollancz, London, 1939), p.20.

88. *Municipal Review* (April 1934), p.196.

89. N.B. All tenants still had to pay rates, which varied from 2s 9d to 6s 3d p.w.

90. *YP*, 1.3.34.

91. *YP*, 16.2.34.

92. Jenkinson, *The Leeds Housing Policy*, p. 44.

93. *Municipal Review* (April 1934), p.196.

94. Ibid.

95. G.D.H. & M.I. Cole, *The Condition of Britain* (Victor Gollancz, London, 1937), p.168.

96. In 1935 the Labour leader Ald. Dobbs claimed that prior to November 1933 'on the whole of the municipal housing estates there was scarcely one poor working-class family living. The houses were largely occupied by the middle class or the better paid working class.' (*YP*, 23.10.35).

97. *Journal of the Leeds Property Owners* (May 1933), p.20.

98. Ibid. (July 1933), p.20.

99. Jenkinson, *The Leeds Housing Policy*, p. 44.

100. *The Yorkshire Post*, *Yorkshire Evening Post* and *Leeds Mercury*, provided the main platform for Labour's opponents; the *Yorkshire Evening News* was the only paper to cover events with any detachment.

101. *YP*, 14.2.34.

102. *YP*, 22.2.34.

103. *YP*, 20.3.34.

104. *YP*, 8.2.34.

105. *YP*, 18.6.34.

106. W.G. Rimmer, 'The Leeds Economy between the Wars', *The Leeds Journal*, no.9 (1959).

107. Letter from Jean Mann, Convenor of Housing, Glasgow Corporation to Ald. Dobbs, dated 25.10.34, in Leeds City Archives, LCA/LP36.

108. *YP*, 18.9.34.

109. *YP*, 13.4.34.

110. *YP*, 17.3.34; 22.10.35.

111. *The Times*, 6.10.34.

112. *YP*, 31.10.35.

113. Wilson, *Rent Rebates*, p. 21.

114. Ibid.

115. Ibid.

116. *YP*, 23.6.39.

117. *YP*, 18.2.36.

118. *YP*, 18.10.37.

119. *Journal of the Leeds Property Owners* (May 1938), p.17.

120. E.g. The Halton Moor estate in east Leeds (already an area of extensive council development) was built as a substitute for Moortown.

121. *YP*, 18.10.37.

122. This theme is also examined in J. Butt, 'Working Class Housing in Glasgow 1900-39', in I. MacDougall (ed.), *Essays in Scottish Labour History* (John Donald, Edinburgh, 1978), pp.143-69.

123. B.B. Gilbert, *British Social Policy* (Batsford, London, 1970), p. 201.

124. Leeds City Council, *Development Plan Survey* (1951), p.10.

125. Wohl, *The Eternal Slum*, p. 29.

126. D. Fraser, *The Evolution of the British Welfare State* (Macmillan, London, 1973), p.188.

127. Leeds City Council, MOH Annual Reports, 1919-39; Improvements Committee Annual Reports, 1919-33; Housing Committee Annual Reports, 1933-9.

128. W. Ashworth, *The Genesis of Modern British Town Planning* (Routledge & Kegan Paul, London, 1954), p.196.

129. S. Glynn & J. Oxborrow, *Inter War Britain: A Social and Economic History* (Geo. Allen & Unwin, London, 1976), p.242.

130. Bowley, *Housing and the State*, p. 177.

131. C.A. Archer & R.K. Wilkinson, 'The Yorkshire Registries of Deeds as Sources of Historical Data on Housing Markets', *Urban History Yearbook* (Leicester UP, 1977), pp. 40-7.

132. I am grateful to Dr Derek Fraser at the University of Bradford, and Jim Morgan at Leeds Polytechnic for their comments on an earlier draft of this essay.

5 CLYDESIDE HOUSING AND THE EVOLUTION OF STATE RENT CONTROL, 1900-1939

Joseph Melling

The history of state rent control has usually been written from the perspective of legislative, legal and administrative innovations with only limited discussion of the social and economic context in which they were framed.[1] Similarly, the history of social movements and labour struggles in areas like Clydeside have been dominated by studies of industrial conflicts and political or revolutionary organisations.[2] Although there are clear connections between local labour markets and housing provisions, the 'labour question' was conceived almost solely in terms of fields, factories and workshops and clearly distinguished from the 'housing problems' as defined by contemporaries and many historians.[3] Yet the history of Clydeside in these years indicates that there was a close relationship between the inadequacies and iniquities of the private housing market and the emergence of labour organisations. The struggles around the issues of housing conditions, rents and property control reached such proportions that state intervention was foreshadowed before 1914 and was forced upon the Government in 1915.

The crisis proceeded not merely from the emergency of war itself, but from the same market conditions which were causing such concern before 1914.[4] The housing market was placed under such strain that the whole fabric of property relations and legal deference was seriously undermined.[5] From the bitter class conflict and the divisions between different propertied interests in 1915 came the first interference with housing rents, and it was the continued failure of the free market which ensured the continuation of controls after 1918. For the war only exacerbated the related problems of overcrowding, insanitation and maldistribution, as well as producing an absolute housing shortage as the building industry languished.

The postwar years brought state subsidies and the gradual revival of a moribund housing market, but the structural and cyclical changes in the British economy changed the character as well as the location of private building.[6] The pattern of regional growth and the distribution of employment and occupations created considerable distortions of housing provision and led to the concentration of certain problems in specific areas. Despite the shifting balance of economic power away

139

from older industrial regions, large industrialists, financiers and officials were anxious to preserve the basic infra-structure of the industries. They were also aware of the social and political consequences of *laissez-faire* during depression and unemployment.[7]

It is in this context that we must see the continuation of rent controls after the First World War, as the building industry turned to providing for owner occupation in the more prosperous areas and the state was increasingly committed to housing the social casualties of regional depression. To remove rent restrictions whilst shortages were so acute only invited the spiralling rents seen in some decontrolled housing after 1923.[8] The results of these difficulties were the continuation of housing and rent struggles in parts of Clydeside and other regions, and the vital importance of the housing issue in local and national politics. Largely on the basis of housing and employment questions, Labour governments were able to take power in 1923 and 1929 and thereby introduce major legislation.[9]

By the 1930s rent controls remained on the majority of working-class houses protected in 1915-19, though their significance was diminished by the impressive building programmes of both private builders and local authorities. The gradual impact of this building, greatly aided in the latter case by the legislation of 1930 and 1935, was to limit and defuse the housing issue in class struggle. After the conflicts of the 1920s and the crisis of Labour in 1931, improving conditions enabled further retreats from rent restriction and the delegation of responsibility for state housing rents from central to local government. The 1938 Rent Act indicated that the rent question had become one for legal decision and local administration rather than for direct action and bitter resistance.

Housing on Clydeside was a subject of considerable interest and concern before 1900, with the housing conditions in the 'second city of the Empire' attracting comments from Engels, Russell, Smart amongst others.[10] Glasgow's housing development followed the contours of economic and social progress very closely, with the property market reflecting the 'life, requirements and dominating characteristics of every unit of the community'.[11] The dependence of local employment on shipbuilding, engineering, and other heavy industries created a close affinity being their vitality and general prosperity.[12] This potential expansion largely determined the growth and flow of population which was itself large enough to dominate housing demand in the years before 1914.[13]

Whilst the supply and demand factors acting upon the building industry are extremely complex,[14] housing demand clearly varied with the level of employment, earnings, expectations and existing rents.[15] The fortunes of local industry and its market orientations help to explain the regional diversities, which were really variations on a national theme, evident at this time.[16] On Clydeside, the focus upon shipbuilding was so pronounced that from the 1860s there can be 'read in the figures of occupied houses some of the violent fluctuations of the shipbuilding industry'.[17] Although rent levels were notoriously eccentric, the relationship between local employment and the demand factors seems evident.[18] Of course the size and the fluidity of local labour markets was itself determined by the changes in the trade cycle, with recurring problems of unemployment and mobility.[19] So we should see the housing market as influenced by local conditions and employment as well as by national cycles and trends. It is the often inverted relationship between the domestic trade cycle and the building cycle, and the eccentric movement of rents, that accounts for the lack of accord between supply and demand in the housing market.[20]

These comments illustrate the two salient features of the private housing market, which provided almost all residential accommodation before 1914: namely, its basic imperfection and its extremely speculative character. Housing booms would continue in the face of rising empties and falling demand until the ratio of empty to occupied housing became so large as to meet existing and forseeable future needs. This was partly due to the fact that general economic activity revived during the burst of speculative building, and rents would frequently continue to climb despite the increasing supply of housing.[21] This would result in shortages followed by periods of considerable oversupply and underconsumption.

The speculative character of the housing industry and the scale of building undertaken, had profound implications for housing supply at this time. For the industry continued to be dominated by a large number of small speculative builders, using traditional techniques and operating with limited resources and skills.[22] In 1914 the Land Enquiry Committee reported that the brunt of building for the working-class fell on these small concerns, the 'bulk of whose capital has been supplied by a local building society, a bank, a solicitor, or the owners of the land'.[23] These small concerns, reminiscent of Tressell's Rushton & Co.,[24] were faced with the constant worry of their capital and credit evaporating as short-term interest rates rose.[25]

Those forwarding the credit were often the prospective purchasers

who provided the long-term investment to the industry and really set
the 'tempo of house construction'.[26] The majority of purchasers appear
to have been small-scale investors, who usually borrowed as much as
two-thirds of their capital on mortgage or bond. There emerged during
the nineteenth century the small urban landlord who 'became the
characteristic entrepreneur in the housing market'.[27] Although the
benefit building societies and the co-operative building societies made
some impact in Scotland before 1914, the great majority of working-
class houses were owned by a large number of private landlords.[28] The
willingness of such investors to place their capital in bricks and mortar
accounts for the rapid expansion of Clydeside building in the 1870s and
1890s, with 40,000 houses built in Glasgow between 1881 and 1901.[29]
At the same time the role of investment trusts, property trusts, brokers
and financial institutions in purchasing housing and (more importantly)
in loaning mortgage capital should not be overlooked.[30] Even those
responsible for the control and agency of housing in Glasgow, the solicitors and factors, appear to have developed substantial holdings in
housing.[31] By the turn of the century there had evolved a complex
network of property and control relationships in working-class housing
on Clydeside which placed the tenant at a considerable distance from
the actual owners of the house he rented.[32]

These contractual and legal relationships presented an outward uni-
formity to what was an extremely sensitive and unstable market. This
became apparent in the 1870s when a frenzy of property speculation
swept over Glasgow, involving all forms of urban property and rents.
Within eight years the rental value of the city rose 60 per cent until
overtaken by the financial panic surrounding the collapse of the City
of Glasgow Bank in 1878.[33] The international repercussions of the
crash suggested the growing importance of the international economy
and of the local and central capital markets. For building investment
was now shaped by overseas investment opportunities and the flows of
labour, capital and credit between countries — hence the draining of
funds during the 1880s.[34]

The perfection of the capital markets meant a growing sensitivity
of investors, whether purchasers, bondholders or brokers, to the availability of money and the rate of interest. Cheap money after 1893
helped to stimulate the long boom of the 1890s, whilst the rising interest rates following the Boer War dampened further the declining
building activity.[35] There was also a pattern of increased domestic
investment following foreign scares and collapses, such as those of the
early 1890s, although the long-term trend of investment was for in-

creasing funds to flow overseas.[36] Partly because of the drain on gold,
the life blood of the international economy, the Bank of England was
periodically called upon to raise its own rate and thereby send up general interest rates. The consequences of these improved opportunities
and rising rates were an erosion of the bonded houseowners' profit
margins and a disincentive to further housing investment. It is estimated
that the owners' margin on Glasgow housing, for example, declined
from a healthy 7 per cent in 1890 to perhaps half that by 1914.[37] Since
between two-thirds and 90 per cent of Glasgow housing was mortgaged
in the pre-war years, the impact must have been considerable.[38]

This supply problem only gives one-half of the answer to Glasgow's
housing difficulties in the pre-war years. For by the 1900s there existed
the paradoxical problems of insanitation, overcrowding *and* over-
housing.[39] In Glasgow proper, there was a housing 'surplus' of 11 per
cent in the housing stock calculated according to families and dwellings, and by 1914 this surplus was still as much as 6 per cent of stock.[40]
Other burghs of Clydeside however, both near and away from the city
itself, experienced acute housing shortages due to their proximity
to shipyards and engineering works. Particularly affected were Clydebank, Partick, Govan and Fairfield with workmen preferring to live
very near their place of work.[41]

Besides this spatial maldistribution of the housing stock, there were
considerable problems of housing distribution and demand between
different grades of workers. Local labour markets suffered from cyclical, seasonal, casual and structural unemployment, with casualisa-
tion affecting 'virtually every industry which used unskilled labour
on a large scale'.[42] Cyclical unemployment was also particularly severe
in those areas dependent on shipbuilding and marine engineering, with
its severe oscillations during these years.[43] Bruce Glasier told the 1890
Presbytery Commission on Housing how this was reinforced in the case
of the unskilled by religion, with the sons of Irish labourers inheriting
the dwellings and poverty of a father who had 'had no trade before
them'.[44] Those with the least skills tended to be the worst housed
therefore, and their incomes in a wide range of local industries were
'too low to allow a man to keep his wife and children in decent accommodation'.[45] This conformed to a national picture of endemic poverty
and insufficient income for good housing.[46]

The position of the skilled artisan workers is somewhat more complex than that of unskilled labourers in poor housing,[47] since it involves
questions of earnings differentials and social distinctions as well as
craft.[48] The City Sanitary Inspector firmly placed the artisans with the

lower middle class when he wrote that:[49]

> The question of the provision of houses for artisans and their famil-
> ies, and people of equal status, is differentiated from the same ques-
> tion in connection with that class of our population which is ben-
> eath them in the social order, and who are usually designated under
> the term 'the poorer classes'. Artisans, clerks, assistant shopkeepers
> have, or ought to have, in normal times, wages which enable them
> to pay as rent a reasonable proportion of the money they receive.

Although there was considerable physical mobility, both to work and
within different grades of the housing stock, this pattern of differentia-
tion seems to have existed in many areas of Clydeside.[50]

Relations of trade, kinship, religion and customs overlapped to
create a series of fluid communities within a shipbuilding area such as
Partick or Fairfield.[51] They enjoyed greater security of employment
and earnings, and were able to patronise savings banks and local rec-
reational institutions.[52] At the same time, changes were affecting their
skills and job control whilst shipbuilding was coming to depend on
naval orders to sustain it during depressions.[53] This was in turn eroding
the more traditional authority structure within engineering and shipbuilding, with recurrent conflicts over managerial prerogatives.[54]
Housing difficulties only increased the employers' difficulties since
many expanding firms were unable to tempt builders into speculative
ventures, despite the obvious needs of local workers. These problems
faced John Brown's of Clydebank, who found that they could never get
sufficient ironworkers (despite the 16,000 men travelling to Clydebank
every day), owing to 'the constant wastage of men leaving us to Govan,
Dumbarton and Partick, where they can live near their work'. The
management went on to relate housing and industrial troubles, inform-
ing the directors in 1914 that:[55]

> a question which is causing us grave concern is that of our Iron-
> worker, Carpenter and Joiner Underforemen. Owing to the great
> fluctuations in the amount of our work in the last ten or twelve
> years, the larger number of these men seem reluctant to throw
> themselves heartily on the side of their Employers on account of not
> knowing . . . when they may be disrated and have to work as mates
> with the men at present under them and with whom they live in
> adjacent flats.

It was the inadequacy of the private housing market, and the strategic considerations of the employers in times of industrial unrest, that accounts for the substantial housing schemes undertaken by many Clydeside shipbuilders in the years 1900 to 1920.[56] Even skilled workmen were not prepared to pay the higher rents of Clydebank, and were reluctant to travel long distances to work.[57]

The housing problems of Clydeside before 1914, therefore, were largely ones of ineffective demand, maldistribution of housing accommodation, growing shortages as investors left the housing market, and uncertain demand as industrial employment and earnings fluctuated. Given the long term trends of declining returns, alternative investments, and high costs of materials,[58] the prospects were bleak. Even if the artisans were able to benefit from the temporary surplus and low rents before 1911, occupying the better working-class housing, the pre-war years showed that they too were being affected by shortages.[59] For Smart had demonstrated that two-thirds of Glasgow's occupied houses in 1902 were of one or two rooms, and in 1911 there were still 60 per cent of the population in this position.[60] Many skilled workers were in such dwellings, though the quality might be much higher than comparable labourers' apartments. As far as they were concerned, the housing market was not merely imperfect: it was grossly inadequate.

It is in this context of market failure and persistent deprivation that we have to locate the rise of the Labour Party in Glasgow before 1914.[61] For in the years after 1906 the growing popularity of the ILP amongst the skilled workers of Glasgow focused on such issues as housing, with Wheatley's cottages scheme creating a solid platform for the party.[62] The intellectual and social composition of the ILP generally may have been steadily reformist,[63] but in Glasgow the housing problem pushed the skilled workers into supporting the socialism of Wheatley, M'Bride and Stewart. Whilst Wheatley was instrumental in securing the support of the Irish vote after 1907,[64] it was Andrew M'Bride who was 'the life and soul of housing reformers' and who set up the Labour Party Housing Committee in 1913.[65] This committee was to marshal the rent strikers during 1915 and again in 1920, and represented every labour organisation in Glasgow.[66] M'Bride and the ILP recognised that 'as private speculators had practically ceased building, and that as many houses were admitted to be unfit for human habitation, we felt we were in easy reach of a famine in housing'.[67] Then in 1914 Mary Laird of the respectable Women's Labour League and Women's Co-operative Guild, joined others in forming the Glasgow Women's Housing Association. She asked a party conference in 1915, how 'can we expect the best possible results while we continue to house our young working-class families in one and two apartment houses?'[68] The speakers there agreed that the underlying problems of inadequate and overcrowded dwellings were merely exacerbated by the collapse of the housing industry.

Pressure was now coming to bear on local government because of the feeble contribution made by state housing in alleviating problems already recognised in the 1860s, when the City Improvement Trust had been established. By the 1900s Glasgow could boast of being 'one of the most municipalised cities in Britain', but the national housing legislation of 1890 made little more contribution than the local enactments earlier.[69] Whilst some local authorities, dominated by progressive businessmen, employers and professionals, fostered local housing in an attempt to maintain stable social relations, Glasgow had done little.[70] Although the Clydeside employers were prepared to accept as much municipal socialism as suited them, and did not infringe on their principal interests, there was no powerful housing civic campaign as in Birmingham. This may have been due to the presence of solicitors, brokers and trustees on the corporation, as some Labour councillors suggested, but it was also due to the small representation of large employers on the corporation.[71]

Under the important legislation of 1890, there were only 150 families rehoused each year to 1913 throughout the whole of Scotland despite the pleas of observers like Smart for a rigorous and unflinching housing gospel.[72] The gradual moves to housing subsidies were needed nowhere more desperately than in Scotland, as the Royal Commission appointed in 1911 was to discover.[73] Those Liberal reforms of 1906-11 did little to redistribute income and so increase effective demand, but the 1909 People's Budget did show investors the 'increasing obligations placed on the house-owner and the value of more profitable industrial or more secure gilt-edged, securities'.[74] Even the House Letting Act of 1911, supported by many Labourists as emancipating the tenant from his annual letting obligations in better types of property, only facilitated monthly rent increases in hard-pressed areas of Clydeside and elsewhere.[75] The actions of the factors (or owners' agents) in raising rents and creaming off the 'odd coppers' in the compounded rents and rates provoked the first serious resistance movement amongst the tenants on Clydeside, in Govan during 1911-12.[76] The complaints of overcharging and dubious accounting became so vocal that an official enquiry, sponsored by the ILP, Councillors at City Chambers, investigated the Govan rent books to find that the great majority of complaints were

justified.[77] An early alliance was formed between the small shopkeepers and tradesmen, and the artisan tenants, both of whom suffered
from the increases in localities like Govan. This continued throughout
1914 and after the First World War broke out, for it was the rents of
better properties which spiralled after 1911, prompting M'Bride to
comment:[78]

> The great expression of disgust at the landlord's action in raising
> rent is not from the Cowcaddens or the slum areas, but from the
> districts in which up to now people thought the housing problem
> only affected the poorer class.

With rents rising in many areas, and industrial unrest affecting both
engineering and shipbuilding, the building trade moribund and the ILP
housing campaign, events were rapidly approaching a crisis in 1914.
As the Labour weekly *Forward* said, an 'epoch seems to be closing.
We are on the threshold of another, and in doubt whither it will lead
us'.[79] It took only one year of war to transform a series of localised
housing problems into a national crisis demanding drastic state action
in the matter of working-class rents. In this transformation Clydeside
was to be instrumental, with an almost unique fusion of industrial,
social and political movements against landlords and the state. The
victory of rent controls in late 1915 brought a fresh impetus to the
industrial movements, whilst stripping them of the support in the local
communities of Clydeside.

The outbreak of war in August 1914 brought an immediate movement of men and resources as thousands enlisted in the services and
fresh labour flooded into the shipbuilding and engineering capital.[80]
All of the available housing in the industrial areas was absorbed, particularly in Fairfield, Govan and Partick, which testified to 'the boom
affecting the shipbuilding and the iron and steel industry'.[81] Those
dwellings around forges and railway works were also affected, with
even some slum dwellings taken over by the immigrant workers.

At the same time the building trade continued to stagnate. The population of Glasgow grew by almost 24,000 in 1914 and required another
5,000 dwellings, of which 373 were actually built.[82] With the 'double
revolution' in credit and commodities, men and materials became too
expensive for potential builders.[83] Meanwhile, the floating of large war
loans increased domestic capital formation whilst forcing up other
interest rates and hence discouraging housing investment.[84] The contradictions between industrial needs, financial interests and insufficient

consumption, which had confronted employers and labour before 1914 had now become a matter of national concern. Munitions workers found themselves paying increasing rent for inadequate accommodation as the rentier bondholders demanded increases in late 1914 and early 1915, even the staid *Govan Press* observed that 'the greatly increased cost of living, combined with high rents and taxes, makes the problem of living a hard one for many at such a time as this . . . the small number of unlet houses in the City gives the factors and "lairds" a monopoly.'[85] It was a monopoly of which factors took advantage, often irrespective of the tenants' ability to pay. Those with low and fixed incomes as well as the dependants of servicemen and casualties were amongst those affected.[86]

Rising prices and rents form the immediate background to the industrial struggles of 1915, with the engineering and shipbuilding trades demanding increases in step with rising living costs.[87] During the year rising rents became the issue on which the resistance to all the living increases focused,[88] with as much as 23 per cent rent rises demanded in Fairfield and Govan.[89] It was in South Govan that the first rent strike broke out in May 1915, in an area inhabited mainly by clerical, supervisory and skilled workers. Many such employees were on fixed upstanding wages at the local yards, and were dependent upon employers to raise incomes. The employers quickly realised the dangers of alienating their key workers and shipbuilders like Stephens refrained from increasing rents on their own properties. Any move which would encourage industrial or local community unrest was to be avoided at a time when massive profits could be earned.[90] Large industrialists had little in common with the housing and financial interests here, and Pirrie's Harland & Wolff supported the Govan strikers, advocating state rent controls immediately.

During the summer the unrest simmered as the government introduced Munitions legislation to restrict free movement of labour and contain wage rises. At the same time the second war loan was raised and the *Glasgow Property Circular* admitted that 'the excessive cost of material, and the increased standard of bond interest, are factors which point to the public being more and more driven into the net of the capitalist'.[91] In August there were simultaneous outbreaks of industrial and tenant unrest in Govan as the Fairfield Coppersmiths and Shipwrights resisted the implementation of the Munitions Act and a local factor notified his tenants of increases. Sectional and community divisions were eroded in a common front against state legal sanctions.[92] Harry Hopkins of Govan Trades Council and Mary Barbour of the

Govan Women's Housing Association emerged as tenant leaders, whilst the ILP umbrella organisations mobilised fresh areas of Clydeside.[93]

By November 1915 there were an estimated 20,000 tenants on strike, with the Women's Housing Association of Glasgow having recruited 3,000 members and local 'vigilance committees' linking the local shipyards and tenants' associations.[94] One newspaper, *The Bulletin*, reported that the Partick strikers (who were now leading the struggle), were occupying:[95]

> tenement houses of a very good class, though consisting of one, two and in a few cases three apartments . . . The large majority of the tenants are of the respectable artisan type — skilled workers employed in the local shipyards and engineering shops.

The skilled workers engaged on vital munitions orders remained the backbone of the strike, although by November there were many different grades of tenant on rest strike.

Throughout all the spring and summer of 1915 the Government did nothing to intervene in the rents controversy, despite the strategic importance of Clydeside in Wartime production. The *Glasgow Advertiser* declared with confidence that the 'State cannot compel a man as to his investments, and no sane man is likely to lock up capital in a venture . . . with the prospect of having the invested capital filched from him by predatory legislation'.[96] Even when the situation was becoming very serious, with weekly prosecutions and eviction attempts resulting in strike threats, nothing was done. For the government itself was heavily dependent on the financial interests and capital markets when raising war loans. Any restriction on interest rates, which were at the root of rising rents, could result in a financial crisis and there was 'no fountain of cash into which the "State" could dip in order to make good to everybody in the chain the loss entailed by tenants refusing to pay rent'.[97] The reluctance of the politicians to act led to the spread of rent strikes across the United Kingdom, with the Glasgow strikers in the forefront.

There were three other sets of interests involved besides those of the bondholders however: namely, the employers, the houseowners, and the other financial interests (including those invested in state loans and securities). The employers were anxious to avoid continued unrest and were demanding either full martial law or concessions to tenants.[98] Powerful figures like Rhondda and Mond were interested in labour questions, with the latter apparently active in the government discussions on the Rent Restriction Bill in November. The owners were largely smaller investors dependent on mortgages,[99] who were caught 'between the devil and the deep sea' with rising interest and striking tenants.[100] Edward Evans of the Property Owners' Association supported intervention providing interest rates were frozen, and Boyton thought the owners would be grateful to Walter Long for his Bill.[101] The stiffest opposition to the measure as finally proposed by the Government, came from the financiers' MPs led by Banbury of the City. These interests included some of the wealthiest men in Britain, drawing massive rentier profits from their urban land holdings.[102] Long apologised to them and other members for tampering with matters affecting 'the value of money and the borrowing of money', but held firm to his intention.[103] But even the financial interests could recognise the dangers of continuing unrest and spiralling inflation which would undermine credit and confidence. For as Mackinder warned them, if bondholders and owners exploited their monopoly position so could labour, and there was:[104]

> no reason why all these values should not go soaring up continuously . . . you are working in a circle, or, rather, a spiral. It is like the thread of a screw. You go round and round and up all the time . . . Therefore, from the point of view of the State, it is essential to bring down the knife somewhere. You have to break the circle somehow.

Here was the crux of the rents issue. So organised and effective were the tenants that they could threaten the operation of the whole war machine by late 1915. The greater interests of both state and capital demanded an immediate sacrifice of certain financial and propertied interests in the form of rent restriction. But the very process of reform implied a restoration of legitimacy and legality without any fundamental change in property or power relations.

This was recognised by the conservative *Glasgow Herald* as early as October 1915, before the government had become seriously committed to legislation in any form, when it argued:[105]

> Should it be found that the situation makes regulation imperative the Government has already created abundant precedents for interference . . . If there are grievances which ought to be removed the interests of the State demand that satisfaction should be given. If on the other hand, the grievances are of that other kind which

are created with sinister purpose to subvert certain war legislation, then the sooner the formulators of the grievances are confronted with the proof of the effectiveness of the Government's weapons the better will it be for all concerned.

Although the strikers were often those very munitions workers resisting labour compulsion under the Munitions Act, they were still deferring to notions of legality albeit translated in community terms. For as the sympathetic Sheriff Lee said at the climax of the strike on 17th November, the tenants were openly defying the landlords not because 'the law was against them but . . . they thought there was no law that had been applied to their case at all'. The real danger to property relations lay in a continued campaign of direct action against the landlords and factors, irrespective of legal or parliamentary rulings.[106]

It is interesting that the programme of action suggested by the *Herald* editorial, should have become government policy over the next few months. After the termination of the strike and the tempestuous visit of Lloyd George to Glasgow in December 1915, the government plans for dilution and emasculation of militancy went ahead with the full support of the employers.[107] M'Bride, Kirkwood and Wheatley went on to build up the Scottish Labour Party Housing Association, but there was not to be the same urgent connection between industrial and housing issues again.

The general effect of the Rent Restriction Act was to seal the fate of private building for letting to working-class tenants. Both Majority and Minority Reports of the Royal Commission on Housing in Scotland agreed that, 'no fact was more general and striking than the coincidence of a considerable, and very frequently an acute, lack of workmen's houses at moderate rents with the entire stoppage of the supply of such houses'.[108] Restricted rents joined high interest, increased costs of building and maintenance, rising rates and taxes, and improved standards in deterring the speculative investor.[109] The commission insisted that the state, via the local authorities, should assume 'full responsibility for housing' for the next decade or more.[110] Despite rent controls industrial unrest continued partly as a result of housing conditions, with one enquiry of 1917 reporting that this discontent could only be allayed by state commitment to a housing problem 'which appears to have grown too great for private enterprise now to meet'.[111] The Royal Commission agreed by stating that before the First World War, 'the demand for better housing had become articulate; to-day, after three years of war, it is too insistent to

be safely disregarded any longer'.[112] There was a growing tendency
during the war for militant trade unionists to take up social and political as well as industrial questions, and to demand a better social wage.
This became clear during the great 1919 troubles in Glasgow, when the
suspended ASE militants voiced a strong feeling that:[113]

> the widespread discussion and repeated promises of postwar Social
> and Industrial Reconstruction were merely nebulous talk, and that
> neither the Government nor apparently the Trade Unions . . . had
> any definite proposals which would give force and direction to the
> workers' efforts.

It was against this background of continuing stagnation and growing
unrest that the government came to review its rent and housing
policies in 1917-19. Addison's Advisory Housing Panel informed him
that Rent Restriction may have been politically necessary, but it placed
the state in a difficult situation when controls were lifted, for:[114]

> on the one hand . . . unless prompt and effective steps are taken to
> remedy the shortage of houses, rents in many places will rise to
> scarcity prices and grave discontent will thereby be caused, and on
> the other . . . its continued existence must be a hindrance to the
> ordinary remedy, namely building by private enterprise.

The panel also recommended that the state must advance large amounts
of capital for housing programmes, in the expectation of considerable
losses on investment.[115]

The Hunter Committee, reviewing rent restrictions in 1919, agreed
with this prognosis and warned that the ending of controls would mean
'that mortgages would be called in everywhere', to the detriment of
owners as well as tenants.[116] Even the financial interests holding
mortgage bonds recognised that a sudden return to free market conditions would precipitate a rents crisis beneficial to no one.[117] Therefore in 1919 both the major housing legislation and further rent controls were introduced by the government.

At this point the Scottish Office estimated that 57,000 new houses
were required for Glasgow alone, all of at least three apartments,
though the Royal Commission recommended 236,000 for Scotland as a
whole.[118] The Glasgow Corporation took advantage of the Addison
Act as well as local builders, although by 1921 only 4,500 new houses
had actually been erected.[119] This serious situation in Glasgow and

elsewhere obviously influenced the Salisbury Committee on rent restrictions, which pointed out that 'the direct result of allowing the Acts to lapse . . . would be the immediate increase in rents beyond the point which public opinion would, in the circumstances, regard as equitable'.[120]

Just how inequitable the 'public' inhabiting controlled houses found it, was demonstrated in 1920 when the government allowed 'some relief to the house owner' with a 15 per cent rise in rents.[121] As the ILP were sweeping local elections on Clydeside, the Scottish Housing Association organised a fresh rent strike under 'district officials'.[122] Although unemployment was looming, the ILP insisted that the tactics of 1915 could defend living standards. Wheatley told the thousands of 1920 strikers:[123]

> On this cost of living question, of which rents are but a part, you cannot avoid a bitter struggle. We are being carried rapidly towards financial confusion, industrial chaos, starvation, and perhaps worse. You alone can change this course. They can starve you into accept-ance of their terms for food but the houses are in your own hand, and, if you fight here, you cannot fail!

Once again it was in those areas traditionally recognisable as largely occupied by artisans that the strike was strongest. The *Voice of Labour* had been exaggerating when in 1907 it described 'the aristocracy of labour . . . in the grip of a merciless class of landlords', but a decade later the indictment had more substance.[124] Skilled workers had seen not only an erosion of craft customs and sectionalism, but also a reduction of privileges and differentials.[125] Bolitho wrote in 1924 that 'the skilled artisan class is the active factor in the Red Clyde', and referred to the primary importance of housing conditions — which had been merely 'inconveniences to the skilled minority before'.[126] The aspirations which had driven them into supporting the ILP housing platform before the war were sharpened by the desperate conditions experienced after 1914, and it was they who supported the ILP in direct struggles and in local elections after 1918.[127]

The campaign of 1920 was continued for some months, despite the feeble attitude of the parliamentary spokesmen, with the centre of the struggle gradually shifting to Clydebank from Glasgow. By 1922 there were again 20,000 tenants on strike, the majority in 'Red Clydebank', as the strike leaders pursued their cause through the law courts as well as the communities.[128] This was eventually to lead the strikers into defeat at the highest judicial institutions of the state, although it did force the owners into some compromises.[129] Moreover, the struggles lacked industrial support and the organised coherence of 1915 as their local leaders concentrated on a variety of defensive tactics.

Although the housing situation was little better than in 1919, and the growing unemployment reduced the prospect of effective housing demand in many areas, the government felt strong enough to introduce a gradual decontrol of rents after the Report of the Onslow Committee in 1923.[130] In the same year Chamberlain's Act was introduced with fond hopes of a rapid revival of private building activity after the postwar crises had passed.

During the same period there were emerging long-term economic trends that were to fundamentally affect the structure of both regional and national economies during the interwar years. Housing was to play a crucial part in these developments, being affected by general economic conditions as well as government economic, financial and social policy; and in turn contributing to economic growth and regional change before 1939. Here again Clydeside became not so much a microcosm of these changes as an indicator of the worst aspects of depression and deprivation, which demanded more extreme solutions.

After the initial postwar boom resulted in the overcapacity of the steel, shipbuilding and heavy engineering trades, areas such as Tyneside, Belfast and Clydeside settled into general stagnation.[131] By 1924 both Beardmores and Armstrongs, which had boomed under imperial expansion and munitions production, were in serious difficulties requiring Bank of England intervention.[132] In the late 1920s the shipbuilding and steel industries were being remodelled by Montagu Norman and the industrial mandarins such as Lithgow.[133]

As the structure of the economy changed, resources, population and occupations shifted to new regions and demanded fresh infrastructural building there.[134] The impact on housing demand and activity was to be very marked, with impressive growth rates in many of the new areas.[135] Many of the salaried, white collar, and higher manual grades were to benefit from this regionalised progress by purchasing housing for owner occupation.[136] It was they who benefited from the availability of building society funds, which expanded from under £128 million in 1925 to over £548 million by 1938.[137]

The supply factors which made this demand effective were low costs of materials and labour, availability of plentiful funds and cheaper money, and state aid subsidies.[138] The intervention of the state in the housing market must be seen at a number of levels here, since its financial policies and economic strategies were frequently as significant as its explicit housing and rents policies. After the Addison Act of 1919, with its direct subsidies and unlimited local authority expenditure, the financial interests of the City and the Bank were pressing for high interest rates and a return to gold. According to Norman, the additional cost to the nation was 'as dust compared with the restoration of free trade and the removal of social unrest and political discontent'.[139] It was only after the passing of such unrest in 1921 that the administrative and financial reactions were carried through.[140]

Depression and unemployment certainly reduced building costs in the 1920s, although the high interest rates dampened speculative construction as large amounts of capital stayed in government and overseas securities. Then in 1930 to 1931 the financial crisis overtook government and finance, and with 'the depreciation of the Pound Sterling goes the prohibition of capital exports . . . foreign loans, the successful Great Conversion'.[141] The latter referred to the conversion of £1,970 million war loans from 5 per cent to 3.5 per cent interest in 1932.[142] The financial panic and the government policies led to the flooding of large sums into the building societies from 1932, facilitating the building boom of 1932 to 1938 in Britain.[144] It is noticeable that the great bulk of building in England and Wales during this thirties boom was undertaken by private enterprise without state assistance.[144] The indirect results of depression and state monetary policies was therefore to stimulate another 'long swing' in the building market and sustain private enterprise.[145]

This expansion of the housing industry was only possible where the local incomes and employment generated a certain degree of prosperity. In depressed areas such as Scotland and the north of England however, the level of real incomes was lower and the level of unemployment higher than elsewhere.[146] Private enterprise was now building for owner occupation rather than for letting at reasonable rents, and the burden placed upon the local authorities was proportionately greater. As the problems of unemployment and poverty grew on Clydeside and elsewhere, debilitating housing conditions continued and worsened.[147]

There were a few thousand houses built in Glasgow under the Addison Act but the advent of the Chamberlain Act led by 1924 'to a marked decline in the number of houses completed'.[148] In these years the disillusionment with liberal policies led to victories of the ILP in Clydeside elections, and in 1924 the first Labour Government passed the important Wheatley Housing Act. Under this measure there were 75,000 houses built in Scotland up to 1934 and the return of the labour politicians in 1929 forestalled the cuts planned in 1928.[149] This was the

other dimension of working-class resistance to bad housing and high
rents, and their electoral power was applied in the return of Labour to
city control at Glasgow in 1931.[150]

Those benefiting from the local authority building which was largely
undertaken after 1924 were generally the more affluent clerical and
skilled workers of Clydeside. Enquiries discovered that these groups
were catered for, rather than the lowest paid and worst housed, because
of the financial constraints placed upon the local authorities to charge
a reasonably 'economic' rent.[151] Those who had formed the backbone
of rents resistance, industrial unrest and Labour support before 1919
were benefiting from the fruits of limited victories.

Despite the inroads of the 1920s, therefore, the chronic problems
identified by the Royal Commission in 1917 were still largely untreat-
ed. The leading issues were then stated to be overcrowding and existing
low standards of housing.[152] The Greenwood Act of 1930 enabled the
local authorities to engage in slum clearance, but it was not until 1935
that legislation was passed which defined and attacked the basic issue of
overcrowding. At this time it was found that one-quarter of all working-
class homes were overcrowded and that Scotland was *six times* as bad as
England in this respect.[153]

The low costs and increased subsidies of the early thirties gave the
Scottish authorities an ideal opportunity for dealing with their worst
problems, and by 1939 two-thirds of the 337,000 interwar houses built
in Scotland were built by local government. Most of the remaining one-
third were built for owner-occupation in the later 1930s, and were
again taken by salaried and higher manual grades.[154] This ratio of public
and private housing was almost exactly the reverse of that in England,
where the private boom surged ahead after 1931.[155]

Consequently there emerged not so much a dualism between private
owner and local authority housing, as a tripartite division between these
two and the remaining private rented sector.[156] The latter were graded
according to standards and rents, though the Marley Committee reported that of the 920,000 dwellings controlled since 1915, only 120,000
had been decontrolled under the 1923 legislation.[157] Those in the higher grades of houses, mainly 'better class artisans' and lower middle class
groups, had been successfully removed from rent control. But for the
broad mass of people in the 'lower rental working-class houses', the decontrol envisaged had not been effective since:[158]

There had been a great deal of friction and some hardship . . . and
the Act has not succeeded in bringing back private enterprise to this

> class of building . . . this partial system of decontrol should cease to
> apply to the lower rented working-class houses.

For the committee discovered that the rents of comparable decontrolled houses had risen much faster than those still under restrictions, with
the result that tenants refused to move from their dwellings to pay
higher rents elsewhere. These occupants were unable to leave the rented
sector because of the high costs of owner-occupation and council housing, and were equally unwilling to leave restricted housing or pay more
rent. Whilst their relative significance became steadily less as new building and decontrol advanced, severe overcrowding was still encouraged
by the system.[159]

During the thirties, the private rented sector was being largely super-
seded by private and local authority building even in the most depressed areas not recovering until rearmament. As the successor of the private landlords, the local authorities were faced with the rent issue themselves and the question of their relationship to the free market. The 1917
Royal Commission had been anxious that the authorities should not
rent housing below 'the standard for similar houses in the neighbourhood', and insisted on strict central control of both grants and rents.[160]
There arose after 1918 a fairly strict control of capital expenditure and
rent levels as central government, very much aware of Treasury advice
and financial interests, stipulated the highest rent practical.[161] Local
authorities had the direct responsibility for building but it was central
government which dictated the tempo of construction and the conditions of letting.

There was a gradual retreat from central supervision during this decade however, as the struggles of the rent strikers and industrial militants passed and the financial crisis of 1931 divided Labour.[162] The
legislation on slum-clearance and overcrowding placed a statutory ob-
ligation on local authorities to deal with cancerous conditions, whilst
the Act of 1935 gave them responsibility for local rent levels. This
measure did specify that council house rents should reflect 'market values', and a memorandum of the act explained that its intention was
that 'persons who can afford to pay for accommodation provided by
private enterprise should not be accommodated in subsidised houses'.[163]
This admirably summed up the purposes of local authority housing in
the interwar years: local government was not to use state subsidies to
compete with or discourage private enterprise in the housing market,
but rather to provide for those who could not present an effective market demand. In this way it could sustain the housing industry and

building capital, whilst maintaining the industrial and social infrastructure for local employers.

There were also political and administrative implications here which
cannot be overlooked. The measure of 1935 removed from central
government the onus for rent increases whilst preserving its powers of
general financial control. This would have the effect of restricting rent
protests to their local representatives and of limiting the local—central
conflicts over rent levels. By this period Labour and Communist councillors were dominant in areas like Clydeside, but the progress of legislation seriously reduced the opportunity for a national campaign on
housing and rents questions.[164]

Meanwhile, rent control in the private sector was draining away as
houses were demolished, again with state compensation, or improved
for higher rents. The Ridley Committee of 1937 recommended that
overcrowding still persisted in many controlled houses, and fixed the
rate of decontrol to the level of overcrowding.[165] It was again up to the
local authorities to rehouse those suffering from overcrowding, thereby
liberating both tenants and private property from the heritage of deprivation.

Conservative economists are able to note with satisfaction the progress of housing during the interwar period, when owner-occupation
boomed on such a scale as to completely revitalise the moribund housing industry. By 1939 the 'housing problem was increasingly a localised one' according to them, whilst the local authorities had shown
themselves 'not very successful in tackling those problems such as overcrowding which they were meant to solve'.[166] Whilst such statements
are certainly correct in some respects, they tend to distort the essential
nature of the problems discussed.

For the same problems of deprivation and underconsumption continued as a major problem during the interwar years, as is shown in
Keynes's 'general theory'. Although there were 4.528 million houses
built to 1940, only 900,000 were available to families with incomes
less than £3 per week and just over half the total were within the means
of families on less than £5 per week.[167] Despite the arguments for 'filtering up', there was little impact in areas like Clydeside because of
depressed economic conditions and the disincentives to leave controlled
dwellings.[168] Relief came for a great many tenants only in the later
thirties, and it is probable that after the downturn of the building boom
from 1938-9 local authorities would have continued their responsibilities in dealing with the casualties of the housing market.[169] Whilst this
building activity itself did much to promote a regeneration of the

economy, it was only the return to armaments and naval construction that brought prosperity back to the backwaters of Victorian imperialism like Clydeside.

This survey of state rent controls during the years 1915 to 1939 suggests the importance of housing struggles and labour conflicts in the formulation of housing policies. These struggles were conducted at many different levels, both within and outside the formal limits of the state. Direct action in rent strikes and tenant resistance was coupled with political campaigns, legal contests, local elections and parliamentary rule. The local support created by Wheatley and M'Bride, gave Labour control of Clydeside administration and minority governments in these years. Under the 1935 Act the Labour pressures for a central housing advisory committee were recognised and provided for.[170]

Yet the same economic problems of pre-1914 did recur again after 1918, but in acute form. The increasing contradictions between working-class perceptions of housing needs and fair rents, and the investors' perception of an adequate return was only resolved by state intervention in 1915. The war converted a series of localised and inarticulate conflicts into a national rents campaign in 1915, but the consequence was not permanent rent control – still less a solution to the housing crisis. Whilst the state retreated from control of the private rented sector, it maintained a stringent rents policy on local authority building which gave improved accommodation to the salaried and skilled worker rather than the worst housed.

In explaining the retention of partial rent restrictions after 1920 and 1923, the resistance of working-class tenants must figure as well as the housing campaigns of the Labour Party. If only by refusing to leave the overcrowded dwellings, these tenants eventually demonstrated the inadequacies of the private housing market. The Marley Committee appointed in 1929 by Labour demonstrated this in 1931, at a time when its initiators were in the throes of the financial crisis that was to divide Labour and stimulate the private boom of the thirties.

With the Second World War came a return of general rent controls, along with the housing shortages and the re-emergence of problems seen earlier.[171] In 1945 the second Ridley Committee recommended that rent control 'cannot be removed immediately and we are satisfied that it must continue for some time after the war'.[172] They reported to Thomas Johnston, editor of *Forward* during the 1915 strike, after hearing Mary Barbour of Govan Women's Housing Association and Dan Rider of the War Rents League, and there was the full expectation that Labour would build 4 million houses.[173]

Therefore, the rent restriction measures must be seen as partial concessions at best and always in the context of other state policies being pursued. Even during full controls, the major industrial and financial interests were little affected by the restrictions and were even willing to support certain controls. Given the financial and political constraints operating after 1921, central and local government catered for the better paid. The 1935 Act really began to deal with the large residuum, whilst insisting that those able to present effective demands for private enterprise should now do so.

As the circulars of 1935 indicated, it was not the intention of state legislation to compete with private enterprise when an 'economic rent' or market price could be paid.

By decentralising the regulation of council rents, the state could give local authorities some practical experience of financial budgeting whilst reducing the potential for wider conflicts over rent levels.[174] Rents were effectively defused as a major social and political issue, and thereafter they became a matter for local administration and judicial arbitration.[175] This is precisely how many historians and social administrators portray them.

Notes

1. Marion Bowley, *Housing and the State, 1919-1944* (George Allen & Unwin, London, 1945); J.B. Cullingworth, *Housing and Local Government in England and Wales* (George Allen & Unwin, London, 1966); R.D. Cramond, *Housing Policy in Scotland, 1919-1964* (Oliver & Boyd, Edinburgh, 1966). But see also Piers Bierne, *Fair Rent and Legal Fiction* (Macmillan, London, 1977).

2. Walter Kendall, *The Revolutionary Movement in Britain, 1900-1921* (Weidenfeld & Nicolson, London, 1969); James Hinton, *The First Shop Steward's Movement* (George Allen & Unwin, London, 1973); Raymond Challinor, *The Origins of British Bolshevism* (Croom Helm, London, 1978). All these works give some discussion of the Glasgow rent strike of 1915.

3. Paul de Rousiers, *The Labour Question in Britain* (Macmillan, London, 1896).

4. Seebohm Rowntree, 'The Question of Providing Housing for the Working Classes at Rents which they can Afford to Pay'; and Pigou, 'The Housing Question', in Rowntree and Pigou, *Housing – The Warburton Lectures* (University of Manchester Press, 1914).

5. This is discussed at considerable length in Joseph Melling, 'The Glasgow Rent Strike of 1915' (University of Glasgow, Sept. 1978). See also Piers Bierne, *Fair Rent*.

6. Sidney Pollard, *The Development of the British Economy 1914-1960* (Edward Arnold, London, 1962); M.J. Elsas, *Housing Before the War and After* (P.S. King, London, 1942).

7. A.M. Robb, 'Shipbuilding and Marine Engineering' in J. Cunnison and J.B.S. Gilfillan (eds.), *The Third Statistical Account of Scotland: Glasgow* (Collins,

Glasgow, 1958).

8. Rising rents after 1923 are discussed in Ministry of Health, *Report of the Inter-Departmental Committee on the Rent Restrictions Acts*. Cmd. 5621 (1937).

9. Excellent survey in Samuel Cooper, 'John Wheatley: a study in Labour Biography' (PhD thesis, University of Glasgow, 1971).

10. Frederik Engels, *The Condition of the Working Class in England* (Panther, London, 1969); James B. Russell, 'On the Comparative Prevalence of Filth-Disease in Town and Country', *Proceedings of the Philosophical Society of Glasgow*, vol.XI, no.1 (1877-8), pp.8-34; William Smart, *The Housing Problem and the Municipality* (University of Glasgow Free Lectures, 1902).

11. *The Glasgow Advertiser and Property Circular* (5 Jan. 1915).

12. James Hamilton Muir, *Glasgow in 1901* (William Hodge and Co., Glasgow, 1901) p.164; Anthony Slaven, *The Development of the West of Scotland* (Routledge & Kegan Paul, London, 1975), p.142; Cunnison and Gilfillan, *The Third Statistical Account*, pp.133-264. For good general survey of Glasgow's housing: John Butt, 'Working-class Housing in Glasgow 1851-1914' in Stanley D. Chapman, *The History of Working-Class Housing* (David & Charles, Newton Abbot, 1971); Robert Baird, 'Housing' in A.K. Cairncross, *The Scottish Economy* (1954) pp.193-212.

13. A.K. Cairncross, *Home and Foreign Investment, 1870-1913* (CUP, 1953), pp.23-5.

14. J. Parry Lewis, *Building Cycles and Britain's Growth* (Macmillan, London, 1965), especially pp.106-86 for general survey.

15. Cairncross, *Home and Foreign Investment*, pp.23-32 for Glasgow context.

16. S.B. Saul, 'House Building in England, 1890-1914', in *Economic History Review*, XV (1962-3), p.123; Parry Lewis, *Building Cycles*, pp.106-7; Bernard Weber, 'A new index of residential construction and long cycles in housebuilding in Great Britain, 1838-1950', in *Scottish Journal of Political Economy*, 2 (1955), pp.111-26 for long cycles.

17. A.K. Cairncross, 'The Glasgow building industry, 1870-1914', in *Review of Economic Studies*, II (1934), p.4. For contrast see R.J. Morris, 'The Friars and Paradise: An Essay in the Building History of Oxford, 1801-1861', in *Oxoniensia*, XXXVI (1971).

18. Cairncross, *Home and Foreign Investment* (1953), pp.4, 13, 25.

19. W.H. Beveridge, *Unemployment, A Problem of Industry* (Longman, London, 1909/30), pp. 86-7.

20. Saul, 'House Building in England', pp.120-1.

21. Cairncross, *Home and Foreign Investment* (1953), pp.28-32.

22. E.W. Cooney, 'The origins of the Victorian Master builders' in *Economic History Review*, VIII (1955-6), p.167; Keith Burgess, *The Origins of British Industrial Relations* (Croom Helm, London, 1975), pp.86-97; UGD 74 1/1, 'Glasgow Building Estimates 1870-7'.

23. Quoted in Saul, 'House Building in England', p.132n.

24. Robert Tressell, *The Ragged Trousered Philanthropists* (Panther, London, 1965).

25. Saul, 'House Building in England', pp.132-3; cf. *Glasgow Dean of Guild Records* (Govan) SRA Ref. 240-310, and Butt, 'Working-class Housing', on Binnie.

26. Cairncross, in *Review of Economic Studies* (1934), p.13.

27. John Greve, *Private Landlords in England* (George Bell, London, 1965), p.9.

28. Scottish Housing Advisory Committee, *The Provision of Houses for Owner Occupation in Scotland*, Cmd. 6741 (1946), pp.5-6; B. Elliot and D. McCrone, 'Landlords in Edinburgh' in *Sociological Review*, vol.23, no.3 (August 1975); cf. Greve, *Private Landlords*, for England.

29. John Butt, 'Working-class Housing', pp.71-4; Cairncross, *Home and Foreign*

Investment (1953), pp.20-1.

30. Enid Gauldie, *Cruel Habitations, A History of Working Class Housing* (George Allen & Unwin, London, 1974), p.192 on shift from employers housing; Caroline Bedale, Chapter 2 above; UGD 80 1/1, *Rules of the Provident Property Investment Company* (1850).

31. Work is continuing in this area by the author and also Mr Paul Watchman, University of Glasgow.

32. This form of 'landlord absenteeism' was condemned by *The Glasgow Herald* as early as 8 February 1849.

33. James Nicol, *Vital Social and Economic Statistics of the City of Glasgow, 1881-1885* (Maclehose, Glasgow, 1885), p.49; S.G. Checkland, *Scottish Banking – A History, 1695-1973* (Collins, 1975), pp.469-71; Parry Lewis, *Building Cycles*, p.109.

34. A.G. Kenwood and A.L. Lougheed, *The Growth of the International Economy, 1820-1960* (George Allen & Unwin, London, 1972), chapters 6-7; Brinley Thomas, 'Demographic determinants of British and American building cycles, 1870-1913', in Donald N. McCloskey (ed.), *Essays on a Mature Economy: Britain after 1840* (Princeton University Press, 1971) for cycles debate.

35. Butt, 'Working-class Housing', pp.71-4.

36. P.L. Cottrell, *British Overseas Investment in the Nineteenth Century* (Macmillan, London, 1975), p.28. Cottrell notes that 40 per cent of life insurance funds or £315 million was being invested overseas by 1913.

37. Cairncross, *Home and Foreign Investment*, p.13.

38. John Wheatley told the Hunter-Scott Committee of Enquiry in November 1915: 'the evidence . . . goes in the direction of proving that about two thirds of the property in Glasgow is owned by bondholders, and they are the real owners as far as revenue is concerned'. *Report of the Committee on alleged increases in rental of small dwellings in Scotland*, Cd. 8111, p.37, Q 933. This little-studied committee is discussed in Joseph Melling, 'The Glasgow Rent Strike'.

39. Ernest Ritson Dewsnup, *The Housing Problem in England – Its statistics, legislation and policy* (Manchester University Press, 1907), p.113.

40. John Butt, 'Working Class Housing in Glasgow, 1900-1939' in Ian MacDougall (ed.), *Essays in Scottish Labour History* (John Donald, Edinburgh, 1979), p.6. I am grateful to Professor Butt for permission to read and cite his draft chapter. He notes that in 1901 there were 134,000 families as against 168,000 houses. In 1915 *The Glasgow Herald* (reporting Cd. 8111) noted that 13,178 dwellings still vacant on eve of war, *The Glasgow Herald* (17 Nov. 1915).

41. Memorandum on the Shortage of Ironworkers at John Brown's, Clydebank. By manager Bell, in UCS 1 23/3. The implications are discussed in Joseph Melling, 'Employers, Labour and the Housing Market on Clydeside, 1880-1920', *SSRC Conference Paper* (Glasgow University, May 1978).

42. J.H. Treble, 'Unemployment and Unemployment Policies in Glasgow, 1890-1905' in Pat Thane (ed.), *The Origins of British Social Policy* (Croom Helm, London, 1978), p.4 of original draft; Beveridge, *Unemployment*.

43. Cunnison and Gilfillan, *The Third Statistical Account*, p.204.

44. The Presbytery of Glasgow, *Report of the Commission on the Housing of the Poor in Relation to their Social Condition* (Maclehose, Glasgow, 1891), pp.16-17.

45. John Butt, 'Working-class Housing in Glasgow 1851-1914', p.82.

46. Pigou, in 'The Housing Question', wrote, 'the failure with which we are confronted is the general fact of poverty, whereof inadequate housing is merely a manifestation', pp.54-5.

47. Rowntree, 'The Question of Providing Housing', pp.5-6; *Royal Commission on the Housing of the Industrial Population in Scotland*. Cd. 8731, pp. 45-51, give comparative situation in Scotland; paragraphs 402-4 give fivefold classification of

tenements from Edinburgh and paragraphs 421-5 discuss this in Glasgow context.

48. This is the subject of a continuing debate. See E.J. Hobsbawm, 'The Aristocracy of Labour Reconsidered', *Seventh International Congress of Economic History* (1978) Edinburgh; H.F. Moorhouse, 'The Marxist theory of the Labour Aristocracy', *Social History*, vol.3, no.1 (1978).

49. Peter Fyfe, 'Report of the Sanitary Inspector of Glasgow on the Proposed Relaxation of Building Regulations' (November 1916), SRA, D TC 8/19/8, pp.7-8.

50. Martin Bulmer (ed.), *Working Class Images of Society* RKP/SSRC (1975); Joseph Melling, 'The Glasgow rent strikes and community protests' (University of Glasgow, 1978).

51. The division of artisan wards and housing generally is discussed by Iain McLean, D. Phil. Oxon., 'Labour in Clydeside Politics, 1914-1922', unpublished thesis (1971), ch.13.

52. Joseph Melling, 'British Employers and the Development of Industrial Welfare: an Industrial and Regional Comparison, c.1880-1920' (Proposed doctoral thesis for University of Glasgow, 1979).

53. Burgess, *The Origins of British Industrial Relations*; J.D. Scott, *Vickers – A History* (Weidenfeld and Nicolson, London, 1962); Duncan Burn, *The Economic History of Steelmaking, 1867-1939* (Cambridge University Press, 1961), pp.183-328; Roy Hay, 'Employers and Social Policy, 1905-1914', *Social History*, vol. 4 (1977).

54. J.R. Richmond, *Some Aspects of Labour in the Engineering Industries* (1916) Glasgow, in UGD 102 3/10, p.6.

55. UCS 1 23/3.

56. Melling, thesis, 'Employers and the Development of Industrial Welfare'.

57. See Gauldie, *Cruel Habitations*, p.192.

58. The problem of 'substantiality' was mentioned by Fyfe, 'Report of the Sanitary Inspector'; the Royal Commission of 1917 noted that because of absence of damp course this only facilitated dampness despite their general solidity. Cd. 8731, paragraphs 481-9.

59. Rowntree, 'The Question of Providing Housing', pp.5-6; Cd. 8731, paragraphs 402 where minority of housing is of 'good artisan class'. R.Q. Gray, 'Styles of Life, the "Labour Aristocracy" and Class Relations in later Nineteenth Century Edinburgh', in *International Review of Social History*, XVIII (1973).

60. Smart, *The Housing Problem and the Municipality*, p.8; Butt, 'Working Class Housing in Glasgow' (1979), p.14.

61. No adequate account exists, but see McLean, *Labour in Clydeside Politics*, and Cooper, *John Wheatley*; S.G. Checkland, *The Upas Tree* (University of Glasgow Press, 1977).

62. Hamish Fraser, 'Municipal Socialism and Social Policy', *SSRC Conference Paper* (May 1978). I am grateful for permission to cite this unpublished paper.

63. Bernard Barker, 'Anatomy of Reformism: the Social and Political Ideas of the Labour Leadership in Yorkshire', *International Review of Social History*, XVIII (1973), p.23; J. Reynolds and K. Laybourn, 'The Emergence of the Independent Labour Party in Bradford', *International Review of Social History*, XX (1975), pp.340-1.

64. Cooper, *John Wheatley*; John Ferguson, *An Address to the Citizens of the 25 Wards* (16 August 1902); William Martin Haddow, *Socialism in Scotland – its Rise and Progress* (ILP Reformers' Bookstall, Glasgow, 1920). James Leatham, *Glasgow in the Limelight: Why did the Second City of the Empire 'Go Labour'?* (Turiff Deveron Press, Glasgow, 1920). I owe the last three references to Mrs Manchester of Baillie's Library, Glasgow, whose unfailing help I acknowledge.

65. *Forward* (4 Dec. 1915).

66. *Minutes of Evidence of the Committee*, Cd. 8154 Q 578-9.

67. Ibid. Q 586.

68. *The Glasgow Herald* (22 Oct. 1915, 25 Oct. 1915).

69. Cooper, *John Wheatley*, p.15.

70. J.F.C. Harrison, *Social Reform in Victorian Leeds* (Thoresby Society Monographs, Leeds, 1954); Callum G. Brown, 'A Civic Gospel for Glasgow?' (University of Glasgow, 1978); Leatham, *Glasgow in the Limelight*, pp.26-7.

71. Leatham, *Glasgow in the Limelight*; Hamilton Muir, *Glasgow in 1901*, p.164.

72. Cramond, *Housing Policy in Scotland*, p.9; Smart, *The Housing Problem and the Municipality*, pp.9-10.

73. The Royal Commission of 1917 noted that war had only brought the housing issue to a crisis but stated: 'of the many social problems which, after the War, will demand treatment and solution, none is more pressing or more vital, in the interests of Welfare not only of the individual but also of the nation, than the housing problem'. Cd. 8731, para. 22.

74. F.E. Fremantle, *The Housing of the Nation* (Philip Allan, London, 1925), p.20; J.R. Hay, *The Origins of the Liberal Welfare Reforms*, p.24.

75. Cd. 8154, Q 70.

76. Ibid. Q 795-8.

77. Ibid.

78. *Forward* (12 June 1915).

79. *Forward* (14 Feb. 1914).

80. Humbert Wolfe, *Labour Supply and Regulation* (Oxford University Press, 1923); W. Scott and J. Cunnison, *The Industries of the Clyde Valley During the War* (Oxford University Press, 1924).

81. *The Glasgow Advertiser* (5 Jan. 1915).

82. Drummond and Lindsay, 'Report of the Town Clerk and City Surveyor on the Proposed Relaxation of Building Restrictions' (12 December 1916) in D TC 8/19/8.

83. W.A. Kirkcaldy (ed.), *Credit, Industry and the War* (British Association, 1915), pp.204-7.

84. W.A. Kirkcaldy (ed.), *Labour, Finance and the War* (British Association, 1916), pp.224-5.

85. *The Govan Press* (8 Oct. 1915).

86. *The Govan Press* (19 Nov. 1915).

87. Joseph Melling, 'The Glasgow rent strike and Clydeside labour – some problems of interpretation', *The Scottish Labour History Society Journal*, no.13 (May 1979).

88. Cd. 8154, Q 592. Andrew M'Bride's evidence.

89. Cd. 8111 *Report* gives figures of 23 per cent for Fairfield Ward.

90. Letter of Dickinson of Harland's reprinted in *Forward* (5 June 1915).

91. *The Glasgow Advertiser* (12 Oct. 1915).

92. *The History of the Ministry of Munitions*, IV, pt. iv. for account of 1915; SRA, TD 54, 'Notes on the visit of Lloyd George to Glasgow'.

93. Melling, *The Glasgow Rent Strike of 1915* (September 1978) for detailed discussion.

94. Beryl Stanley, 'Women in Unrest, 1914-1918', *Labour Monthly*, vol.22, no.8 (1940), pp.460-1.

95. *The Bulletin* (29 Sept. 1915); Cd. 8154, Q 586-9.

96. *The Glasgow Advertiser* (4 May 1915).

97. Ibid.; *The Bulletin* (8 Oct. 1915).

98. Melling, thesis, 'British Employers'.

99. *Parliamentary Debates*, LXXVI (1915) CI. 726, Tudor Walters stated: 'Rich men are not foolish enough to invest their money in small house property.'

100. Ibid., Cl. 461, Mackinder's phrase.

101. Ibid., Cl. 438, Boyton.

102. H.W. Singer, 'An index of urban land rents and house rents in England and Wales, 1845-1913', *Econometrica*, 9 (1941), pp.223-8; W.D. Rubinstein, 'The Victorian Middle Classes: Wealth, Occupation and Geography', *Economic History Review* (1978).

103. *Parliamentary Debates*, Cl. 421, Walter Long.

104. Ibid., Cl. 461-2, Long to Hohler.

105. *The Glasgow Herald* (18 Nov. 1915).

106. This interpretation can be compared with David Byrne and Seán Damer, 'The State, the Balance of Class Forces and Early Working Class Housing Legislation', *CSE Conference Paper* (March 1978).

107. Melling, 'The Glasgow Rent Strike and Clydeside Labour' (May 1979).

108. Cd. 8731, Minority Report, p.356, para 9.

109. Ibid., p.358, para 19.

110. Ibid., *Majority Report*, p.348, para. 2242.

111. *The Committee of Enquiry into Industrial Unrest: No. 8 Scotland*, Cd. 8669 (1917) p.4, para. 8; Walker Smith, Cd. 8154, Q 69; *Parliamentary Debates*, Cl. 798-9. Dundas White on housing problem.

112. Cd. 8731, p.346, para 2230; Cramond, *Housing Policy in Scotland*, pp. 94-5.

113. Letter of suspended ASE Committee to Executive, in UGD 102 4/10; G.D.H. Cole, *Trade Unionism and Munitions* (Oxford University Press, 1923), pp.2-4.

114. Ministry of Reconstruction, *Memorandum by the Advisory Housing Panel on the Emergency Problem*, Cd. 9087, para 2.

115. Ibid. paras 4-12.

116. Ministry of Health, *Report of the Departmental Committee on the Increase of Rent and Mortgage Interest Restriction Acts*, Cd. 9235 (1919) para 15.

117. Ibid.

118. Cd. 8731, pp.346-7, para 2233.

119. John Butt, 'Working-Class Housing in Glasgow, 1900-1939', pp.8-17; Cramond, *Housing Policy in Scotland*, pp.14-15.

120. Ministry of Health, 'Report of the Committee on the Increase of Rent and Mortgage Interest Acts', Cmd. 658 (1920), para 4.

121. Iain McLean, 'Labour in Clydeside Politics', p. 263; John Wheatley, *The New Rent Act – a reply to the rent raisers*. Scottish Labour Party Housing Association (1920) Glasgow, p.2. Wheatley argues that the real impact of the Act would be a 30 per cent rise.

122. Iain McLean, 'Labour in Clydeside Politics', pp. 254-64.

123. Wheatley, *The New Rent Act*, p.8.

124. *The Voice of Labour* (18 Jan. 1907).

125. UGD 102 4/10; Bernard Waites, 'The effects of the First World War on the economic and social structure of the English working class', *Scottish Labour History Society Journal*, no.12.

126. William Bolitho, *The Cancer of Empire* (Glasgow, 1924), pp.57-9.

127. Iain McLean, *Labour in Clydeside Politics*, p.254 gives a good analysis.

128. Bert Moorhouse, *et al.*, 'Rent Strikes – Direct Action and the Working Class', *Socialist Register* (1972), pp.136-7.

129. Ibid. for the development of this Clydebank strike.

130. Ministry of Health, *Report of the Inter-Departmental Committee*, Cmd. 3911 (1931), para 10.

131. P.L. Payne, 'Rationality and Personality: A Study of Mergers in the Scottish Iron and Steel Industry, 1916-1936', *Business History*, XIX, no.2 (July 1977)

132. Sir Henry Clay, *Lord Norman* (Macmillan, London, 1957), pp.318-22.

133. Ibid. pp.325-31, 339-41; Payne, 'Rationality and Personality', pp.171-81.

134. C.H. Lee, *Regional economic growth in the United Kingdom since the 1880s* (McGraw-Hill, New York, 1971), pp.70-1.

135. Pollard, *The Development of the British Economy*, p.240; Arthur Peter Becker, 'Housing in England and Wales during the Business Depression of the 1930s', *Economic History Review* (1953), pp. 327-8.

136. W.F. Stolper, 'British Monetary Policy and the Housing Boom of the 1930s', *Quarterly Journal of Economics*, vol.56, no.1, pt. ii (Nov. 1941).

137. J.L. Marshall, 'The Pattern of Housebuilding in the Inter-War Period in England and Wales', *The Scottish Journal of Political Economy* (June 1968), p.188; Stolper, 'British Monetary Policy', p.115; Becker, 'Housing in England and Wales', p.333; Pollard, *The Development of the British Economy*, pp.239, 260.

138. Becker, 'Housing in England and Wales', pp.331-7 for survey of supply factors.

139. Andrew Boyle, *Montagu Norman* (Macmillan, London, 1973), quoted p.182.

140. Rodney Lowe, 'The Erosion of State Intervention in Britain, 1917-1924', *Economic History Review*, XXXI, no.2 (May 1978), p.273.

141. Stolper, 'British Monetary Policy', pp.108-11, 148.

142. Pollard, *The Development of the British Economy*, p.213; cf. p.239 where Pollard doubts importance of cheap money on building boom.

143. Becker, 'Housing in England and Wales', p.322 defines boom as dating from 1932.

144. Ibid. for figures.

145. Weber, 'A New Index of Residential Construction', pp.110-13 for long cycles.

146. Marshall, 'The Pattern of Housebuilding', p.186.

147. Cd. 8731, para. 2232 for Scottish housing conditions.

148. John Butt, 'Working Class Housing in Glasgow, 1900-1939', p.25.

149. Cramond, *Housing Policy in Scotland*, pp.15-17.

150. Checkland, *The Upas Tree*.

151. Cramond, *Housing Policy in Scotland*, pp.64-6.

152. Cd. 8731, para 2233-4.

153. Cramond, *Housing Policy in Scotland*, p.22; Becker, 'Housing in England and Wales', p.339 also identified key problem as overcrowding.

154. Cramond, *Housing Policy in Scotland*, pp.51, 99.

155. Becker, 'Housing in England and Wales', p.322.

156. John Butt, 'Working Class Housing in Glasgow, 1900-1939' (1979), p.31 for 'dialism' in market.

157. Cmd. 3911, para 24.

158. Ibid. para 48.

159. Cullingworth, *Housing and Local Government*, pp.25-6.

160. Cd. 8731, para 1988.

161. Cramond, *Housing Policy in Scotland*, pp.64-6.

162. Keith Burgess, *The Challenge of Labour* (Croom Helm, London, 1980). I am grateful to Keith for allowing me to read and cite his draft chapters.

163. Cramond, *Housing Policy in Scotland*, quoted pp.68-9.

164. Compare with Stuart MacIntyre, 'Unemployment Policies in the Vale of Leven, 1918-39', *SSRC Conference Paper* (May 1978).

165. Ministry of Health, 'Report of the Inter-Departmental Committee on the Rent Restrictions Acts', Cmd. 5621 (1937); Cullingworth, *Housing and Local Government*, pp.26-7.

166. Marshall, *Pattern of Housebuilding*, p.188.

167. R.L. Reiss, *Municipal and Private Enterprise Housing* (J.M. Dent, London, 1945), pp.68-9.

168. Ibid. p.43.

169. M.J. Elsas, *Housing Before the War and After* (P.S. King, London, 1942), p.19.

170. Becker, 'Housing in England and Wales', p.339.

171. Elsas, *Housing Before the War*, p.58.

172. Scottish Office, *Report of the Inter-Departmental Committee on Rent Control*, Cmd. 6621 (1945), para 17.

173. Derek Fraser, *The Evolution of the British Welfare State* (Macmillan, London, 1973), p.209.

174. Cynthia Cockburn, *The Local State – The Management of Cities and People* (Pluto Press, London, 1977).

175. For example: The Department of Health for Scotland, *Report by Mr. C.J.D. Shaw, Q.C. on the Local Inquiry in the matter of a review of the rents of Corporation houses* (HMSO, Edinburgh, 1958).

6 THE STANDARD OF COUNCIL HOUSING IN INTER-WAR NORTH SHIELDS – A CASE STUDY IN THE POLITICS OF REPRODUCTION

David Byrne

Introduction

This essay is concerned with the politics of reproduction in a society in which the state in both its national and local manifestations has had a mass-democratic character throughout the period under consideration. If mass democracy in urban England is dated from the second major extension of the franchise (a male orientation) then the essay is concerned with the second quarter of the first half of the life of that political system. It is a study of a locality and of the events surrounding one major issue, the role of the local authority, as the local manifestation of the state, in *providing* housing. The objective is not anecdotal. Rather the sketchy case history presented here is intended to serve as a framework for a discussion of the character of class politics in relation to reproductive issues in a mass-democratic context. I want to focus upon one particular event – the dispute about the standard of local authority housing for slum-clearance tenants which occurred in 1931. A general account of the overall development of housing in this area is given in the first volume of the final report of North Tyneside Community Development Project.[1] Here the purpose of the more focused account is to assist in the clarification of the relationship between class structure, the political form *and* content of the state, and class conflict.

The concern of this study is with an issue of reproduction, simply put in Marxist terms, with an aspect of the capitalist system of relations of production which lies outside the process of production itself but which is essential to the maintenance of that set of relations of production. Reproduction here has two aspects. The first is the physical reproduction of the working class, or in other words meeting the requirements of urban industrial workers for accommodation which reproduces the labour power of the existing work-force, of its successors (children), and of the domestic workers who maintain it and them (wives and mothers). The second relates to the specific form of the relationship between the working class and the state in a mass democracy or more precisely to the relationship between the working class and the capitalist system of relations of production as mediated through political process in a mass democracy. Here reproduction covers ideological reproduction, the representation of existing arrange-

168

ments as legitimate, and accommodation with organised class power. These two aspects are not separate as processes. Indeed the focus of this essay will, to a considerable degree, be upon the unitary process of legitimation and accommodation in relation to the democratic political system. The notion of reproduction is well clarified in Cockburn's recent book, *The Local State*,[2] although the present writer by no means accepts all the implications of her discussion. Indeed a major point of difference relates to an analysis of reproduction in relation to mass-democratic political forms and processes. So far the term 'mass-democratic' has been used repeatedly without definition. That is quite deliberate. I now want to turn to a discussion of this notion in relation to the politics of reproduction.

Let me begin with two quotations from Anderson's important recent essay on 'The Antinomies of Antonio Gramsci':[3]

For the peculiarity of the historical consent won from the masses within modern capitalist social formations is by no means to be found in its mere secular reference or technical awe. The novelty of this consent is that it takes the form of a belief by the masses that *they exercise an ultimate self-determination* within the existing social order. It is thus not acceptance of the superiority of an acknowledged ruling class (feudal ideology), but credence in the democratic equality of all citizens in the government of the nation — in other words, disbelief in the existence of any ruling class.[4]

And again:

By comparison, the economic improvements won by reforms within the framework of the representative state — apparently more material — have typically left less ideological mark on the masses in the West. The steady rise in the standard of living of the working-class for twenty-five years after the Second World War, in the leading imperialist countries, has been a critical element in the political stability of metropolitan capitalism. Yet the material component of popular assent to it, the subject of traditional polemics over the effects of reformism, is inherently unstable and volatile, since it tends to create a constant progression of expectations which no national capitalist economy can totally ensure, even during long waves of international boom, let alone phases of recession; its very 'dynamism' is thus potentially destabilizing and capable of provoking crisis when growth fluctuates or stalls. By contrast the juridico-political component of consent induced by the parliamentary state is much more stable: the capitalist polity is not subject to the same conjunctural vicissitudes. The historical occasions on which it has been actively questioned by working-class struggles have been infinitely fewer in the West. In other words, the ideology of bourgeois democracy is far more potent than that of any welfare reformism, and forms the permanent syntax of the consensus instilled by the capitalist State.[5]

There are two things wrong with Anderson's analysis (an analysis presented through these quotations presisely because it has great force and importance). The first is that Anderson regards the social formations of modern capitalism as comparatively constant within the capitalist era. In other words his contrast for mass democracy, that phase within which the masses *'believe* [my emphasis] that they exercise an ultimate self-determination'., is feudalism and not the era of capitalist social arrangements characteristic of most of the nineteenth century in Britain in which the masses certainly did not either believe in or actually exercise a political self-determination. The capitalist state, even in Britain, has not always been even formally (and no claim is made here that mass democracy goes beyond enormously important formal status. The state is a capitalist state), mass democratic. The episode being examined is from its early middle period in that form and covers the period of consolidation of appropriate forms and processes for the mass-democratic local state.

The other error I identify in Anderson's formulation is his separation of the 'consent of the exploited' from 'welfare reformism'. I have argued elsewhere at some length[6] that the importance of bourgeois mass democracy as an ideological form derives from the fact that it is not simply a con-mechanism. Rather, reformist politics (defined as reformist by their characteristic participation in the political processes of the mass-democratic capitalist state) have involved real working-class gains of however contradictory a kind. The system has legitimacy because, partially and never permanently or simply, it has produced some of the goods. Anderson is absolutely right to point to the dynamically destabilising character of welfare capitalism in advanced industrial societies, but the most important aspect here is that the crisis of legitimacy is produced in very large part by the destruction of expectations itself. For the purposes of this essay this is a side issue, or rather an issue which relates to the post 1945 developments, the origins of which are the subject of this study. The purpose of the Anderson quotations here is to raise the issue of the emergence of mass-democratic local politics as an arena of class conflict and identify this issue as of crucial importance for the understanding of early twentieth-century reproductive politics.

And this brings me to a central theme of this piece which is the contention that in examining reproductive politics as an arena of class conflict at any level and in seeking to understand the course of events and their contemporary implications we have to take account of the other side, of the bourgeoisie and of the structure of that class, of its fractions, and of the interests of those fractions. This essay is constructed as a sandwich. The introduction is a thin slice of abstract preliminaries; the filling is a thick slice of account; the base will be the discussion of the relationship of bourgeois class fractions to reproductive and political processes and the importance of this for understanding actual events and developments. I postpone this discussion to that place but here state that it will occur as a preparation for the account.

Balkwell versus Meadowell – Housing for the Poor in the 1930s

The actual events which resulted in the building of much inferior local authority dwellings in the 1930s to those built in the 1920s have to be seen as part of a continuing series which dates from the development of urban industrial capitalism on Tyneside in the late eighteenth and early nineteenth centuries. In other words they have to be located in relation to the problem of the reproduction of the working class under the conditions of urban industrial capitalism and the role of the state, fractions of the bourgeoisie and the politically emergent working class. I propose to give a schematic account of all this as a background to the events of the 1920s and 1930s which will be described in more detail in a moment. Although North Shields is an old town, it was transformed in the nineteenth century by developments associated with its role as a major coal shipping port and with associated shipbuilding and ship-repairing. In 1801 the total population of the area which was later to become Tynemouth Municipal and then County Borough, was about 13,000. By 1901 it was 51,000 and continued to grow to 65,000 by 1931. The first census to record numbers of dwellings was, significantly, 1841. Then the population was over 25,000 and there were 4,400 dwellings. In 1901 there were 6,779 dwellings and in 1931, 13,338. For purposes of comparison it is worth noting that in 1971 the population was 69,000 and there were almost 24,000 dwellings. These sorts of figures are typical for old industrial towns in Britain and Northern Ireland. What they reflect is urbanisation in the sense of population concentration in the nineteenth century and urban development in the sense of massive housing construction in the twentieth century.

Urbanisation produced a major problem for simple physical

reproduction of the working classes. In the 1840s the Health of Towns Committee indicated in effect that there was a real danger of the industrial working class being used up in a couple of generations. It was from the state bodies established to deal with the problems of sanitation etc., originally at the iniative of private local industrial capital, that the core of urban local government emerged. Thus in North Shields the Town Improvement Commissioners, established with rating powers by private act of parliament in 1819, were succeeded by the Municipal Borough of 1848, which was in turn succeeded by the County Borough of 1903. It is worth stressing that it was the body concerned with urban sanitation and public health which was to serve as the core around which local government was organised. Other local bodies administering the poor law and education were assimilated to it. In any event by the 1860s a body of local building regulations and public health requirements existed which effectively gave a local authority control, subject to the national imposition of minimum standards, over the standard of new housebuilding in its area. Regulation of the standard of existing stock came later and much depended on the use made of permissive powers by any given local authority. In North Shields the first generalised concern with the quality of existing housing was prompted by the 1890 Housing of the Working Classes legislation. This important measure provided local authorities with permissive powers to clear areas and to build for rent. The politics of housing in North Shields in the years between 1900 and 1914 were essentially about whether or not Tynemouth County Borough should make use of precisely these powers.

There is an additional factor which has to be considered in relation to working-class housing during these years, one by no means separate from that of the role of the local state, and that is the operation of private capital. After 1860 or so, the building and renting of working-class housing (and incidentally this is certainly among the first purpose built urban working-class housing anywhere in the world, ever), was an important locale for the operation of private capital. A system for the production and realisation of rented housing (to use the tenure form as a label) emerged, involving land developers, builders, landlords, and investors in housing. Building societies, originating as co-operative ventures by skilled artisans seeking to become owner-occupiers, were taken over by the agents of this system, notably solicitors and estate agents, and became in effect specialist banks. The state's involvement with this system was confined to regulation of the quality of production with some minimal involvement in control of the quality of rented stock. I propose to use the label 'urban capitalist' to describe those involved in this process of production and realisation of urban working-class housing. The actual relationship between production and realisation of housing is complex in the extreme, not least because of the crucial role of land, and for the purposes of this article a review of rent and revenue theory is not necessary.[7] Suffice it to say that in the 1900s North Shields experienced its own version of the general crisis in housing production and that, partly as a consequence of this crisis, housing became the crucial issue through which the emergent labour movement related to the electorate at the time of elections to the local council.[8]

Although this article is about the events of the 1930s those years cannot be understood without some discussion of the pre-1914 debate. And that debate at that time has to be seen in relation to the association between the local authority, the responsible local executive of the state, and private capitalists involved in the processes of housing production and realisation. The elements of the housing system in North Shields at this time have already been delineated. The system was well and coherently organised although it was vulnerable to disruption because of the character of the link between urban capital and finance capital. That degree of organisation was not simply a matter of market and trading relationships. It intimately involved the local state in the form of the local authority, that is to say precisely the body which was concerned with regulating the private capitalist provision of housing so that the general capitalist interest in the maintenance of the working class could be preserved. The actual connection was through the elected representatives. By 1900 Tynemouth Council had a few Lib-Lab working men and sympathetic supporters as members but the great bulk of the Aldermen and Councillors were unequivocally bourgeois, and moreover closely connected with the urban bourgeois as such.

In 1913-14 at the height of local disputes about the direct provision of housing by Tynemouth County Borough, 16 out of 33 members of the local council were one or more of the following: landlords, building society directors, estate agents or builders. Of the remaining seventeen one was a radical liberal, and four were Lib-Lab manual workers or trade union officials. The radical liberal was a building society director, but was not otherwise involved in the property world. These five were the proposers of LA housing. It has to be stressed that only for builders and estate agents was the role of urban capitalist an exclusive one. Others involved in a partial fashion either as landlords or as building society directors or both, included three shopkeepers, two architects and four local industrial or shipping capitalists of varying sizes. Clearly the fractional interest of the group corresponding to those engaged in urban capitalism was not precise but nonetheless real.

However it is not adequate simply to examine the composition of the local bourgeoisie in North Shields. The housing issues of the 1920s and 1930s also had to do with the character of the working class and particularly the divisions within it between skilled artisans on the one hand and labourers on the other.[9] This division was one of income and of consequent housing form and area of residence. A 1908 Board of Trade report showed that on Tyneside the average weekly wages of skilled workers were between 35s and 40s. Labourers in contrast tended to earn 20s to 25s per week. Thus the skilled worker was earning about 40 per cent more than the unskilled. Rents for working-class dwellings ranged from 2s 6d for one tenement room to 6s 6d for a four roomed flat. The result was simple if not exact. Labourers and their families lived in one or two roomed tenements on the banksides. The by-law Tyneside flats built after 1860 on the bank-tops were predominantly an artisan preserve. Segregation was not total in that labourers and seamen did live in flats, although hardly any skilled workers lived in tenement property, but the relationship between rents and wages was crucial.

I have argued elsewhere that it was the relationship between 'cost-rents' (i.e. the minimum rent required to service debt, pay management costs, and provide an acceptable return to the landlords in relation to other investment opportunities) and labourers' wage levels which was the determinant factor in the production crisis which occured after 1908. Be that as it may the rent paying or, more precisely, the housing costs paying capacity of artisans as compared with labourers was to be of great importance for inter-war developments.

The emergent state of the labour movement around political issues in general and the housing issue in particular was crucial during this period. In 1901 the local trades council had sponsored a conference together with the National Housing Reform Council and the Durham and Northumberland Land and Labour Committee, to consider what action could be taken on housing in North Shields. The resultant Shields and District Housing Council brought pressure to bear on both Tynemouth and South Shields Borough Councils in an effort to force them to use their discretionary powers under the 1890 Act and build houses to rent. For example in February 1902 Tynemouth Council received petitions from the Trades Council, the Trades Protection Society, the National Seamen's Federated Union, the National Amalgamated Union of Labour and the North Shields Tailors' Society requesting that the local authority set in hand the building of houses to rent. Significantly the individual unions were not skilled craft unions. The matter was raised at a full council meeting and a proposal to build 20 units to rent as an experiment was defeated by 14 votes to 5.[10]

The refusal to new build was paralleled by the sustained refusal of Tynemouth Borough to use its powers under Part 1 of the 1890 Act. These amounted in essentials to the power to clear unhealthy areas as opposed to individual unfit houses. In 1893 the Sanitary Committee had recommended to the full council that it should be: 'resolved that it was impracticable to deal with part 1 of the act ... The chairman would see Mr Wheeler, the Duke of Northumberland's Commissioner, to urge upon him the necessity of putting more land into the market for dwelling houses for workmen.'[11] The Sanitary Committee had eight members. Six of them were identifiable landlords including Alderman Elliot, a very large builder and owner of tenement property on the banksides, and Councillor Spencer, another large slum landlord. This episode was interesting not just because of the naked display of self-interest (not naked in the sense of public. The committee met in private and the identities of actual landlords in North Shields at this time was seldom known to the public. See the appendix to this chapter), but also because of the alternative proposed instead of slum clearance, i.e. the extensive building of new working-class housing by private enterprise. Alderman Elliot and Councillor Holden, another prominent member of the committee, were both participating to the full in the general local boom in construction. Table 6.1 gives the figures for housing construction in Tynemouth County (and Municipal) Borough for the years 1894 to 1914.

Table 6.1: Housebuilding in Tynemouth Borough, 1894-1914

1894	75	1905	227
1895	78	1906	162
1896	101	1907	160
1897	127	1908	43
1898	78	1909	43
1899	145	1910	7
1900	99	1911	61
1901	232	1912	36
1902	250	1913	38
1903	151	1914	39
1904	148		

Source: Borough Surveyors' Records

Kenwood has prepared an index for urban housebuilding in the North East as a whole during these years. This rose (average 1901-10 = 100)

from 71.1 in 1894 to 128.1 in 1898, fell back with the Boer War and
the shortage of crucial short-term credits[12] and rose again to 126.1 by
1903 whence it declined more or less steadily to 36.0 by 1913.[13] Thus
1893 was the start of a boom in building to rent, and 1902 was the
start of a recovery in building to rent. Jack Common's comments on the
situation are well worth reproducing.

> People believed in houses as the best investment for a bit of cash.
> You could see where your money was if you owned a house; it was
> safe, safe as houses, the very phrase, and you couldn't say safer than
> that unless you brought in the Bank of England which was too big
> altogether for the local men and their well-warmed nest eggs. Build-
> ers kept putting them up in response to a demand which seems now
> oddly lop-sided. It was largely a demand from landlords, would be,
> not from would-be tenants.[14]

Indeed Common hits the nail of the post-1908 problem firmly on
the head. It is usual to assert that the 1909 Finance Act 'dried up' the
supply of building land[15] and that this constraint outside the profit
and loss economics of the housing process itself was responsible for the
collapse of construction in the years immediately before the 1914 war.
I consider this to be flatly wrong. Weber and Cairncross[16] both investigated the profitability using the elements described by Parry-Lewis
when he remarked:

> It would be wrong to think of rent as being the only measure of
> income from property. There is always the possibility of capital gain
> through selling at an inflated price, and property values reflect this
> as well as such almost unpredictable variables as site values.[17]

On Weber's index the profitability of house-ownership declined by over
30 per cent between 1901 and 1910 and Cairncross found that whereas
in 1901 a house was typically purchased for 15.8 times its annual gross
rental, by 1909 this was down to 13.2 years. This does not correspond
with a picture of short supply of building land, which would of course
have had the effect of increasing the capital value of existing houses,
but rather with a reality of a surplus of available stock to rent.

Clearly the rents of houses bear in theory a relationship in the short-
or even medium-term to the relationship between vacancies and demand,
rather than simply to amount of new production and demand. If
demand dries up, then why build? Especially why build if the effect of

adding to stock is to create a situation in which rent levels will fall in existing houses for vacancies mean easy movement and rapid rent-level adjustment. All the indications are that between 1901 and 1906/7 there was a speculative boom in housebuilding with a scramble to buy. Prices rose in response to speculative pressure. Then, vacancies and the bottom fell out of the boom. At this time landlords were over-geared. Their money was laid out and they had borrowed. National Building Society assets rose from £61 million in 1900 to £77 million by 1910 after which they were badly affected by the withdrawals which followed the collapse of the Birkbeck. Indeed a surplus of assets over mortgage assets of 40 per cent in 1910 fell back to just 7 per cent the next year. This squeezing of building society liquidity obviously did not help the position. Assets fell from £77.5 million in 1910 to £64.5 million the next year, but advances continued to run at about £9 million a year. There were bankruptcies, e.g. one of the Easton brothers in North Shields (a prominent pair of local builder developers, the other one of whom was to become controller of production for housing in the post-1918 Ministry of Reconstruction), who went bankrupt owing £20,000-plus. The bankruptcy hearing was informed that this was due to a 10 per cent decline in the value of properties he owned.[18]

In such a situation the vital thing was to hold rents at least at their current level and on Weber's figures[19] this seems to have been done. However, all new competitive supply had to be held off. On the private provision side this was not a problem. Who would want to build houses when there were vacancies in the existing stock and where would they borrow the money given the crisis in the Building Societies? However public sector supply was a horse of another colour, particularly when there was the possibility of cheap land as in North Shields where the Balkwell estate, acquired for the building of a smallpox hospital, provided ample land for development at a very low site-cost per dwelling. And of course in a situation of collapse of housebuilding and an apparent housing crisis, the demands of the ILP and others for council house building were given added force and relevance. However it was not only the working-class organisers who were concerned. Colin Barker has recently given us a very pertinent reminder of the error of an approach which

> treats the state as if it existed only in the singular. Capitalism, however, is a world system of states, and the form that the capitalist state takes is the nation state form. Any discussion, therefore, of the capitalist state form must take account of the state *both* as

apparatus of class domination *and* as an apparatus of competition between segments of the bourgeoisie.[20]

In the years just before the 1914-18 war the truth of this assertion is undeniable, although in the 1970s it is perhaps rather more complex than Barker suggests. Anyhow one of the vehicles of competition between nation-states is war and for war you need soldiers. The Inter-departmental Committee on the Physical Deterioration of The Working Classes[21] had, in the aftermath of the evidence of working-class health given to the nation state by the condition of the volunteers for the Boer War, produced a report suggesting that something had to be done. Social Imperialism coupled with unease at the growth of socialism was the motivation for national attempts at action.

What all this amounts to is that whereas in the 1890s and the early 1900s the local urban bourgeoisie were well placed to standoff labour pressures because their private enterprise system (which hinged on new building and upward filtration) could be represented as working, post-1910 they were not in the same fortunate position. Instead building collapsed, in North Shields as elsewhere, and houses stood empty while the rents demanded for them were beyond the capacity of labourers to pay. In the circumstances, a phrase which covers both local and national context, it is not surprising that the labour movement returned to the housing fray in 1913 and 1914. The episode is described in full elsewhere but two quotations are in order here.[22]

> The opposition will consist of Liberal and Tory alike, of those who feel interested in preventing the Corporation from building cheap and healthy dwellings to compete with the highly rented and unhealthy dwellings of themselves and their friends (Stephen Walsh, ILP).[23]
>
> To put houses on the market at a rent nobody could compete with was not fair to the owners of property . . . The scheme was not at all fair to the middle class people, the owners of property and the share-holders in Building Societies. (Councillor Plummer, landlord).[24]

All this is if you like a specific reiteration of Englander's general point in his discussion of these issues; that, at a local level, the urban bourgeoisie exercised considerable power to shape policies and events to their interests. However that power was contextual and in a particular context vulnerable to the specifically anti-landlord campaign of the emergent labour movement. My final point on this period is this. The housing campaigns in North Shields before the First World War were explicitly socialist, to the extent that they were explicitly hostile to the private system of housing provision. Until 1914 the campaigns were unsuccessful; the left were merely as it were knocking at the gate of the local state. However they had a *programme* that was specifically different from existing policies on housing, a programme moreover based on an analysis of the housing system which tended towards a prescription of the abolition of rent. This almost certainly owed more to Shaw and Henry George than to Marx but it was politics of quite a new order. This was to be in marked contrast to the position of the Labour Party in the 1930s, a theme to which I shall return. The upshot of the 1913-14 dispute was that the Council agreed to a pilot scheme for the building of an estate on the Balkwell farm. This was shelved on the outbreak of war but was to reappear as the nucleus of action under the 1919 Addison Act.

The passing of the 1919 Act found Tynemouth Council the owner of substantial amounts of good building land including the Balkwell, the Hunt Hill estate and various smaller sites. The schemes which had been shelved in 1914 were brought out and dusted off, and the basis of Tynemouth's programme under the 1919 act was to proceed with these schemes on a larger scale. Table 6.2 gives details of housebuilding at this time. The 490 dwellings built between 1920 and 1923 were the core of the Balkwell estate as it is today plus some smaller groups of houses in the east end of the town. By 1923 the Local Authority's total capital expenditure on housing was £407,923 which gives an average cost of about £830 per dwelling including liable development costs. These houses were substantial dwellings. There were three basic forms viz. type A2 with living room, scullery and two bedrooms, type A which was three-bedroomed and type B which had three bedrooms and two living-rooms. The layout was in terrace of six to eight dwellings with back and front gardens. In 1921 rents were set at 8s per week for type A2, 10s per week for type A, and 12s 6d for type B. All these included rates. These rents were well below those it had originally been intended to charge. In 1920 the authority had thought in terms of rents of 14s per week exclusive of rates for the type B dwellings and the borough surveyor had produced a report indicating that for a dwelling costing £1,000 and taking into account central government's view that rents should cover two-thirds of costs, the annual rent inclusive of rates would be £68 15s. A private builder obtaining the maximum £150 grant under the 1919 Additional Powers Act could not rent the dwelling at less than £81 per annum, inclusive.[25]

There was no opposition to local authority building until 1921 when Smith was elected councillor for the Linskill ward on a platform which included opposition to any further LA building. By September 1922, seven of the urban capitalist members were attempting to block any further local authority building at East Howden. Gregg, the radical liberal, described them as 'the same old reactionaries'. However the important shift came in November 1923 when, in response to the Chamberlain Act the Housing Committee established a sub-committee with the intent of encouraging building by private enterprise in North Shields and Tynemouth. (Incidentally North Shields had about two-thirds of the total population of the Tynemouth CB area.) The strategy was threefold and involved the encouraging of building of houses with the subsidy of £85 under the 1923 Act attached to each dwelling. Tynemouth added to the national minimum subsidy from the rates. The other two elements were the selling of Balkwell, Hunt Hill and Cullercoats land *after development*, cheaply to local builders in small lots and the guaranteeing of mortgages with local building societies. Attempts to sell purpose built LA houses were blocked by the district valuer who set the prices too high. The operation at Hunt Hill, which was entirely disposed of for private building, was typical. This 7¾-acre site was sold at 8s 6d per square yard inclusive of street works and drains to local builders. All the 120 dwellings built were given the £85 subsidy under the 1923 Act and many were purchased with guaranteed mortgages. The Local authority's crucial initiative was its function as developer which enabled small builders to avoid tying up their cash in land. Most of the houses built on these sites were built in lots of ten to twenty. It was clearly recognised that this was speculative building for sale. A substantial proportion of Balkwell land and a 20-acre site at Cullercoats were developed in the same fashion. Between 1925 when subsidised building in the private sector was first separately recorded by the LA and 1930, when the subsidies were withdrawn, of the 1,053 dwellings privately constructed 70 per cent were built with the subsidy. The local authority was a crucial enabler in this establishment of the whole owner-occupied system in the area.

After 1923 this private development was the major interest of the Housing Committee. More housing was built at the Balkwell under the Wheatley Act. The average cost of the 444 LA dwellings built between 1924 and 1930 was just over £600. This reduction in cost was in part due to the very cheap 60-odd tenements constructed for the first slum clearance scheme but can be assigned in the main to reduced building costs.[26] The slum-clearance scheme, consisted of 22 pairs of flats at

Percy Square at an all in cost of £370 and a further twenty tenements in Bell Street and Pant Street at around the same cost. The building of these dwellings was a kind of pilot scheme for the building of the Meadowell estate and the background is worth noting. These dwellings were built to replace the tenements at Pant Street and Adamson's buildings, cleared after an enquiry in 1924 under the 1890 Act. This was Tynemouth's first use of this legislation to clear an area. In all, 95 tenement dwellings housing 373 people were cleared. Proposals for the scheme dated back to 1923 and the clear intention to build low quality dwellings was indicated by the designs produced at that time. These were lauded by Dr Harrison, a Tory councillor, who was quoted in the local paper, the *Shields Daily News*, describing the new designs as: 'houses of two, three and four rooms – houses which they could furnish and pay rent for. He went among them in their houses and knew exactly what they wanted.' The editorial supported him and went on:

> It is probable that a great deal more could have been done to cope with the housing difficulty if action had been taken along these lines previously ... In so pressing a situation it is not a wise policy to press for unattainable housing ideals. The practical measures now adopted of closing the old Pant Street and neighbourhood property and substituting modest but nice houses at Percy Square is, in our opinion, altogether to be commended.[27]

The position was clear. The Balkwell houses at 8s to 12s 6d per week were too expensive for slum dwellers. In contrast these flats and tenements were rented out at 4s per week for 2 rooms and 5s per week for three rooms. Despite this scheme the bulk of local authority building in the late 1920s was of good quality stock at the Balkwell. However this was seen as a reducing commitment, and in October 1928 the housing committee of the authority was actually wound up, not re-appearing until 1930. Before turning to the events of 1930 to 1932 it is worth looking at the overall housing context in North Shields and at the changing political situation.

Whereas in 1914 there had been just two significant forms of housing for manual workers, by-law flats and tenements, by 1930 there were four. These were, in descending order of amenity, status and cost, the Balkwell and other LA construction, the by-law flats, the council tenements and the river-bank tenements. The last block, from which over 9,000 people were rehoused in the clearance programme of 1932-6, had been effectively written off, although it stood for 40 years longer than comparable areas in Liverpool or some other cities. The failure of Tynemouth CB to engage in any clearance by area under the 1890 Act until 34 years after the act became effective, is a tribute to the strength of the urban bourgeoisie on the council. As 'Overcrowded' observed in a letter to the *Shields Daily News* of 19 June 1931: 'Many of our prominent townsmen would not care for a census to be taken of the owners of slum property.' However by 1930 the writing was on the wall for this stock and the only real opposition to the clearance came from owners who were engaging in delaying tactics or who would have preferred clearance or closing orders, which would have left them as owners of the land, to outright compulsory purchase. This meant that the significant forms of housing with long future lives were by-law stock, high quality LA stock and LA tenements. Part of the 'interest' key lay in this first stock. Writers on housing frequently seem to assert that private renting was crippled by the introduction of rent control in 1915 and was without significance thereafter. This is not even true of building to rent, as we shall see, but it is completely untrue for the tenure form. Not until the 1950s did private unfurnished letting cease to be the dominant tenure form in North Shields and very little by-law stock passed into owner-occupation (as opposed to that proportion which had always been so owned) until the 1957 Rent Act.

Table 6.2: Housebuilding in Tynemouth CB 1919-20

	LA	Private		Total
		With sub.	Without sub.	
1919	—		6	6
1920	71		8	79
1921	172		8	180
1922	219		40	259
1923	28		76	104
1924	35		100	135
1925	46	108	80	234
1926	84	95	62	241
1927	139	233	59	431
1928	112	154	44	310
1929	4	156	62	222
1930	14	—	161	175

Source: Annual Reports MOH Tynemouth CB

Rent control had not meant a rent standstill. An increase of 40 per cent in controlled rents had been permitted by various measures and since 1923 all property was automatically decontrolled on possession.

The resulting pattern identified by the Marley Committee in 1931 was one where a dwelling which had had a 1914 inclusive rent of 6s per week, the average for a by-law flat in North Shields, would be renting, if controlled, at about 9s per week and about 11s 3d if decontrolled.[28] Rate register dates from North Shields suggest that these sorts of figures were about right for the town. All this accommodation was still in existence and still an important locale of investment. There is some evidence to suggest that during the 1930s this stock was coming to be owned by property companies or by property professionals.[29] In any event this very large bastion of private landlordism existed which could be contrasted with the very much better local authority houses. The last 104 houses built at the Balkwell under the 1924 Act were rented at 11s 6d per week inclusive, i.e. at about the same rental as decontrolled by-law flats with fewer rooms, no gardens, no bathrooms, no internal WC and so on. The comparison was not flattering to the private sector.

Evidence from local directories in the 1930s suggests that the occupants of the Balkwell estate were from just the same stratum as the occupants of the better by-law stock. The directories are not complete but, for example, in 1933 in Balkwell Green where 41 out of 84 heads of households had occupations recorded, 20 were skilled craftsmen, 6 were bus-drivers, 5 were seamen or fishermen, 2 were shopkeepers, 1 was a policeman, 1 was a marine engineer, 2 were labourers, 1 was a widow and the rest were clerks. The proportion for streets such as Chirton Green or Yeoman Street which were good by-law housing, were much the same. Significantly, the occupations of residents on the bankside stairs and, later, on the Meadowell were never recorded by the directories.

Clearly the LA construction in the 1920s was not available to the poorest section of the population. Rather it was locally considered that it relieved conditions by filtration. Higher paid manual workers who moved into LA stock made cheaper by-law flats available to the unskilled and slum dwellers. There is some evidence that this happened. In 1931 the proportion of private families living at more than two persons per room as recorded by the census of that year was, at 15.9 per cent, less than two thirds of the equivalent figure in 1921. Filtration could only work by a process which involved the depression of rents in privately rented accommodation below that they would otherwise have been. This would not operate simply, given the complexities of rent control and decontrol, but in the long run that would be the tendency. This was not to the advantage of private landlords and their associates.

However economic interests are not completely described by a comparison between the LA stock and privately rented stock. During the 1920s building costs fell far faster than the real incomes of those who remained in employment. By 1930 building costs were at least 40 per cent down on their level of nine years earlier.[30] This meant that whereas in 1924 the average sort of semi-detached house being sold by local builders was costing about £550 to £600 *after* the £85 subsidy under the 1923 Act had been applied, by 1931 unsubsidised houses (the subsidies were withdrawn in 1929) were selling at £475 or about 12s 9d per week at 20 years purchase.[31] This figure was of course exclusive of rates but the point was that owner-occupation was now coming within the reach of most white-collar workers and some higher paid manual workers who could rely on regular employment. It has to be remembered that in the 1930s there was no significant inflation to erode the value of the original debt. Housing cost for owner-occupiers would stay constant so a weekly cost of about 16s a week with rates for buying a house had to be compared with 11s 6d for renting one that was broadly comparable in amenity, with repairs and structural insurance not being the liability of the tenant. The attraction was not that massive for someone who might reasonably expect to obtain a council tenancy. This period was of course a period of massive suburbanisation. Between 1920 and 1940, 4,094 private houses were built in Tynemouth CB, i.e. roughly about 30 per cent again over the total number of dwellings that existed in the borough in 1921. Some of these, especially in the 1930s were built to rent at rents of between 16s and 18s per week, inclusive. Almost all were built with building society finance. During this period the mortgage assets of building societies nationally increased massively. In 1923 it was £99 million. By 1928 it was £208 million and by 1939 it was over £800 million. The total funds invested in mortgaged property rose by an average of 13.2 per cent per year between 1919 and 1939.[32] The development of new private housing in Tynemouth and North Shields between 1920 and 1939 was financed by just this boom, and the shift in the emphasis of interests of property professionals and urban capitalists from private renting towards involvement with owner-occupation was well under way. In the local council of 1931-2, the urban capitalists were much less well represented than they had been at the time of the dispute about whether to undertake LA building which had occurred 20 years earlier. In a council of 34 members there were 10 labour or Lib-Lab members. (The Labour Party in Tynemouth was only to achieve real control over elected representatives after 1945.) Of the remaining 24, 4 were identifiable landlords. There were 2 builders and 8 were directors of building societies.

This then was the local background to the decisions of 1931 which determined the form of the Meadowell dwellings. The national background was of course the stimulus of the 1930 Greenwood Act. Until 30 April 1934 the Wheatley subsidy of £7 10s (the rate fixed in 1927) was still available and, at the time that decisions were being taken about housing form on the Meadowell, there was no foreknowledge that this would be eliminated for houses completed after that date. The key decisions about the standards of housing built on the Meadowell were taken at the design phase in 1931 and were substantially local. The contrast between 1920s and 1930s LA housing stock is far sharper in North Shields than in Newcastle for example. This extra sharpness is a *local* factor.

The actual forum of debate seems to have been the letters column of the local paper. Once a decision had been taken to begin a substantial programme of slum clearance and to build a replacement estate on the Ridges farm, J. Wallace-Black, a prominent local Tory businessman, wrote a letter asserting that houses of the kind built on the Balkwell were too expensive for slum clearance tenants to afford. He wanted a scheme involving block flats. Wallace-Black, whose letter campaign received substantial editorial support, in this and subsequent letters, cited schemes elsewhere ranging from South Shields to Vienna, which showed the practicability of block flats for these sorts of tenants. The basic reason for this was the financial one. Housing of the Balkwell standard was expensive and could not, contended Wallace-Black, be afforded without high levels of subsidy. And high levels of subsidy were to be avoided at all costs. In an editorial the *Shields Daily News* of 26 March 1932 waxed full on the evils of subsidised housing which could: 'only be justified in exceptional circumstances', citing the distorted market at the end of the First World War as such circumstances. In a normal situation, the argument ran, then as now, the market would adequately provide. This was not all Wallace-Black had to say. In his first letter of the 19 June 1931 he also asserted that:

> they [the local authority] must get rid of the idea that slum dwellers want to live in villas. They don't. To put them there would make them miserable. They like to be together. They have told me so.

Wallace-Black's opponent in this letter writing debate was the extremely respectable and moderate Labour vice-chairman of the Housing Committee the retired school master J. Hunter. Hunter quite correctly

pointed out that 'The Housing [Financial Provisions] act of 1924 and
the Housing Act of 1930 must be worked in combination because they
are part of one single policy'.[33] In other words with the combined subsidies, and by implication the fall in building costs since the early 1920s,
rents could be low enough on standard houses of the Balkwell kind for
the slum dwellers to afford. At the time of writing Hunter was in fact
correct. The debate continued, with J.W. Ancrum another local worthy
putting in his oar in general support of Wallace-Black. The series of
letters is, in fact, fascinating. The issue was quite thoroughly thrashed
out at a technical level and the letters are an invaluable source of information about the local housing market. What is most remarkable about
them however is the absence of political debate. Hunter wrote as a
member of the Housing Committee about the technical possibilities
inherent in a local authority's use of subsidy legislation. The apolitical
character of his stance is in complete contrast with the letters of ILP
members in 1913 and 1914, who asserted the class nature of the local
authority and the self-interest which lay behind its opposition to council
housing. Nowhere does Hunter say that slum-dwellers are entitled to
good houses and should have them by whatever means. Perhaps it is not
surprising that at the next local elections 25 per cent of the vote in one
of the bankside wards went to a communist candidate.

In the end the Meadowell, or Ridges as it was to be called for the
next 35 years, was built on the flatted pattern of the smaller Deans
estate in South Shields. In all there were 2,141 LA dwellings built by
the authority during the 1930s, the vast bulk on the Meadowell, at an
average cost of about £350. This contrasts with the average £750 all-in-
cost of 1920s construction. Part of the difference is of course assignable
to falling building costs. However the 444 dwellings built in the years
after 1923 averaged £600 each as against £870 for the 468 built before
that date. By 1923 costs were well down, so the drop in standards is
perhaps indicated by a contrast between £600 and £350, i.e. a drop of
about 40 per cent. Certainly this was how later opinion was to regard
them.[34] The immediate consequences were that about 9,000 people or
15 per cent of the total population of the area were housed in dwellings
which, while they were certainly sanitarily adequate and of a standard
which allowed for the physical reproduction of the working classes, were
far below the target standard established for decent working-class housing by earlier class action. True rents were lower than on the Balkwell
at 6s 6d for three rooms, 7s 1d for four rooms, 7s 10d for five rooms.[35]
These were about the same as for by-law housing. Private renting had
had a potential competitor controlled as had nascent owner-occupation.

A triumph for the economic interest of the urban bourgeoisie. Surely, but is that all?

Reproduction, Class and State

At one level, an account is accurate which asserts that the actions of the local state in relation to housing policy were a product of conflict between working-class interests and those of a local urban bourgeoisie and that the drastic reduction in LA construction standards was a consequence of general working-class political weakness in 1931-2. However it is by no means adequate. It is not all. My own view is that to produce an adequate account we have to look at things in a rather different way. In particular we have to attempt to understand the operations of the bourgeoisie and the character of the bourgeoisie in relation to the politics of reproduction in a mass-democratic context. Theorists of the state action have not paid much attention to this. Indeed, apart from Marxist tinged variants of élite theory and studies of resource distribution, the only real attention to the character of the bourgeoisie had been in an industrial context, and in particular in relation to the form of monopoly capital. Now if we regard reproduction as an arena of class conflict just as production is, and I for one wholeheartedly endorse such a position, then we have to look at the antagonists and at the political forms in which they function.

The first such form is of course the local state itself. And a premiss of the argument that follows is that the state is not 'neutral' but rather an unequivocally capitalist institution, which is not to say that in the course of class conflict the actions of the local state may not be to the advantage of the working class and represent real gains by it. It seems obvious that the local state is a capitalist form emerging under capitalism in its urban industrial phase to cope precisely with the problems of reproduction of a working class. Here the issue of fractions of capital becomes important because the only adequate way to describe many developments that have occurred in reproductive politics is one which involves the notion of fractions of capital. Clarke has recently undertaken an extensive and critical review of Poulantzian style employment of this notion.[36] It is hard to disagree with his rejection of the hegomonic fraction directing the relatively autonomous state and equally hard to see how he copes with the need of capitalism as system for the regulation of particular capitalist activities in order to survive. I put this simply, deliberately. It seems clear to me that much of the action of the capitalist state in relation to reproduction in the era of capitalism which preceded mass democracy, while it owed something to the role of emergent proletarian political pressure was self-regulating. The 9-hour day was in large part a function of proletarian class pressure. Public health regulation was not. It is against the interests of slum landlords to have the houses they own demolished with minimal compensation. It is in general interest of capitalism (and just what constitutes a slum is historically specific as well). In the era of mass democracy few developments have been at the level of simple physical reproduction. They have been political responses to proletarian demands and have gone beyond physical reproduction in direct relation to the strength of proletarian organisation at a particular time. In this context and contest there have been times when particular capital interests, usually but not invariably interests lying outside the direct process of production, have been sacrificed at least in part or temporarily. The only basis, and the traditional one greatly predates and does not imply Poulantzian usage, for descr.)-tion here is in terms of fractions of capital because these divisions do correspond to particular definable processes in capitalist production and circulation.

This brings us back to the problem of state action under conditions of mass democracy, conditions not always extant in advanced industrial capitalist societies but uniquely and specifically important in Britain where long-established mass-political democracy coexisted with class organised parties and no, even traditionally, revolutionary party. A good deal of attention has been paid to the composition of local labour parties, usually in relation to the accounts of parliamentarian degeneracy, and fair enough. But what about the bourgeois parties, or, as in the case of the local state in North Shields in the 1930s, the representation of bourgeois interests without formal parties. In a parliamentary state the positions of the bourgeoisie must have some representation as a part of the democratic process. If they are simply imposed, not seen as a part of the democratic form, then there are major difficulties in the effective functioning of what Perry Anderson has quite rightly identified as the major bourgeois ideological apparatus. This is why it has been in many ways ideologically disturbing for local labour councils to impose cuts in public expenditure at the behest of international capitalism. If the Tories had done it, well that is after all what they stand for. In other words the Tories represent a bourgeois position through the democratic process. Labour does not, and for Labour to act against its formal position is to diminish the credibility of parliamentary democracy. This is a far more important phenomenon when Labour is not only ceasing to be socialist but even reformist.

What I am arguing is that it is of very great importance in a mass-democratic political system for the bourgeois (and note the use of the class label rather than the economic label of capitalist) position to be adequately represented at all levels. But who is to do this? We know both logically and empirically that the great capitals eat up the small ones. The role of developing monopoly has in the past, notably in advanced agrarian societies, led to the creation of small capitalist movements. If the logic of capitalist accumulation in production is antithetical to the small productive bourgeoisie, who is to represent the class interest in the local democratic process? Clearly that question is not simply answered and indeed one of the purposes of this paper is to suggest that we need very detailed studies of bourgeois political forms, as well as of the character of parliamentary socialism. However one answer in the 1930s was that the local representation of the bourgeois political position was through the local small bourgeoisie, by this time seldom a productive bourgeoisie because the control of manufacturing, the coal trade and shipping interests were predominantly delocalised, but a reproductive bourgeoisie and that part of the bourgeoisie concerned with the related and technically old-fashioned, business of housebuilding. In other words, the fraction of capital concerned with the process of private housing provision generated a section of the bourgeoisie that had considerable political importance. This fraction was certainly knocked back by rent control, although the inter-war years saw that particular battle refought. However it was also intimately associated with one of the major policies in the bourgeois ideological armoury, owner-occupation. Thus the events in 1931 cannot be described simply in terms of the triumph of the interests of a fraction of capital. They have to be examined in relation to the local and the general significance of the section of the bourgeoisie associated with that fraction.

And, of course, in reviewing any episode of this sort, attention has to be paid to both sides in detail and in temporal context. I have described the episode of the reduction in the housing standards as one in class politics, yet it could be fairly remarked that the working class appear only through the assumed relationship between them and the Labour Party. This substitution of party for class is not just an artifact of description: it relates to the real core of events. This is best understood by thinking about the contrast between the events of 1930 and those of 1914. In 1914 the labour movement in North Shields stood outside the state and the process of administration of reproduction through the local authority. The local situation corresponded with the national in that the labour movement was scarcely developed as a parliamentary party and had never participated in the government. This meant that the political programmes developed could be critical of the structural arrangements. I am not asserting here that anybody in North Shields or even in Glasgow was proposing a revolution as a solution for housing difficulties. The actual contents of the proposal was that the local authority should make use of powers granted to it by Parliament. However the proposals were located in relation to a socialist critique of the private market in housing and involved an explicit recognition of the class nature of the state at the crucial local level. This meant that the relationship between the labour movement and the working class was one which centred on agitation. The outsiders had to raise the steam to force the insiders to change. They could only do this by making an appeal to the class in the terms of the class content of the issue. This is what they did through the bourgeois democratic process, including, in particular, the letters column of the local paper. This may seem a strange vehicle for class agitation but the historic association between the Tyneside press and the revolutionary liberalism seems to have given this medium particular importance.

The situation in 1930 was quite different. By this time the Labour Party was a central part of the political framework of the mass-democratic state. The current housing policies its policies. The Party had achieved representative status and functioned through the electoral process. This is not to say that the proponents of reform in 1914 were armed revolutionaries; the difference lay in the acceptance of power and the parliamentary framework for the exercise of that power. By 1930 the Labour Party related to the working class through the organisational medium of elections. In 1914 the labour movement had related to the class through the agitational medium of propaganda. At both times the actions and proposals could be described as reformist, but to use that term is to realise just what sub-classifications of it are necessary. Reformism in 1914 hinged on the presentation of an alternative based on a critique of what was. Reform in 1930 hinged on Labour control of state institutions given to it by the class vote but not under scrutiny in relation to the class content of detailed issues. In contemporary terms the debate between Wallace-Black and Hunter seems almost a model of democratic procedure. Reasoned alternatives for policy decisions were presented to the public at large. However there was no explicit perception of class interest; the issue remained administrative.

This can be contrasted not only with the character of the housing debates fifteen years earlier but with the immediately contemporary conflict over the payment of the public assistance to the North Shields unemployed.[37] Here there was non-parliamentary direct action under the explicitly revolutionary leadership of the communist-dominated North Shields branch of The National Unemployed Workers Movement. It was not just that the mode of action of the NUWM was through demonstration and class mobilisation. The presentation of issues was system critical, i.e. it depended on a location of the origins of the problems of unemployment in relation to the capitalist relations of production themselves. Often the modes of action of the NUWM were reformist. Their only actual riot arose out of an attempt to present a petition to the Public Assistance Committee of Tynemouth County Borough Council. The demands were all reformist and boiled down to less objectionable treatment and higher rates of payment of assistance. These were threatening demands precisely because they were outside demands expressed through not just letters to the paper (although letters to the paper remained a crucial mode for the NUWM's presentation of arguments), but through mass demonstrations on the streets. The NUWM appealed to the class on issues. The Labour Party appealed only in general terms which were of course issue-derived, but did not involve the class at the point of specific decision-making.

Now all this should not be interpreted as a general critique of the reformist mode of operation of the Labour Party in North Shields. Fifteen years later and without a Labour majority on the council their participation in the process of the administration of reproduction by the local state was to result in the largest programme of building of good council housing for general needs that there has ever been in North Shields.[38] The differences of course derive from the wider political context and the balance of class forces specifically in relation to mass-democratic institutions in 1945 as compared with 1930. It would be folly indeed to hang a general critique of parliamentary reformism on the discussion of one episode in the reproductive politics of one small town. All I want to do here is to assert the relevance of this sort of grounded analysis to the discussion of these issues.

In summary the only general point I want to make relates to the way in which the ground of political struggle over reproductive issues has influenced the form and outcome of those struggles. Because reproduction has been the affair of the state, both local and national, the ground has been the ground of political participation in the processes of the mass-democratic state. However, the enormous influence this has had on the character of reproductive struggles should not mislead us into thinking that the relationship is all one way. If Anderson is correct in his identification of the democratic form of the state as crucial to the contemporary character of politics in societies like Britain, and if he is wrong about the independence of welfare capitalism and the mass-democratic state form, then we are moving into very interesting times. The situation in the monetarist political economy, as distinct from the Keynesian, appears to be one in which the capitalist relations of production preclude any significant degree of reform and improvement in reproductive spheres.

Appendix – Some Brief Notes on Method and Sources

This chapter is based on work carried out when I was working for North Tyneside Community Development Project. The historical account is drawn from a variety of sources including in particular the Minutes of Tynemouth Council, the local paper – the *Shields Daily News*, and the other papers of the Council held in the Local Studies Library in North Shields. Of particular importance have been the deeds of properties acquired for clearance which give details of ownership of land and houses, together with records or mortgages on the properties. These together with the Borough Rate Registers enable landlords to be positively identified, something which contemporaries without access to these confidential documents were unable to achieve, much to their expressed chagrin. Association with building societies was established from the adverts of the societies at the time of their annual general meetings in which lists of directors were usually included. As with all CDP historical work in Shields I am much in debt to John Bell and Alex Robson for access to their memoirs and for conversations on the history of the local labour movement. The reports of the borough surveyor to the housing committee are the source of information on housing plans. I have relied heavily on letters to the local paper for expression of political debate. In these years this does seem to have been a major medium for such disputes. I have also used the evidence of local witnesses to various national enquiries. Detailed reference to these has not been made, especially where I have written elsewhere on the subject. I must finally note my dependence on and gratitude to my colleagues on CDP. The presentation in this chapter is mine but the work was ours, collectively.

Notes

1. *North Shields: Working Class Politics and Housing 1900-1977* (N. Tyneside CDP, 1978).
2. C. Cockburn, *The Local State* (Pluto, London, 1977), especially ch. 2.

3. Perry Anderson, 'The Antinomies of Antonio Gramsci', *New Left Review*, p. 100.

4. Ibid., p. 24.

5. Ibid.

6. The North Tyneside CDP, *North Shields: Organising for Change in a Working Class Area* (1978); also, D.S. Byrne, 'Reproduction, Class and Politics', *Ulster Polytechnic Working Papers in Social Policy*, no. 1.

7. See the two volumes published by the Political Economy of Housing Workshop (PEHW); *Political Economy and the Housing Question* (1975), and *Housing in Class in Britain* (1977), for a number of articles on this theme.

8. See North Tyneside CDP, *North Shields: Working Class Politics and Housing – 1900-1977* (1978).

9. See *Report of an Enquiry of the Board of Trade into Working-Class Wages, Housing Rents and Retail Prices in the Principal Industrial Towns of the U.K.* (HMSO, 1908), Ch. 3864.

10. *Shields Daily News* (14 Feb. 1902).

11. *Tynemouth Municipal Borough Minutes* (Sanitary Committee Report to Council, 25 Jan. 1893).

12. A.T. Kenwood, 'Residential Building Activity in North Eastern England 1853-1913', *The Manchester School*, vol. XXXI (1963).

13. Ibid.

14. Jack Common, *Kiddar's Luck* (Frank Graham, Yorks, 1974), p. 86.

15. Eg.P. Wilding, 'Towards Exchequer Subsidies for Housing 1906-1914', *Social and Economic Administration*, vol. 6, no. 1 (Jan. 1972).

16. See the discussion in I. Parry Lewis, *Building Cycles and Britain's Growth* (Macmillan, London, 1965), Ch. 6.

17. Ibid., p. 158.

18. *Shields Daily News* (14 Feb. 1902).

19. See note 16 above.

20. C. Barker in *Capital and Class*, no. 4 (1978).

21. Report of the Inter-departmental Committee on Physical Deterioration (1904).

22. In note 1 above.

23. *Shields Daily News* (5 Oct. 1914).

24. *Shields Daily News* (6 Oct. 1914).

25. Tynemouth Borough Surveyor's Reports (1920).

26. See K. Maywald's index reproduced in B.R. Mitchell, *Abstract of British Historical Statistics* (Cambridge UP, Cambridge, 1962).

27. *Shields Daily News* (27 Sept. 1923).

28. Cmd 3911.

29. See 'The Property World in and around North Shields', in *Some Housing and Town Planning Issues in North Tyneside* (North Tyneside CDP, 1975).

30. See Maywald's index.

31. Letter of R.W. Ancrum, *Shields Daily News* (6 July 1931).

32. See A.A. Nevitt, *Housing, Taxation and Subsidies* (Nelson, Sunbury on Thames, 1966), p. 87.

33. Letter in *Shields Daily News* (24 June 1931).

34. See 'Council Housing, the attributes of estates', in note 1 above and 'The Meadowell, the history of a 1930s estate', in note 13 above.

35. Tynemouth CB Council *Minutes* (27 Sept. 1933).

36. C. Clarke, 'Capital, Fractions of Capital and the State', in *Capital and Class* no. 5 (Summer 1978).

37. See note 1 above, pp. 25-33.

38. Ibid. Page 41 onwards.

7 CLASS STRUGGLE, SOCIAL POLICY AND STATE STRUCTURE: CENTRAL-LOCAL RELATIONS AND HOUSING POLICY, 1919-1939

Jennifer Dale

This chapter forms a contribution to debates about the character and role of the state at local level. The empirical material relates to housing policy between the two world wars. We are therefore dealing with the phenomenon of the modern welfare state. The very use of the term 'welfare state' begs many questions about the precise character of the activities of the state, and the extent to which a clear dividing line can be drawn between 'welfare' and other activities. Nevertheless the term points to two key features of the contemporary state: its growing interventionism — the sharp separation between the economic and political spheres characteristic of capitalism in its liberal moment is increasingly eroded; and the manner in which the state influences, redirects and in some cases replaces market forces so as to meet certain social needs and relieve what are perceived to be social problems.

The Liberal reforms of 1906 to 1911 were a watershed in the transition from limited, ad hoc initiatives characteristic of the nineteenth century — often brought in on a purely local basis, and apparently concerned primarily with social control and the pure physical reproduction of the workforce — to the emergence of the modern welfare state in the twentieth century.[1]

This paper is thus concerned with a period when the local authorities were not initiating social policies purely, or largely in response to local conditions, but rather because they had been entrusted with responsibilities under national legislation — legislation whose passage had been shaped by national political and economic conditions. This is not to deny that local factors could continue to be influential in pressure for changes at national level; nor that there were not important local differences in the implementation of policy. Nevertheless, with policies increasingly national in scope, and with the central government having a keen interest in their implementation, the central-local dimension becomes increasingly important, and this is the focus of this chapter.

Does Local Government Matter?

Within orthodox political science and social administration, discussion of local government evokes a series of different responses, and the starting point for analysis varies. On the one hand writers such as Robson evince passionate concern at the supposed decline of the institution linked to statements of faith in its importance as part of a system of representative democracy.[2] In a less polemical strain, many authors have examined the formal characteristics of the governmental system and concluded that local government is singularly and increasingly hamstrung in what it can do.[3] Against this authors such as Boaden have suggested that this produces a misleading impression of centralisation based on an appraisal of the formal means of control of the central government rather than the extent to which they are used.[4] Such a critique has been extended by Dearlove through an examination of policy-making at local level.[5]

Whilst within political science, debate tends to centre on the character of the central-local relationship in the context of the democratic system, within social administration, concern has more often been with the impact of local discretion on policy output. In particular, Bleddyn Davies has pioneered the use of regression analysis to discover the extent of variation between the services in local areas which is not attributable to differences in the level of need.[6]

This essay does not aim to make any significant addition to the impressive empirical material which already exists in these two areas. Instead it suggests a different starting-point from that of orthodox political science or social administration. Whilst it is not insignificant to ask whether or not the existence of elected local institutions makes any difference in, for example, access to public housing for A living in Leeds as compared to B living in Manchester, this type of question tends to stem from an approach which sees aspects of the operation of institutions as possible problems in the quest for successful social engineering.[7]

The more fundamental issue, it is argued here, is the impact of local government on society as a whole, and to come to grips with this, we have to ask the question whether the existence of a particular state structure involving separate *political* as well as administrative institutions at local level, affects the overall relations between classes in society.

In posing such a question we are clearly adopting a particular theoretical model of society. Briefly stated the framework is that suggested by Mishra: 'social institutions must be analysed as part of a wider social system and that the latter is best seen in terms of a distinctive mode of production.'[8] The use of the concept of mode of production implies that great weight is being given to the economic level in determining social relations generally, although since institutions are the product of history, and human action is mediated by values and ideology, social life cannot necessarily be directly and mechanistically reduced to the economic level.

This framework enables us to view society as a structure — the system of production entails a set of social relationships which people have not consciously created, which they enter regardless of their own wishes, and which largely determines their role in society; but at the same time it avoids the determination inherent in the other main structuralism, namely functionalism.

Under capitalism society is divided into social classes defined by their relationship to the means of production: on the one hand those who own or control the means of production, and on the other, those who sell their labour power and neither own nor control the means of production.[9] These classes are placed in an antagonistic relationship: the very essence of the capitalist mode of production is the production of commodities for sale for no reason other than accumulation, a process entailing the exploitation of those who sell their labour power. It is this exploitation which is the basis of *systematic* conflict between labour and capital. On the one hand the class struggle can be seen as something determined by the impersonal logic of capitalist accumulation; on the other hand, people's collective class action is the means by which they come to shape society and ultimately to transform it. To understand the class struggle it is necessary both to examine people's objective position within the social system of production, and the ideologies and values which fashion their perception of their own situation and the possibilities for their conscious acting upon that situation.

To develop an answer to the question posed earlier, we must first locate the state as a whole within the capitalist mode of production and consider what functions it performs. This will not, however, constitute an answer as to the origins of specific capitalist nation states — to suppose that it would is to lapse into a functionalist methodology. Rather it will be argued that the form of the state is the product of the class struggle — past and present — and that this provides an avenue leading to consideration of whether the form of the state in a particular country affects the underlying balance of class forces. This line of analysis is suggested by Esping-Anderson and others: 'the internal structure of the state is simultaneously a product, an object and a determinant of class struggle.'[10] Unfortunately they do not develop this theme, a task to which this paper makes a very meagre beginning.

To analyse the nature and role of the state in advanced capitalism we can most fruitfully turn to recent Marxist literature dealing with the contentious questions of the relationship between the economically dominant class, the dynamics of the capitalist economy and the state. Space does not permit any detailed discussion of the various debates in this area,[11] but the various elements of the approach adopted here will be briefly set out.

The particular character of the capitalist state derives in the first place from a unique feature of the capitalist mode of production: the separation of the economic and political spheres. Exploitation takes place in the economic sphere without any direct coercion, but simply through the operation of the market. This very aspect of capitalism means, however, that the capitalist class is fragmented: capitalists are in competition with each other and different market situations lead to conflicts of immediate interest. The state, then, is the organ which can pursue the interests of the capitalist class *as a whole*. To do this it needs to maintain a *relative* autonomy from that class both in order to retain legitimacy and to avoid being dominated by the sectional interests of particular fractions of capital.

There are however important disagreements on the precise character of the state. Miliband[12] defines it in terms of a set of institutions which function to maintain class domination through the personnel controlling them, the role of ideology and the bias of the economic system. These features are common to capitalist states although there are also important differences, for example in the degree of independence of the state apparatus. Poulantzas[13] on the other hand criticises this approach for stressing personnel rather than structures. The state here is seen as an expression of the relationship between classes rather than something that exercises power in its own right. It is defined in terms of a set of functions rather than institutions.

Miliband's work can legitimately be criticised for lapsing into a form of conspiracy theory through over-stressing the conscious manipulation of the state by the capitalist class as opposed to the production and reproduction of ideologies which reinforce class power, but without those involved in applying those views necessarily being aware of this process.[14] Nevertheless on the basic question of the state as institutions versus the state as a function, the former approach is adopted here. The latter is relatively barren when we come to analyse the manner in which the state organises reform. The notion of the state as an expression of class power enables one to draw out the way in which the actions of the state reproduce the dominance of the ruling class but not how the state can be forced to grant major concessions under the impact of class struggle, how the conflicts between class fractions are reproduced in the state apparatus leading to all sorts of vacillations over policy, and how indeed the state can introduce policies which have altogether contradictory and unintended consequences.

A rejection of functionalism does not of course imply that the state does not carry out certain functions which are necessary aspects of the maintenance of ruling-class power. The functions that the state must perform in order to pursue the interests of capital have been variously described, in particular by Cockburn[15] and O'Connor.[16] Cockburn divides the functions of the state into two main areas: reproduction and production. State policies in the former area are concerned with the reproduction of the labour force (ensuring that workers' needs are satisfied to the extent that they are ready and willing to labour anew each day, and that their skills and other attributes conform to the requirements of the labour process); and the reproduction of the relations of production (the engineering of compliance both through attempts to shape values, or the employment of means of repression). In the sphere of production, the state aids accumulation directly.

O'Connor divides these two functions slightly differently into those concerned with accumulation and those with legitimation. This two-fold division enables him to place a focus on the contradictions inherent in the state's attempt to meet both these requirements.

The specific origins of *particular* capitalist nation states are not, however, reducible to the *general* analysis of the functions of the state in capitalist society. To understand the particular form of the state we must look at the historical unfolding of the class struggle. Comparing capitalist states, for example, we can note that British local government allows for greater autonomy than the French system, whilst in the United States there is a picture of unsurpassed localism.

Markusen[17] explains these differences by reference to historical differences in the period of emergent capitalism. In Britain, for example, she suggests that an ideology of local autonomy became established as a result of the antagonism between the rising mercantile capitalist class, based in the towns, and the rural-based class of feudal landowners. In this case the capitalist class required a degree of city autonomy to pursue their interests.

The dominance of a laissez-faire ideology in the nineteenth century sustained the tradition of local autonomy during an era when the capitalist class had managed to gain national political dominance. The gradual erosion of that autonomy in the twentieth century can be related to developments at both the economic and political level which have led to attempts by the state to act in a more concerted way.[18]

Whilst class struggle affects the form of the state, the chain of determination may also be reversed. It has been suggested that the character of political institutions may affect the way in which class struggle is conducted. Markusen[19] again argues that in the United States the intense localism and fragmented system of local government reinforces sub-class identification based on attempts to use place of residence as a means to avoid paying higher taxes for social expenditure in the inner city. This argument is only of relevance to the period when access to social services and the distribution of welfare expenditures have been major issues. In Britain major differences in the level of local taxation existed during the inter-war years due to problems of financing poor relief, yet there is little evidence that this in itself was a divisive element in the working class: rather it was the distinction between areas of economic growth and those of decline. More recently the growing centralisation of local government finance has reduced variations and made the phenomena of 'fiscal struggle' of marginal significance.

Nevertheless local government has not been irrelevant to the working class, and there are many examples of class struggle focusing on the state at local level. Where this has taken the form of struggles for the extension of municipal ownership it has often been referred to as 'municipal socialism'.[20] This term is often used rather loosely, however, to refer either simply to the extension of municipal services in a particular local area, or to an ideology. In its latter form it can mean either that in a socialist society common ownership should be exercised by locally elected bodies, or that municipalisation is a route to a socialist society.

The uneven development of class struggle, and the greater accessibility of local government to working-class representation has led to significant reforms being gained at local level, which have then been transposed to the national political arena.[21] On the other hand, the ideology of municipal socialism, in its second sense, would constitute a barrier to the development of class struggle since it is at national level that class conflicts must ultimately be resolved. There is little evidence, however, that working-class militants have seen municipal enterprise as the route to socialism. The ideology has always been most strongly associated with the Fabians, a predominantly middle-class group, strongly influenced by ideologies of national efficiency and hostile to working-class self-organisation. Fraser, in his study of Glasgow, concludes:

It was however Liberals and Progressives, not the working class, that had any real faith that municipal enterprise could be a kind of socialism. It seemed often to stem from an optimism that social problems could be solved relatively easily and cheaply by municipal activities, with the minimum interference with individual rights. The working-class organisations had, on the whole, a further grasp of the immensity of the social problems and the need for a perspective that went beyond the town hall.[22]

Studies such as Fraser's, highlighting the way in which reforms could be won at local level generally, deal with a period earlier than the one which is the subject of this chapter. Since the First World War there have been fewer examples of services being introduced in a locality and later being taken up at national level. The class struggle has been directed more towards improving the social services through changes in national legislation. Nevertheless there has been an important and continuing tradition of local struggles in defence of social services against national cutbacks or attempts to shift the burden of financing services onto the consumer. Three examples in particular stand out: the Poplar Guardians defiance of the Local Government Board's attempts in 1906 and 1921-2 to force through a more restrictive administration of the Poor Law; the disputes over the payment of transitional benefit during the 1930s, which led to the Ministry of Labour displacing two authorities and threatening others; more recently, the refusal of the Clay Cross councillors to implement the 1972 Housing Finance Act. In this case, again, the councillors were suspended and replaced by a government-appointed housing commissioner. Local resistance is a weapon, but one which is not often used, and has many pitfalls: increasing centralisation has shifted power more and more away from the locality, and lack of support from other areas may leave councils isolated.

If we turn from consideration of how the working class conducts its struggle, to how the state attempts to fulfil its functions we may find that this particular form of the state is more or less conducive to the pursuit of the twin goals of facilitating accumulation and maintaining legitimacy. Accepting O'Connor's point, however, that these functions are in fact to some degree contradictory, we should not expect to find that any particular institutional arrangement is 'ideal' from the point of view of the state as a whole.

Local government can, in abstract, be seen as having possibly contradictory implications, since on the one hand it potentially serves a legitimating function, but on the other hand there may be disfunctions in a fragmented state structure.

The legitimating function of local government is accepted implicitly by the passionate defenders of local government referred to at the beginning of this chapter, and there is an influential tradition which sees local government as an important element in a pluralist state.[23] It is also suggested for example by Cockburn that local government is perceived differently from the rest of the state: 'We have been taught to think of local government as a kind of humane official charity, a service that looks after us "from the cradle to the grave"'.[24] This attitude derives from certain features of local government in the context of the welfare state. In the first place local government is both democratically elected and *local*. The reform of the local government system has gone hand in hand with extensions of the franchise nationally, and locally elected institutions provide an additional point of access to the state within a system of representative government — a system which may be regarded as the most functional from the point of view of the maintenance of ruling-class dominance without provoking a crisis of legitimacy.[25]

In the second place, local government has been given the main responsibility for the provision of those items of collective consumption from which ordinary people benefit: housing, education, personal social services and health were either administered from the beginning by local authorities, or were transferred to them as the state gradually took over responsibilities which previously it had delegated to approved voluntary or private bodies.[26] Whilst local authorities have now lost their functions in the sphere of personal health care, their other services have continued to expand enormously.

On the other hand local autonomy may give rise to conflicts within the state apparatus which are disfunctional. The interests of the capitalist class as a whole may be said to lie in the state conceding reforms necessary to contain working-class struggle and maintain the legitimacy of capitalist social relations, but at the same time not jeopardising the accumulation process, which will be hampered if, for example, rising social expenditure and taxation fuels wage demands which eat into surplus value. If local authorities fail actually to implement reforms granted nationally, the credibility of the government is undermined. On the other hand, services provided on too generous a scale may lead either to rising taxation locally (or, if central government grants are calculated according to a sliding scale, nationally) or to instability in particular markets. In this latter case it may be that only certain fractions of capital are affected. Whether or not this group can exert a decisive influence on the course of policy depends on their relative weight in the capitalist class as a whole, the strength of particular ideologies, and the manner in which conflicts between fractions of capital are reproduced within the state apparatus.

How likely is it that conflicts between central and local government will cause major problems for the state as a whole? In Britain it has already been argued that the working class has rarely used local government as a vehicle for political struggle. Nevertheless, conflicts do arise, and they tend to centre around three issues related to the reproduction of labour power with which most local authorities are concerned:

(i)   What should be the *level of reproduction*? The notion of the reproduction of labour power denotes a level of subsistence which is enlarged under the impact of working-class struggle. National policies embody historically changing definitions of subsistence which may be more or less acceptable to individual local authorities.

(ii) Should items of collective consumption be provided equally for all or for particular groups? This can be illustrated by reference to a service such as public housing which may be provided for all in need, or limited to particular groups – e.g. rehousing families under slum clearance schemes.

(iii) How should the *costs of reproduction be distributed*? This concerns the way in which finance should be raised – should the burden fall on the consumer, the local taxpayer or the national taxpayer. Generally local authorities tend to favour shifting the cost onto nationally raised revenues.

Within the context of these disputes, local authorities may be seen to be either more backward than central government – favouring a lower level of reproduction for a smaller section of the population – or ahead, stressing high standards for all. These two possible scenarios derive from two possible causes of conflicts within the state apparatus.

In the first place, local authorities may be dominated by particular fractions of the bourgeoisie: in effect the state at local level may lose its relative autonomy and come directly to represent the short-term interests of one particular section of the capitalist class. This situation may threaten the long-term interests of the class as a whole because of the loss of legitimacy involved. This situation has arisen in its starkest form in Northern Ireland, where Unionist control has left a legacy of inadequate services compared with mainland Britain, allocated in a discriminatory way. Here the effects of the loss of legitimacy were so disruptive that central government has removed the most sensitive services from local authority control. At a less dramatic level, Byrne in his chapter identifies a local 'urban bourgeoisie' with particular interests in property which is resistant to the extension of social services such as housing.

Whilst Byrne refers to the resistance of many local authorities to providing improved housing for the working class, it is also the case that many local authorities – not even necessarily Labour-controlled – have consistently wanted to do more than was permitted within the financial and administrative limitations of central government policy. To explain this it is not enough to refer to particular immediate class interests: the mediations of ideology must also be taken into account. The role of local middle-class political leaderships in pressing for schemes of municipal reform has been noted in relation to cities such as Birmingham from the Victorian era. Briggs[27] refers to a 'civic gospel' and the pride of the city fathers in their aspirations to be the best governed city. There is a tendency then for particular areas to seek legitimacy through providing high standards of service, and asserting their authority and independence from central government. This lays the basis for endemic conflicts between central and local government over the level of reproduction, the distribution of costs, and the extent of central government intervention. These disputes remain, however, within fairly narrow bounds, and neither the demands nor the conduct of the struggle, such as it is, are much threat to the overall unity of the state.

The remainder of this chapter takes the form of a case study of housing in inter-war Britain, with particular reference to Manchester. This both illustrates the arguments outlined above, as well as suggesting some ways in which focus on central-local relations helps understand the nature of state intervention in the housing field.

National Policies Towards Public Housing 1919-1930

An analysis of changing national housing policies, and the extent to which attempts were made to enforce changes of direction, is the starting-point for an empirical examination of central-local relations. This section attempts to show how the class-conflict model of society discussed above in relation to the character of the state, can be used to explain the overall limits of debate in social policy, changes in the direction of national policy within those limits, and the extent of discretion allowed to local authorities in whether, or how they implement them.

A class-conflict model implies a framework which stresses firstly the struggles of the working class on the one hand, and on the other the needs of capital for social harmony and continued capital accumulation; and secondly the manner in which the actions of both classes are mediated by dominant ideologies and perceptions of rationality and feasibility. The approach here is close to that adopted in this collection by Damer who argues that the balance of class forces is crucial in understanding state social policy. The pluralist, incrementalist approach of Bowley[28] and Wilding[29] is rejected. Whilst Wilding, for example, is able to provide an interesting insight into the nitty gritties of the form of policy, he, in common with other adherents of pluralism is not able to give a general account of the emergence of housing policy. Clearly differences in the outlook and influence of the various individuals, government departments and pressure groups involved in what political scientists refer to as the policy-making process are important factors shaping the final form of policies: but they enter at the final curtain, when the stage has already been set by the class struggle within the context of dominant ideologies.

Applying this model to national housing policy and central-local relations we can argue that under the impact of a working-class offensive the state will grant considerable concessions, which may later be whittled away and partially, although never totally, withdrawn. The extent to which these changes are forced on local authorities will depend on the severity of the political crisis which precipitated the initial concession, the extent to which reforms are then seen as threatening dominant interests, and changes in the overall balance of class forces.

Before proceeding to discuss changes in national housing policy in more detail, it is necessary to consider further the notion of a 'concession'. It would clearly be wrong to erect a simple yardstick to denote the magnitude of a concession: nevertheless a crucial factor is the extent to which production and consumption are removed from the sphere of commodity relationships. The interests of building, finance and landlord capital all come under threat if housing is financed out of taxation and built by the state. In practice, clear limits have been set to the incursion of the state in the housing market: rent control and the growth of the local authority rented sector have led to the gradual squeezing of the private landlord out of the housing market, but housing remains largely built and financed by private capital.[30]

Nevertheless, within these limits, there have been important differences of degree in national policy, of significance both to the working class and fractions of capital. In particular periods of heightened class struggle, particularly after the two world wars, coinciding with disarray in the housing market, have led to major extensions in the role of the state in housing: in particular, new building has been almost entirely commissioned by local authorities, rather than being undertaken on a speculative basis, the standard of houses built has been raised considerably whilst rent control has covered most working-class housing in the private sector. This concession has subsequently been whittled away as the class struggle has ebbed, and pressures for a contraction of the state's role have come from fractions of capital, finance capital especially. Changes in policy have involved the reduction in the standard of public housing, cuts in the resources devoted to this sector, and the limitation of local authorities to a residual, slum-clearance role.

Whilst it is important to stress the role of class pressure from capital based on immediate economic interests in this process, it is also necessary to bring in the ideological dimension. Mike Ball[31] argues that encouragement of the local authority sector is, in economic terms, the most rational housing policy from the point of view of capital since it minimises both the costs of the reproduction of labour power and the amount of surplus value creamed off by unproductive finance capital: nevertheless owner-occupation tends to be the more favoured tenure category since it reinforces the values of individualism and private property. Whilst stressing the way in which the state at times deliberately fosters owner-occupation, it is also important to stress the other half of the equation: the absence of high quality, cheap and genuinely democratically controlled public housing makes owner-occupation appear the most desirable alternative to those who can afford it, since it offers economic advantages and security, and enables the family to keep their private domain relatively more free from external intervention. The great extension of owner-occupation during the 1930s was thus the beginning of a phenomenon which has massively affected the politics of housing.

Looking in more detail at the inter-war period,[32] the ebbs and flows of the class struggle led to some major policy changes which were enforced on local authorities to varying degrees. It may be useful to examine housing policy in terms of three periods.

The first phase saw the introduction of the first system of exchequer subsidies for housing in 1919, and ends with the premature ending of the scheme in 1921. This period was dominated by the extra-parliamentary class struggle, which led to a temporary agreement in the government on the need for concessions of an emergency character. Subsidies were introduced relieving local authorities of all losses on schemes above a penny rate and strong pressure was put on local authorities to get house-building underway. The standard of housing was greatly increased.

Against this, the scheme was intended to be for three years only, and the production of housing remained dominated by commodity relationships: all but the smaller authorities had to raise their finance from the money market and a system of building licensing was rejected. The result was a tremendous demand for capital and inflation in house-building costs, which produced a backlash against the scheme, led by finance capital. As the working-class offensive subsided, and the first post-war defeats occurred, the government moved in July 1921 to bring the scheme to an end.

Nevertheless, this was not the end of housing policy, and during the second phase up to 1933, local-authority building became established under the 1924 Housing (Financial Provisions) Act, brought in by the short-lived minority Labour Government, which provided a fixed subsidy of £9 per house for 40 years. Private enterprise was also subsidised under Conservative-inspired legislation of 1923 which gave local authorities a fixed subsidy of £6 for 20 years, but stipulated that their first option must be to subsidise private enterprise.

Local authorities in many ways enjoyed much greater freedom during this period since the fixed subsidy avoided any threatening escalation of costs. On the other hand, the working class was largely on the defensive during this period, although its organisation remained intact, so that there was no great pressure as there had been in 1919, to get building underway.

Nevertheless central government influences were brought to bear on the localities. The 1924 Act was administered, apart from the years 1929-31, by Conservative governments who were reluctant to see subsidies continue beyond the minimum necessary time. Similarly it was felt that high-quality public housing brought local authorities into competition with private enterprise. In 1926, therefore, it was decided to cut the level of subsidy and urge local authorities to build smaller houses. A similar decision was taken again two years later, although it was never implemented due to the return of a Labour government.

This reliance on the price mechanism to influence local authorities, rather than the use of draconian administrative action as in 1921, was to become characteristic of central-local relations, apart from a brief change in 1931. After the financial crisis of that year and the fall of the Labour Government, the new National Government immediately made drastic cuts in the level of house approvals and adopted a much tougher stance towards local authorities who continued to build houses of a generous standard.

In the third phase of policy from 1933, there was a return to reliance on the price mechanism, but with much more restrictive consequences than previously. Legislation in that year brought the 1924 Act subsidy to an end, leaving state assistance confined to the slum-clearance subsidy introduced in 1930. Local authorities were to leave the provision of additional housing to private enterprise, confining themselves to a residual role which did not compete with private enterprise, and in any case was intended to be complete, according to the government, in five years.

This discussion of housing policy has been largely concerned with the question of house production, showing changes in the degree to which housebuilding was encouraged, and the way in which standards have been raised or depressed. The question of the consumption of housing received far less attention from central government: under the general needs scheme only the most rudimentary guidelines were suggested for allocation criteria. Rents of local authority houses were subjected to slightly more control, especially under the 1919 scheme, where the exchequer had a direct financial interest in the level of rents as they affected the amount of loss of any scheme. In this case the Ministry established a rent tribunal to arbitrate between central and local government in cases where it thought rents were too low. Under the 1924 Act rents were intended to be set, on average, at the 'appropriate normal rent' for pre-war housing. No attempt was made, however, to enforce this, and local authorities were given virtually total freedom in rent setting after 1933, when all housing subsidies were consolidated. Despite considerable discussion of the merits of rent rebates, no official viewpoint on the matter was adopted, let alone enforced.

Housing in Manchester: 1919-39

The final section of this paper forms a case study of the implementation of housing policy in one particular locality, illustrating both the degree of local initiative which was possible, the areas in which there was disagreement between the central government and Manchester City Council, and the manner in which disputes over these issues was conducted.

Use of a single case study clearly poses major problems for making any points of general validity. Suffice it to say that Manchester provides several points of interest. Rapid urban growth in the early nineteenth century had produced a legacy of appalling slums in the core of the city. Unlike the adjacent Lancashire towns, however, it had always had a fairly diversified economic structure. As early as 1844 Engels[33] had noted that Manchester had a clearly defined central business district which served as a commercial centre for the surrounding towns, whose

economies were based almost entirely on cotton manufacture. As the
cotton industry declined, Manchester was able to make the transition
from an economy based on textile manufacture to one based on engineering and commerce. This process was by no means unique to
Manchester: by 1921 more male workers were employed in engineering
than textiles in Lancashire as a whole, and employment in textiles
tended to be concentrated in the smaller towns rather than the county
boroughs.[34] Nevertheless Manchester remained the dominant commercial centre.

The economic history of the city can be seen in its social structure.
Ward[35] noted the large strata of white-collar workers in Manchester as
compared with other provincial cities as early as *c.* 1850. In 1921 Manchester had the highest percentage of clerks amongst county boroughs
in Lancashire, and the third highest percentage of other commercial
and professional workers after the seaside resorts of Blackpool and
Southport. The largest single occupational category for males, on the
other hand, was metal workers who comprised 15.7 per cent of males
aged 12 years and over.[36]

The occupational structure of the city is an important factor in
understanding the development of the housing market. As a major industrial city, the solid core of its population was working class, housed
at the time of the First World War in the ring of working-class housing
around the city centre, extending northwards and eastwards. To the
south, however, Manchester had experienced suburban growth based
on the development of estates for the upper and lower middle class.
Exclusive estates such as Victoria Park were built for the wealthy of the
early years of the nineteenth century, whilst from 1860 areas such as
Moss Side were developed with superior terraced houses for the growing
strata of commercial workers. Finally, during the 1930s, new owner-
occupied estates were built further out towards Cheshire, and areas such
as Moss Side became notorious as areas of 'farmed' or multi-occupied
housing.

Manchester has a long tradition of labour organisation, in which the
engineering unions have played a prominent role. The local trades council was formed in 1866, and attention turned to national politics when
the Manchester Labour Representation Committee was formed in 1903.
Labour made consistent gains in local elections prior to the First World
War, and made something of a breakthrough in November 1919 when it
increased its representation from 17 to 36. Whilst never gaining outright
control, it maintained a consistent presence during the inter-war period.
There was a strong Liberal presence on the council including the

prominent housing reformer, Sir Ernest Simon. Both he and a fellow Liberal Sir Miles Mitchell were chairmen of the City's Housing Committee, and the latter was also chairman of the Housing Committee of the Association of Municipal Corporations (AMC).

These factors were reflected in a vigorous municipal building programme, which exceeded the output of private enterprise during the inter-war period. (The latter built 24,160 houses compared with the corporation's 27,447.)[37]

Manchester was thus an authority with the severe housing problems of an old industrial city, but with the added complexities of residential succession which are typical of metropolitan cities. It was therefore to find the restriction of government policy more problematic than authorities such as Leeds whose problems were more straightforwardly those of physical obsolescence. The authority took a fairly forward-looking stance on housing. A study of the occupations and political stances of councillors does not immediately suggest that the city was dominated by a local 'urban bourgeoisie' with particular interests in property.

On the other hand we shall see in the next section that although Manchester was often in the forefront of disputes with central government, these were limited to particular issues, mainly that of housing standards, and the degree of actual conflict was very limited, in part because the labour movement seems to have been relatively uninvolved. During the 1920s, for example, the Trades Council seems to have given only limited attention to housing, although reports of a Tenants Defence Association, concerned with private sector rents, are included in the Council's Annual Reports. In 1930 the Council itself became more actively involved, but again the focus was on the private sector and providing a rent advice service for tenants.[38]

Before 1914 the main activities of Manchester City Council had been to establish by-laws and attempt to improve the existing stock by closing cellar dwellings and eliminating back-to-back houses. A few tenement blocks had been built as part of slum-clearance schemes, and in 1900 the council agreed to buy a site in Blackley to build 1,800 cottages. However, in this case property interests represented on the council were sufficiently strong to stymie actual building, and only 150 houses had been put up by 1914.[39]

The situation in 1918 was, however, rather different. Apart from the influence of national political developments, the city council was confronted by a local labour movement which had grown in strength during the First World War. In particular, Manchester's main industry engineering had been affected by the development of the shop stewards' movement and wartime struggles over dilution. The city council decided to act on the housing question for, as Sir Ernest Simon pointed out 'public opinion insisted that houses must be built somehow'.[40]

The 1919 Act

Manchester had already acquired sites for housing before the end of the First World War. The further purchase of land in 1919 provided sites sufficient for 7,706 houses.[41] The total three-year programme of building under the act was agreed with the regional housing commissioner as 17,727 houses.

Progress in meeting this target was extremely slow however, and, in all, only 3,900 houses were ever completed. This was in part due to local market problems — builders found it more profitable to tender for other work, so that contracts were difficult to obtain, whilst two firms which became involved in the programme went bankrupt in the early stages of developing sites, and in part due to central government restrictions.

The Ministry's desire to achieve cost control, whilst leaving local authorities at the mercy of inflationary market forces, led to many delays. Local authorities were supervised at every stage of their activity, a task which the state apparatus found difficult to achieve speedily. Simon complained that 20 weeks was the minimum time in which a scheme could be approved.[42] At the same time, the Ministry decided to attempt to keep prices down through direct negotiations with builders. Manchester was therefore asked to delay seeking tenders for one of its first estates, Blackley, until discussions between the housing commissioner and the local builders' federation were complete. In the absence of any sanctions available to the state, these negotiations inevitably broke down, leaving Manchester back at square one at the end of February 1920. It was not until mid-1920 that the Housing Committee reported that the Ministry was accepting tenders on a cost price basis, which Manchester regarded as the only feasible way of getting firms to tender. As regards labour, the shortage was a seriously inhibiting factor. Again Manchester pressed for changes in national policy — calling for a tightening up of the law enabling local authorities to ban luxury building, and supporting the faction in the cabinet which favoured a national agreement with the building trade unions whereby concessions would be given if the trade unions allowed an increase in the entry of unskilled men.

An alternative method of meeting these difficulties would have been to by-pass the private contractor altogether. The use of direct works was particularly inimical to property interests. Nevertheless despite opposition from this group on the council, the city took a pragmatic approach. A works department was set up, and a more extensive use was made of it than by any other authority.[43] The local Building Guild, a co-operative venture under the auspices of the District Committee of the National Federation of Building Trade Operatives (NFBTO), also offered to build 2,000 houses for the corporation. After considerable prevarication, it was eventually invited to tender for the 426 houses on the Clayton Estate. In the event, however, a contract for only 100 houses was agreed in October 1920.

Despite these developments, however, the majority of houses were built by private firms. In some cases — Gorton Mount and Newton Heath, for example — direct works only became involved when private firms went bankrupt in the early stages of a scheme. The largest estate, Wilbraham Road, was constructed by McAlpines. Large-scale regional and national capital was thus involved in the programme, as much as the small local builder.

On the question of housing standards, the vast improvements recommended in the Tudor Walters Report were adopted nationally and taken up enthusiastically in Manchester. The new minimum floor area for a three-bedroomed house was set at 760 square feet. The majority of houses built were three- and four-bedroomed houses with parlours being in the majority. Proposals by the Minister of Health to modify certain elements of the design and specifications so as to reduce costs were largely resisted. In mid-1921, members of the Housing Committee visited Leeds to examine the cheaper houses being built there, but came out against adopting Leeds' policy.

The system of open-ended central government subsidy under the 1919 scheme meant that rents were of direct concern to the central government, and in general authorities attempted to set rents lower than the level favoured by central government. In fact, whilst the Ministry wanted rents set at 10s to 12s 6d for three-bedroomed houses, the central Rent Tribunal set up to arbitrate disputes, was awarding lower rents, around 8s and 10s. In the case of Manchester the authority does not seem to have come into conflict over this issue, and high rents were accepted. In October 1920 gross rents varied from 13s 7d to 25s, and were higher than other similarly placed authorities.[44] There appears to have been fairly wide variations between authorities as to the percentage of expenditure that was met by rents. In Manchester in the year 1920 to 1921, rents accounted for 40 per cent.[45] Whilst such figures were undoubtedly difficult to stomach to those inured to the idea that housing costs should be met out of wages, the tremendous post-war inflation, which the state had taken no steps to control, meant that in fact the higher standards of post-war housing were to a large extent being met by the tenants themselves.

High rents led to difficulties in housing management. The authority's allocation policy was based on giving preference to ex-servicemen and no account was taken of income. Added to this, the suburban location of most estates made them unattractive to low-paid workers. Prior to 1924 just under half the houses built were let to manual workers, with 'clerks' forming a substantial category of tenants.[46] Nevertheless, the Public Health Committee which was responsible for lettings pointed out that the majority of applicants wanted the smaller, cheaper houses.[47]

In the spring of 1921, reaction in the Cabinet against the housing programme was reflected in the ousting of Addison from the Ministry of Health and his replacement by Sir Alfred Mond. Manchester councillors commented on a definite change of attitude at the Ministry, and this was soon manifested in a refusal to allow the council to accept tenders for 650 houses. Furthermore the council was told that no invitations for tenders should be made for six weeks, and that of the 300 houses which Manchester wanted to build by direct labour, only 150 were approved. The Ministry reserved the right to terminate this later programme if costs exceeded the original estimate by more than 2½ per cent.

This heavy-handed treatment was undoubtedly resented, but no real opposition to it was shown. Tenders for small groups of houses were accepted in dribs and drabs as the Ministry gave permission during the ensuing months, and in August 1921 the Ministry and the city council came to an agreement on Manchester's total programme being fixed at 3,500 houses. Whilst Manchester was able to maintain the standard of housing, it seemed neither able or willing to do anything about the larger question of the size of its programme. Resignation was clearly more acceptable than any confrontation.

The 1923-4 schemes

The 1923 Act in some ways gave local authorities far more freedom from central supervision than the earlier 1919 Act. The fixed subsidy meant that the Ministry need no longer be involved in the supervision of expenditure, since its interests were already protected. In addition, the intention of the act was to inject capital into the building industry rather than meet working-class housing needs, so that there was no further need to impress a sense of urgency on the more backward local authorities. The large supervisory apparatus of the Ministry of Health, including the system of regional housing commissioners was, therefore, abandoned in 1921 and not subsequently reactivated.

On the other hand, the act stipulated that local authorities must subsidise private enterprise as their first option. In practice this does not appear to have been a major problem: the Ministry agreed to allow the city to go ahead with plans to build 690 houses itself before it had drawn up plans to assist private enterprise. Plans to provide both a lump sum of up to £100 and loans to private builders were not agreed until September. Altogether more than 8,000 houses built by private enterprise — something like a third of those built during the inter-war years — received some form of assistance from the corporation. The city itself built 1,352 houses under the 1923 Act.

With the passage of new legislation granting higher subsidies, Manchester, like most authorities, switched to building under the 1924 Act, which formed the basis for more than half of all dwellings built by the authority between the wars (16,277 houses out of a total of 27,447).[48] The pace of building tended, however, to be somewhat erratic due both to local blockages in the building process and the manner in which these intersected with changes in government policy.

In the first place Manchester seems to have been fairly slow to get construction underway. By March 1927, three years after the new legislation had been passed, only 861 houses had been completed. In 1927, however, the subsidy was cut, and local authorities generally made a concerted attempt to get houses complete before the deadline at the end of September. In the year 1927/8, 2,379 houses were finished. This tremendous rate of activity was in fact surpassed in the following year, after which building by the city declined, recovering only in the final year of the scheme, 1933/4.

This decline in building after 1928 was paradoxical, since building costs generally were falling, and the decision by the 1929 Labour Government not to implement the second subsidy cut proposed by the outgoing Conservative Government meant that the overall housing cost-subsidy relationship was quite favourable after 1929. The answer probably lies in three factors: the lack of confidence that had been engendered by the cut in subsidy and the general uncertainty in the aftermath of the 1931 crisis; the pressure to reduce expenditure after 1931 exemplified in restrictive government policies and the appointment and recommendations of the Ray Committee on Local Expenditure;[49] and finally local difficulties, which were only resolved just when government policy was entering its restrictive phase.

These local problems centred particularly on the development of Wythenshawe, a large privately owned estate in Cheshire adjoining the city's southern boundaries. The city council had decided to purchase the estate in 1926 because of the shortage of housing sites within the city boundary. Although purchase was completed in 1927, further development was delayed, since Manchester was not responsible for the public services. It was not until 1930, when the area was incorporated into the city, that progress could be made — just prior to the time when the 1931 crisis was to precipitate more restrictive national policies.

Nevertheless, Wythenshawe was the centrepiece of the city's building programme under the act, accounting for more than a third of the total, and it was over the question of how the estate should be developed that disputes with the central government once more came to a head. The estate was intended to form a 'satellite town' — largely residential, although with some industry — and such a large-scale, self-contained development offered full scope to the implementation of the popular garden city planning ideology. The Housing Committee reported:

> If laid out on sound and broad town planning lines it would form one of the finest garden cities in the United Kingdom, affording a residential district of the working and other classes of Manchester, sufficiently removed from the smoky atmosphere of a large industrial centre, yet within access, where the people would be housed in delightful surroundings and in such a position that the prevailing south-westerly winds would prevent the smoke and fumes from Manchester and Stockport polluting the air.[50]

The statement suggests a certain municipal pride — the expectation that Manchester could produce a scheme to rival semi-private ventures such as Letchworth. The report displays an anti-urbanism characteristic of much British town-planning thought, which goes back to the nineteenth-century fear of the city as the place which harboured not only the typhoid bacillus, but the more insidious forces of moral and physical degeneration.[51] Wythenshawe was thus to be a low-density estate with a semi-rural environment. There was to be social mix — both because of the superior quality of the estate and because sites would be leased to private developers. The implicit assumption was that social harmony could be achieved if only the right physical environment were provided. In the development of Wythenshawe was encapsulated all the zeal of the particular brand of liberal reformism that was dominant in Manchester's housing policy.

Unfortunately for the city council, its plans to embark on a high-standard development coincided with national moves to force local authorities to build smaller houses. This question had been simmering for some time. Conservative governments from 1924 favoured a reduction in housing standards and the city built fewer parlour houses after 1924 than under the 1919 scheme. At the same time there was some internal pressure to build smaller houses and the Housing Committee discussed the matter on several occasions: in 1927 the chairman visited Birmingham to see the smaller cheaper houses being built there, and in October 1930 the Council set up a Cost of Housing Special Committee which engaged a Wolverhampton quantity surveyor to report on a comparison of costs between Manchester, Birmingham, Liverpool and Nottingham. In both cases the committee came down in favour of retaining the higher standards prevailing in Manchester.

The formation of the National Government in 1931, however, led to a heavy-handed approach from central government. The Housing Committee proposed in April 1931 an initial instalment of 1,000 houses, of which 319 would be begun immediately. The distribution of house types was:

A1	A2	A3	B3	B4
	small	large		
16	45	66	134	46	12

The Ministry simply informed Manchester that larger A3 and parlour (B) houses would not be regarded as eligible for subsidy.[52] Coming as it did in September 1931 when Manchester's plans were in an advanced stage, the city council was understandably upset. Miles Mitchell, chairman of the City's Housing Committee, used his position as chairman of the AMC's Housing Committee to further Manchester's case, and in December managed to get a meeting arranged between the Ministry and the AMC Housing Committee. Miles Mitchell argued in particular for the right of local authorities to build in relation to local conditions and for social mix on estates such as Wythenshawe which were attempting to build for whole new communities.

These delays, coming at a time of high unemployment in the building industry, were of particular concern to local building workers, who raised the matter in Parliament via George Hicks MP, who was also the General Secretary of the Amalgamated Union of Building Trade Workers (AUBTW).[53] This action indicates that the AUBTW clearly grasped where power lay in the central-local relationship! Whilst they raised the matter nationally through a parliamentary question, the NFBTO made the more radical suggestion to the local authority that they simply ignore the Ministry[54] — a rather futile gesture perhaps given the Conservative majority on the council.

Despite resolutions re-affirming the original layout, the council reached a compromise with the Ministry in December 1931 whereby the Council agreed to reduce the number of A2 and B3 houses, and build all A3 houses to the small specification.

When putting forward proposals for a second batch of houses, in March 1932, the Housing Committee appears to have abided by the Ministry's guidelines, since only 10 per cent of the houses were B type, and all the A3 houses were of the smaller design with bathroom downstairs. Apart from Wythenshawe, no plans for building houses with parlours were put forward after 1931. Even four-bedroomed houses were of the non-parlour (A) design, something that would have been unthinkable in 1919.

Building under the 1924 Act was virtually complete by March 1934, and thereafter the city concentrated almost entirely on slum-clearance under the 1930 Act. Prior to the passage of that act, Manchester's slum-clearance activities had been confined to the demolition of 200 houses in the Medlock Street Improvement Scheme. In 1930 local authorities were asked to submit five-year programmes of action under both the 1930 and 1924 Acts. The city had put forward a programme of 12,000 houses, divided equally between the two acts. Such a policy of maintaining both the slum-clearance and general need programmmes was consistent with the housing situation faced by the city. Whilst there was an undoubted problem of slum housing which was not being touched by the city's housing programme, there was also a severe shortage of accommodation which could only be exacerbated by a single-minded policy of clearance. The deficiency of dwellings occupied in relation to families was considerably greater in 1931 than it had been in 1921.[55] Private-enterprise building was erratic, and only at a consistently high level during the second half of the 1930s. Even then, much of the building was for owner-occupation and in suburban locations. It did not touch the inner-city housing problem.

It would be instructive to pause here to draw a parallel between Manchester and Leeds. In the case of Leeds, Bob Finnegan argues that the city used the 1930 legislation to pursue a comprehensive policy of transforming housing into a social service. In the case of Manchester the narrow confines of national policy confronted with the diversity of housing problems meant that the city could not adopt a comprehensive approach. It could not deal with the shortage of housing which was leading to increasing multi-occupation in former middle-class areas such as Moss Side. As Simon and Inman pointed out:

> The worst slums in Manchester are, however, not the two-up and two-down houses. Unfortunately there are not enough of these houses to meet the needs of Manchester families, and the surplus population is forced to overflow into houses let in lodgings. These are generally respectable, old, middle class houses, with say, eight or ten good-sized rooms: as the neighbourhood goes down and the pressure for housing accommodation increases, single houses such as this sort are let off to a number of families, generally one room to each family.[56]

Conditions such as these could not be dealt with under any existing policy.

The pressure to undertake slum clearance should not however be regarded as entirely negative — only the limitations inherent in the government's change of policy. Manchester showed itself reluctant and ill prepared to undertake this task — perhaps because it feared the disruption to its administrative machine that would be caused by having to deal with the poorest families' housing — and some external pressure was clearly required.

In dealing with its first clearance area in Hulme the city showed itself to be extremely undecided on central questions such as rehousing. An initial report in July 1931 seemed concerned that clearance should provide the minimum inconvenience to the council: demolition was to be carried out by houseowners themselves and it was suggested that rehousing from this inner city area be in existing suburban estates. Discussion was deferred twice, but eventually it was agreed that rehousing be on ordinary estates, apart from a scheme of 130 cottage flats on the Anson estate.

This policy gradually gave way, however, and rehousing began to be undertaken in the cleared areas. The need to build at higher densities led to a similar re-appraisal of the policy of building cottages. In 1933 it was decided to build the first block of residential flats at Smedley Road, Cheetham.

The question of the rent-paying capacity of these families was clearly very important: a survey by the Housing Committee found that in Hulme, 223 families out of 1,257 would, if rehoused in ordinary estates, have a deficiency on the family budget based on the 1914 Rowntree

'Human Needs' standard adjusted for changes in the cost of living. Of these, 133 were non-earners who were excluded from consideration! (Unemployment was around 20 per cent in Manchester in 1931.)[57]

We have already seen that Manchester rents tended to be relatively high. In the private sector tenants were generally paying under 10s for rent and rates for the typical two-up two-down house in inner Manchester.[58] Figures for corporation rents are available for mid-1936 and show that most *net* rents fell within the range 6s to 8s.[59] For a three-bedroom house, a further 4s or 5s would have to be added to cover rates. All these considerations led the corporation to begin to differentiate between slum clearance and other tenants. The Anson flat development was first placed in a separate rent pool and subsequently a rent-rebate scheme was introduced for all families compulsorily rehoused under slum clearance and later overcrowding legislation. In 1939, 840 families were in receipt of rent rebate.[60] (The city then owned around 30,000 houses of which about one-fifth had been built under slum-clearance subsidies.)

By 1939 Manchester had experienced some major changes in policy from providing high-quality suburban estates for the better paid workers, or at least those with regular jobs, to building blocks of flats for inner-city former slum dwellers. Few of these changes were the result solely of administrative pressure from the central government: this aspect was only really dominant in the period 1919 to 1921, and for a short period in 1931. More typical of central government pressure was the manipulation of the level of subsidy, and restrictions on its availability, such that local authorities were left to draw their own conclusions about what type of housing could feasibly be built in the context of building costs and the rent-paying capacity of working-class families. This highlights clearly the contradiction between local authorities providing good housing for all, whilst leaving most commodity relationships intact.

Conclusion

In conclusion, perhaps three points about central-local relations should be briefly stressed. In the first place, the Manchester case study illustrated the fact that disagreements between central and local government do cut across party lines — Conservative governments do come into collision, for example, with predominantly Conservative local authorities. Our particular illustration was concerned with a relatively progressive authority which was concerned to maintain housing standards. Its opposition to central government policy can best be explained in terms of a certain municipal ideology: a desire to provide well designed and laid out housing estates which would be attractive to a broad spectrum of workers rather than limited to the poor. Issues such as the use of direct labour rather than private construction firms, and limited state control of the house-building industry were approached pragmatically: the council was ready to contemplate such measures if they were essential to keeping the housing programme going, but arguments by a minority of councillors for exclusive use of direct labour were rejected.

In these respects, Manchester's ideology was closer to the social democracy of the 1945 Labour Government than to traditional Conservative or Liberal Party approaches. This phenomenon can perhaps best be explained in terms both of the particular politics of a relatively prosperous large industrial authority, and the specific position of local authorities within the overall state apparatus.

Nevertheless, the disagreements illustrated by our case study were very limited in scope, centring mainly on the question of housing standards. Fundamental questions about the production of housing within a system of commodity relationships were never raised, so that Manchester was eventually forced to compromise its policy of high standards because high costs of production placed rents out of the reach of families. In this respect, it was more often economic pressures rather than central government control which was decisive in causing a change of policy. Apart from questions of housing standards, the main areas in which central government attempted to control local authorities were in the number of houses built, and whether they were for slum clearance or general needs. In neither case did Manchester, or for that matter any other authorities, seriously attempt to challenge central government policy.

The final point to stress about central-local relations is that the central government avoided so far as possible any direct administrative confrontation with the local authorities such as occurred in 1921 and 1931. If central government action takes this form it is highly visible: the more usual situation is one in which central control is far more opaque. A framework is created in which financial and other pressures constantly confront local authorities in their day-to-day work and cause them to direct their activities in particular directions. This is achieved largely through central government manipulation of the subsidy system: in particular changes in the level of subsidies in relation to costs and limitations on the types of activity which are eligible. The only way in which local authorities could be freed from these pressures would be through a massive reduction in the cost of house construction which could only be achieved through an increase in productivity in the building industry and prising the finance of housing away from finance capital — policies to achieve such aims could only be won through prolonged struggle on a national scale.

Returning to our question about whether local government matters, brings us back to the issue of whether local government, which has its origins in the pre-capitalist era, aids the capitalist state in the performance of its functions. In 1919 it could be argued that the existence of a degree of local autonomy was problematic since it meant that an extremely generous open-ended subsidy had to be given in order to guarantee a generalised local response to the demands of the new act that local authorities consider the housing needs of their areas. Nevertheless, 1919 to 1921 was an exceptional period. At times when political and economic conditions have been more stable, local government appears both to provide a measure of legitimation but at the same time the central government is, in most cases, able to ensure that they carry out at least the necessary minimum of activity, but that services are not provided at a level which might affect the basic dynamics of capital accumulation. Nevertheless the situation does not remain free of contradiction: the conflicting demands of legitimation and accumulation continue to make themselves felt in the continuing debate about local government reorganisation and the difficulty facing the state in reconciling the demands of 'democracy' and 'efficiency'.

Notes

1. See J.R. Hay, *The Origins of the Liberal Welfare Reforms 1906-1914* (Macmillan, London, 1975); Derek Fraser, *The Evolution of the British Welfare State* (Macmillan, London, 1973). For a comparative perspective see Ramesh Mishra, *Society and Social Policy: Theoretical Perspectives on Welfare* (Macmillan, London, 1977) and G.V.Rimlinger, *Welfare Policy and Industrialisation in Europe, America and Russia* (Wiley, New York, 1971).

2. For example, 'I must reaffirm my belief in the virtues of a sound and healthy system of local government'. W.H. Robson, *Local Government in Crisis* (Allen & Unwin, London, 1968), p. 51.

3. For a useful summary of such literature see John Dearlove, *The Politics of Policy in Local Government* (Cambridge UP, London, 1972), ch. 2.

4. Noel Boaden, 'Central Departments and Local Authorities: the Relationship Examined' in *Political Studies*, vol. XVIII, no. 2 (1970).

5. Dearlove, *Policy in Local Government*.

6. In particular B. Davies, *Social Needs and Resources in Local Services* (Joseph, London, 1968).

7. Davies is frankly normative in his approach which is concerned with specifying an 'ideal resource distribution'. Davies, *Social Needs and Resources*, p. 16.

8. Mishra, *Society and Social Policy*.

9. The theory of class has remained relatively undeveloped in Marxist theory. A recent attempt by Olin Wright to take account of the growth of managerial, technical and other white-collar workers, whilst yet retaining an essentially dichotomous model of classes has led to the notion of 'contradictory class locations': in other words many occupational groups cannot be unambiguously assigned to either of the two major social classes associated with the capitalist mode of production, nor to the remnants of the pre-capitalist petty bourgeoisie. This approach implies that it is the process of class struggle itself which ultimately determines class locations, as those occupying ambiguous positions veer in the direction of one or other of the two major social classes. See Erik Olin Wright, 'Class Boundaries in Advanced Capitalist Society', *New Left Review*, 98 (July-August 1976).

10. Gosta Esping-Anderson, Roger Friedland, Erik Olin Wright, 'Modes of Class Struggle and the Capitalist State' in *Kapitalistate*, 4-5 (Summer, 1976), p. 191.

11. For a useful discussion of this literature and a stimulating discussion of various debates on the state see Ian Gough's forthcoming book, *The Political Economy of the Welfare State* to be published by Macmillan. I am grateful to Ian for showing me a manuscript copy.

12. R. Miliband, *The State in Capitalist Society* (Weidenfeld and Nicolson, London, 1969).

13. N. Poulantzas, *Political Power and Social Classes* (New Left Books, London, 1973).

14. More recently Miliband has made some criticisms of his earlier work on this issue of the mediations between the capitalist class and the state. See R. Miliband, *Marxism and Politics* (Oxford UP, London, 1977).

15. Cynthia Cockburn, *The Local State: Management of Cities and People* (Pluto Press, London, 1977).

16. James O'Connor, *The Fiscal Crisis of the State* (St James Press, London, 1973).

17. Anne Markusen, 'Class and Urban Expenditures: a Local Theory of the State', in *Kapitalistate*, 4-5 (Summer, 1976).

18. This process of centralisation appears to be common to capitalist states, see O'Connor, *Fiscal Crisis* in relation to the United States, and H. Glennerster, *Social Service Budgets and Social Policy* (Allen & Unwin, London, 1975), in relation to Britain and the US.

19. Markusen, 'Class and Urban Expenditures'.

20. See, for example, H.W. Fraser, 'Municipal Socialism and Social Policy' (unpublished paper to the University of Glasgow/SSRC conference on Social Policy and the Locality: order conflict and social control, June 1978).

21. See chapters by Seán Damer and Joseph Melling in this collection.

22. Fraser, *Municipal Socialism*, pp. 20-1.

23. For an overview of this question see Dilys Hill, *Democratic Theory and Local Government* (Penguin, London, 1974).

24. Cockburn, *Local State*.

25. Nevertheless, the capitalist class has only granted universal suffrage with great reluctance. For an impressive historical and comparative survey see G. Therborn, 'The Rule of Capital and the Rise of Democracy', *New Left Review*, 103 (1977).

26. The exception to local administration of the social services is the insurance and assistance services which were set up outside the Poor Law (pensions, unemployment and sickness insurance and means tested assistance). This can perhaps best be explained with reference to the fact that they were established in opposition to the much hated Poor Law which was locally administered, and because a strong tradition of equal treatment underpinned the final break with the Poor

Law, so that assistance was brought within the ambit of central government, whilst in most other European countries parts of it at least remain locally administered.

27. Asa Briggs, *Victorian Cities* (Pelican, London, 1963).

28. Marion Bowley, *Housing and the State* (Allen & Unwin, London, 1945).

29. B. Wilding, 'Towards Exchequer Subsidies for Housing 1906-1914', *Social and Economic Administration*, vol. 6, no. 1 (1972).

30. See Joseph Melling's chapter for a discussion of the way in which the interests of private landlords have been sacrificed through rent control.

31. Mike Ball, *British Housing Policy and the Housebuilding Industry* (unpublished paper to the Political Economy of Housing Workshop of the Conference of Socialist Economists).

32. The remainder of this section is a short summary of chapters III to V of my unpublished University of London PhD thesis 'Public Housing in England and Wales 1919-1939', which draws on both primary and secondary sources dealing with central-local relations and housing policy.

33. Frederick Engels, *The Condition of the Working Class in England* (Panther, London, 1969).

34. Census Office, *Census of England and Wales 1921* (HMSO).

35. Robin Ward, 'Residential Succession and Race Relations in Moss Side', (unpublished University of Manchester PhD thesis, 1975).

36. Census Office, *Census 1921*.

37. Figures from A. Redford, *The History of Local Government in Manchester*, vol. III (Longman Green, 1940).

38. See Manchester and Salford Trades and Labour Council, *Annual Reports* 1918-1938/9. The Trades Council was also involved in the setting up of the Manchester and Salford Better Housing Council in 1930. This was hardly a labour movement body, however, consisting mainly of voluntary groups involved in housing survey work, and organisations such as the Women Citizens' Association and the Social Services Group of the Auxiliary Movement (an offshoot of the Student Christian Movement).

39. E.D. Simon, *A City Council from Within* (Longman Green, London, 1926).

40. Ibid., p. 40. Nevertheless, the 'simmering dislike of municipal housing' found an outlet when discussion turned to the question of staffing the newly formed Housing Department, and this issue was not satisfactorily concluded until December 1921. Ibid., p. 46-7.

41. This and other data on Manchester's housing programme is, unless otherwise indicated, taken from *Manchester City Council Minutes* (three volumes, annual) or *Housing Committee Proceedings* (annual).

42. Simon, *City Council from Within*.

43. 500 houses were completed by direct labour up to 1925: ibid. Between 1923 and 1928, 1,540 were built. The next largest figure was 753 completed by Bradford Direct Works Department. Figures supplied by the library of the Trades Union Congress, London.

44. Average net rents in, for example, Pudsey, Yorkshire were 5s per house whose average floor area was 620 square feet. In Manchester the corresponding figures were 9s and 760 square feet. (The figures are for 1928.) Since rates were also above average in Manchester, the disparities between gross rents in Manchester and other towns were even greater. See E.D. Simon, *How to Abolish the Slums* (Longman Green, London, 1929).

45. Calculated from Ministry of Health, *Local Taxation Return* (HMSO, Annual).

46. Redford, *History of Local Government*.

47. This curious division between the Housing Committee and the Public Health Committee persisted until recent years.

48. Figures from ibid.

49. Ministry of Health *Report of the Committee on Local Expenditure*, Cmd 4200 (HMSO, 1932).

50. Manchester City Council, *Council Minutes* Appendix, 3/12/1926, p. 206.

51. For a discussion of anti-urbanism see G. Stedman Jones, *Outcast London* (Clarendon Press, Oxford, 1971).

52. Public Record Office (PRO) HLG 52/885.

53. *Minutes of the Manchester District Committee of the AUBTW*. 26/11/1931 and *Parliamentary Debates*, vol. 259, col. 1010, 19/11/1931 and col. 1170, 20/11/1931.

54. Ibid.

55. *Census*, 1921 and 1931.

56. E.D. Simon and J. Inman, *The Rebuilding of Manchester* (Longman, London, 1935), pp. 64-5.

57. Ministry of Labour, *Local Unemployment Index* (HMSO).

58. See Manchester University Settlement, *Housing Needs of Ancoats in Relation to the Greenwood Act*, 1930, and Manchester and Salford Better Housing Council, *Angel Meadow and Red Bank*, 1931.

59. Ministry of Health, *The Rents of Houses Owned by Local Authorities*, Cmd 5527 (HMSO, 1937).

60. *A Short History of Manchester Housing* (City of Manchester, undated).

CONTRIBUTORS

Caroline Bedale has worked as a research assistant for a number of years at the University of Manchester, and is currently employed as a research officer in Oldham.

David Byrne spent some years researching in the North East of England and is now Principal Lecturer at the Polytechnic of Ulster. He is at present working on housing in Northern Ireland.

Jennifer Dale has been a Lecturer in Social Administration at the University of Manchester for the past few years and is engaged on theoretical as well as empirical studies into housing provision.

Seán Damer did research in Glasgow and lectured at Trinity College, Dublin, before joining the Department of Sociology at Manchester. He is at present working on a fresh study of Glasgow housing and is preparing a research project on property relations.

Robert Finnegan has been researching at the University of Bradford for the past three years, and is at present a Temporary Lecturer with the School of Social Studies and Humanities at Leeds Polytechnic.

Joseph Melling has spent a number of years researching at the University of Glasgow, and is presently occupied on the economic and social history of British employers. He is preparing a research project for a further local study at the moment.

SELECTED DATES IN THE HISTORY OF HOUSING REFORM, 1868-1946

Formal titles are followed by the more popular names attached to legislation and committees.

1868	Artizans and Labourers' Dwellings Act 1868, 'Torrens Act'
1874	Working Men's Dwellings Act 1874, 'Housing (Corporation Building) Act'
1875	Artizans and Labourers' Dwellings Improvement Act 1875, 'Cross Act'
1879	Artizans and Labourers' Dwellings Improvement Act 1879, 'Second Cross Act'
	Artizans and Labourers' Dwellings Act (1868) Amendment Act 1879, 'Second Torrens Act'
1884-5	Royal Commission on the Housing of the Working Classes, 'Dilke Commission'
1885	Housing of the Working Classes Act 1885
1890	Housing of the Working Classes Act 1890
1905	Liberal Government in power
1907	Committee on House-Letting in Scotland, 'Guthrie Committee'
1909	Finance Act 1909
	Housing, Town Planning, etc., Act 1909, 'Housing and Town Planning Act of 1909'
	House Letting (Scotland) Act 1909
1911	House Letting and Rating (Scotland) Act 1911
	Housing unrest in coal-mining areas of Scotland
1912-17	Royal Commission on the Housing of the Industrial Population in Scotland, Rural and Urban, 'Ballantyne Commission'
1914	Outbreak of First World War
	Defence of the Realm Act implemented
1915	Industrial and housing unrest in munitions areas
	Munitions of War Act
	Commission of Enquiry into Clyde Munitions Workers, 'Balfour-Macassey Commission'
	Committee on the Alleged Increases in the Rental of Small Dwellings, 'Hunter Committee'
	Rent and Mortgage Interest (War Restrictions) Act, 'Rent and

Mortgage Restriction Act of 1915'

1916   Defeat of the Clyde Workers' Committee and dilution of
            engineering works

1917   Reports by the Commissioners on Industrial Unrest
            Report by the Royal Commission on the Housing of the
            Industrial Population in Scotland, 'Ballantyne Report'

1917-18   Advisory Housing Panel of Ministry of Reconstruction and
            Memorandum on Emergency Problem, 'Salisbury Panel'

1918   Committee on Building Construction in Connection with the
            Provision of Dwellings for the Working Classes, 'Tudor Walters
            Committee'
            Committee on the Increase of Rent and Mortgage Interest
            (War Restrictions) Acts, 'Second Hunter Committee'

1919   Royal Commission on the Coal Industry, 'Sankey Commission'
            Housing and Town Planning, etc., Act 1919, 'Addison Act'
            Ministry of Health Act 1919

1920   Report of the Committee on the Increase of Rent and Mortgage
            Interest (War Restrictions) Acts, 'Salisbury Committee'
            Increase of Rent and Mortgage Interest (Restrictions) Act
            1920, 'Rent and Mortgage Restriction Act of 1920'

1923   Housing Act 1923, 'Chamberlain Act'
            Report of the Committee of the Increase of Rent and Mort-
            gage Interest (Restrictions) Act 1920, 'Onslow Committee'
            Rent and Mortgage Interest Restrictions Act 1923, 'Rent and
            Mortgage Restriction Act of 1923'

1924   First Labour Government
            Housing (Financial Provisions) Act 1924, 'Wheatley Act'
            Clydebank rent protests
            Prevention of Eviction Act 1924

1925   Committee on the Rent Restriction Acts, 'Constable
            Committee'
            Rent and Mortgage Interest (Restrictions Continuation) Act
            1925, 'Rent and Mortgage Restriction Act of 1925'

1926   Royal Commission on the Coal Industry, 'Samuel Commission'
            General Strike

1929   Second Labour Government

1930   Housing Act 1930, 'Greenwood Act' or 'Slum Clearance Act'
            Housing (Scotland) Act 1930

1931   Report of the Committee on National Expenditure, 'May
            Committee Report'
            Financial crisis

Fall of Labour Government and first National Government
Committee on the Rent Restriction Acts, 'Marley Committee'
1932   Committee on Local Expenditure in England and Wales, 'Ray
       Committee'
1932-6 Housing boom in England and Wales
1933 · Rent and Mortgage Interest Restrictions (Amendment) Act
       1933, 'Rent and Mortgage Restriction Act of 1933'
1935   Housing Act 1935, 'Overcrowding Act'
1936   Housing (Consolidation) Act 1936
       Housing (Scotland) Act 1936, 'Scottish Overcrowding Act'
1937   Committee on the Rent Restriction Acts, 'Ridley Committee'
1938   Increase of Rent and Mortgage Interest (Restrictions) Act 1938,
       'Rent and Mortgage Restriction Act of 1938'
       Housing (Financial Provisions) Act 1938
1939   Outbreak of Second World War
       Imposition of full rent controls
1945   Report of the Committee on Rent Controls, 'Second Ridley
       Committee'
1946   Housing (Financial and Miscellaneous Provisions) Act 1946

INDEX

Acts of Parliament: Factory Acts 56;
Finance Act 1909 21-2, 176;
Housing (Municipal Corporation
Building) Act 1874 51; Housing of
the Working Classes Act 1890 41,
45, 146, 175, 181; Housing, Town
Planning, etc., Act 1909 45, 75;
Housing and Town Planning, etc.,
Act 1919 11-12, 24-5, 27-8, 41,
62, 66, 114-16, 152, 155, 179,
205-7, 210-12; Housing (Addi-
tional Powers) Act 1919 179;
Housing Act 1923 66, 116, 128,
180, 212, 216; Housing (Financial
Provisions) Act 1924 27, 64, 117-20,
155, 180, 186, 206-7, 212-13;
Housing Act 1930 115, 120, 122,
127-9, 156, 185, 216; Housing Act
1935 125, 132, 156, 159; Housing
Finance Act 1972 200; Increase of
Rent and Mortgage Interest
(Restrictions) Act 1938 140;
'Munitions Acts' see Ministry of
Munitions Act 1915 and Munitions
of War Act 1915; Ministry of
Munitions Act 1915 23; Munitions
of War Act 1915 23, 105, 148, 151;
Public Health Acts 64; Rent and
Mortgage Interest (War Restrictions)
Bill 1915 101, 177; Rent and
Mortgage Interest (War Restrictions)
Act 1915 23, 75, 102, 151; Rent
Act 1957 182; 'Rent Restriction
Acts' and 'Rent and Mortgage
Restriction Acts' see under specific
rent legislation
'Addison Act' see Acts of Parliament
and Housing and Town Planning
Act 1919
Addison, Christopher 11, 102, 152
Advisory Housing Panel of the
Ministry of Reconstruction 152
Albion Motor Works 104
Amalgamated Society of Engineers
(ASE) 91
Amalgamated Union of Building
Trade Workers (AUBTW) 215
Aman, D.L., Baron Marley see Marley

Ancrum, J.W. 186
Anderson, Perry 169-70, 188, 191-2
Armstrongs, W.G., Ltd 154
artisans 24, 144, 156, 174, 183
Askwith, G.R. 20, 22
Asquith, H.H. 100
Asquith Government 22
Association of Municipal Corporations
(AMC) 209, 215

Baldwin, Stanley 124
Balkwell Estate (North Shields) 29,
171, 177, 179, 186
Ball, Michael 69, 205
Ballantyne, Henry 23-4 see also
'Ballantyne Commission'
'Ballantyne Commission' see Royal
Commission on the Housing of
the Industrial Population in
Scotland
Ballantyne Report see Report of the
Royal Commission on the Housing
of the Industrial Population in
Scotland (1917)
Banbury, Sir Frederick George 150
Bank of England 20, 25, 143
Barbour, Jean 103-5
Barbour, Mrs Mary 148, 159
Barker, C. 177
Barr and Stroud Ltd 104
Bateson, H. 48
Baxter Bros 50
Beardmores, William 154
Belfast 154
Bell, John 192
Bell, Tom 104
Binnie, Thomas 89, 96
Birkbeck Building Society 177
Birmingham 118, 146, 203, 215
Blackfriars (Glasgow) 93
Blackpool 208
Boaden, Noel 195
Board of Trade, Report of an Enquiry
. . . into Working Class Rents,
Housing and Retail Prices (1908)
48-9, 55
Boer War 21, 79, 142, 178
Bolitho, Hector 153

228